BREAKING THROUGH
THE NOISE

STUDIES IN THE MODERN PRESIDENCY

A series edited by Shirley Anne Warshaw

Studies in the Modern Presidency is an innovative new book series that brings together established and emerging voices in modern presidential research, from the Nixon administration to the present. While works on the modern Congress abound, this series seeks to expand the literature available on the presidency and the executive branch.

Scholars and journalists alike are increasingly writing and reporting on issues such as presidential rhetoric, executive-legislative relations, executive privilege, signing statements, and so on. We are committed to publishing outstanding research and analysis that reaches beyond conventional approaches to provide scholars, students, and the general public with insightful investigations into presidential politics and power.

This series will feature short and incisive books that chart new territory, offer a range of perspectives, and frame the intellectual debate on the modern presidency.

A list of the books in this series can be found online at
http://www.sup.org/modernpresidency.

BREAKING THROUGH THE NOISE

PRESIDENTIAL LEADERSHIP, PUBLIC OPINION, AND THE NEWS MEDIA

Matthew Eshbaugh-Soha and
Jeffrey S. Peake

STANFORD UNIVERSITY PRESS
Stanford, California

Stanford University Press
Stanford, California

Printed in the United States of America on acid-free, archival-quality
paper

Library of Congress Cataloging-in-Publication Data

Eshbaugh-Soha, Matthew, 1972– author.
Breaking through the noise : presidential leadership, public opinion,
and the news media / Matthew Eshbaugh-Soha and Jeffrey S. Peake.
pages cm.—(Studies in the modern presidency)
Includes bibliographical references and index.
ISBN 978-0-8047-7705-6 (cloth : alk. paper) —
ISBN 978-0-8047-7706-3 (pbk. : alk. paper)
1. Presidents—United States. 2. Presidents—Press coverage—United
States. 3. Government and the press—United States. 4. Press and
politics—United States. 5. Communication in politics—United States.
6. Public relations and politics—United States. 7. Political leadership—
United States. 8. Public opinion—United States. I. Peake, Jeffrey S.,
1970– author. II. Title. III. Series: Studies in the modern presidency.
JK554.E73 2011
352.23'60973—dc22
2011017095

Typeset by Thompson Type in 10/15 Sabon

For my parents, Joe and Susan Soha
—Matthew Eshbaugh-Soha

For Jacob and Nathan
—Jeffrey S. Peake

Contents

Acknowledgments

Breaking through the Noise is the culmination of a lengthy collaboration that we began in 2002. Although we have written several conference papers and published a few articles on the presidency and media, we had avoided tackling the more difficult questions surrounding presidential leadership and responsiveness in regards to the public. Once we refined our ambitions to presidential agenda-setting and realized that we needed more than a couple of articles to make our mark, we turned our ideas into this book. We have arrived at the end of this project, not without a few bumps in the road, but as better scholars for having taken the journey.

Along the way, we have had help from many scholars and graduate students. George Edwards's research and guidance has been instrumental not only in this book but also in our general approach to studying the presidency. Jeff Cohen commented on our initial idea and was instrumental in helping us focus our research question. Dan Wood's methodological approach to study the dynamics of the American presidency has clearly inspired this book. It is the ideas of these three giants in the subfield of presidential politics that drove much of this book's research.

Others deserve thanks for helping, in both large and small ways, our ideas become this book. Matt's colleagues at the University of North Texas were both patient and supportive. To name a few, Paul Collins answered myriad questions about methods, case selection, and theoretical framing, Tetsuya Matsubayashi helped explore other possible causal modeling strategies, Mathieu Turgeon commented on our conception of public opinion processing, and Jim Meernik, when department chair, fostered an environment conducive to writing a book. Thanks also to the Office of Research and Economic Development at the University of North Texas for a small grant that we used to help defray the cost of indexing the book. Jeff's colleagues at Bowling Green were great sounding boards for ideas. Especially helpful were David Jackson, Neal Jesse, and Melissa Miller. We thank

Ryan Salzman, Jun-deh Wu, Chris Linebarger, and Tom Miles, at UNT, and Kate Bresnan, Cody Koch, and Yuanliang Wang, at Bowling Green, for help with research assistance. Conversations with Johanna Dunaway about media and with Brandon Rottinghaus about the presidency and public opinion were most helpful. Discussions with Martha Kumar were especially encouraging and helpful in shaping our ideas on public relations in the White House. John Geer provided supportive comments on an earlier version of the paper that encouraged us to pursue a book-length project. Others have offered comments, through informal conversations or as panel discussants, over the long course of this project. They include Steve Forde, Andrew Enterline, Lori Cox Han, Diane Heith, Karen Hoffman, Chuck Walcott, Jim Pfiffner, Paul Quirk, and Eric Juenke. Thanks are also due to Justin Vaughn, Ken Meier, and seminar participants at Texas A&M University, where Matt presented an earlier version of Chapter 5. Several suggestions by two anonymous reviewers were vital to improving the presentation of the book and addressing limitations to our findings and conclusions according to the policies we examine. Thanks go as well to John Woolley and Gerhard Peters for the American Presidency Project, an indispensible resource for public presidency research.

Everyone at Stanford University Press has been helpful. Series editor Shirley Anne Warshaw provided encouragement and important suggestions at the initial stages of the project. Stacy Wagner saw enough promise in our proposal to send it out for review. She has offered valuable suggestions reflected in a much improved final manuscript. We appreciate that Jessica Walsh kept us apprised of our manuscript status during review and assisted us with completing the publication paperwork. Emily Smith and the production team at the Press were outstanding to work with. Finally, Margaret Pinette's help was instrumental in putting the final touches on the book.

Our deepest and most sincere thanks go to our families. Although Ethan and Rowan's control of the Force has surely helped push this book to fruition, and Shelly provides essential inspiration, Matt dedicates this book to his parents, Joe and Susan Soha, for teaching him the importance of education and giving him the freedom to pursue his own path. Jacob and Nathan forced Jeff to devote at least some of his free time to play, rather than work, and Lori's patience, strength, and love provided him much needed encouragement.

BREAKING THROUGH
THE NOISE

CHAPTER I

Introduction

CALLED THE "GREAT COMMUNICATOR" for his remarkable oratorical skill, President Ronald Reagan purportedly could sway the public to support him, using television to engage, motivate, and inspire the viewing audience.[1] Decades after the end of his presidency, journalists recall with nostalgia Reagan's mystic ability to connect emotionally with and thus lead the American people by saying "a few simple things passionately" (Packer 2010; see also Cannon 2004; Hansen 2004). Reagan's alleged public relations prowess has become the standard to which subsequent presidents are compared. The expectation of effective presidential leadership is furthered by contemporary presidents who have marshaled an extensive White House public relations operation to lead the public and news media (Kumar 2007). A failure of leadership for contemporary presidents, therefore, is often reduced to a failure of communication.[2] Despite this conventional understanding of presidential leadership that pervades Washington, D.C., systematic evidence of effective presidential leadership of the public proves illusive, even for the "great communicator" (Edwards 2003). In this book we are guided by the following puzzle: Why has presidential leadership of the public been unimpressive, even as the presidency retains substantial institutional tools to lead the public and news media?

The importance of this question is illustrated with two examples from both Reagan and Obama who, despite being perceived as powerful orators by their contemporaries, struggled in their efforts to lead the public. One of President Reagan's top policy priorities concerned relations with Central America. Reagan's public relations strategy centered on convincing the American people that the communist threat in Central America was real and that adequately funding the Nicaraguan Contras, an anticommunist guerilla force, was the best strategy to confront it. Reagan raised the issue many times with the American people, as he sought

I

congressional support to fund the Contras who opposed the communist Sandinista government of Nicaragua. President Reagan spoke on aid to the Contras in twenty-five speeches in 1985 and thirty speeches in 1986, the peak of his attention to the issue (Edwards 2003, 132). In addition to mentioning the issue regularly in his public statements, Reagan delivered eight nationally televised addresses on Nicaragua and the Contras during his presidency (Edwards 2003, 30–31), with four of these occurring before the disclosure of the Iran-Contra scandal in 1986.

Despite the extent to which Reagan spoke publicly about Central America, public opinion did not move toward Reagan's position. According to numerous polls reviewed by Edwards (2003, 52–54), support for aid to the Contras ranged between 22 and 42 percent during the period 1985 through March 1988, with opposition always substantially outweighing support. Moreover, the country consistently viewed Reagan's handling of Central America negatively, averaging nearly 61 percent disapproval between 1983 and 1988 (Edwards 2003, 55). Most telling of all, President Reagan considered his public leadership efforts on aid to the Contras a significant failure of his presidency. In his memoirs, the president writes, "Time and again, I would speak on television, to a joint session of Congress, or to other audiences about the problems in Central America . . . But the polls usually found that large numbers of Americans care little or not at all about what happened in Central America" (quoted in Edwards 2003, 53). Reagan believed his policy failed precisely because he was unable to lead the public on the issue.[3]

Like Reagan, President Barack Obama used his speaking skills and the "bully pulpit" throughout his first year in office (see Goldstein 2009; Hornick 2008) and especially as part of his effort to pass comprehensive health care reform. From May 2009 through March 2010, the Obama White House marshaled the full resources of its communications operation to build public support for health care reform. To sell reform, the president held a prime-time televised press conference, delivered a nationally televised address before a joint session of Congress, conducted a nationally televised town hall meeting, and travelled extensively throughout the nation delivering campaign-style addresses. All in all, the president mentioned health care reform in over 200 speeches during his first year in office. In addition to the president's own efforts, members of the administration flooded news programs for months attempting to sell health care reform to the American people.

These efforts notwithstanding, the public did not move to support the president's plans for reforming health care. After his national address on September 9, 2009, for example, Obama received just a one-point increase in the percentage of Americans who felt he had explained his position but no other bump in public support.[4] Throughout the fall of 2009, as Obama went public on health care reform and the Senate debated it in committee and on the Senate floor, public support barely moved from a consistent baseline of 40 percent approval.[5] At the same time, Obama's handling of health care reform continued to decline, dropping to 43 percent after his nationally televised State of the Union address in January 2010.[6]

Given these failures to move public opinion, why did Presidents Reagan and Obama speak so frequently on these top policy priorities in the face of overwhelming evidence that their efforts were not paying dividends? Why have other presidents, such as Bill Clinton on health care reform in 1993 or George W. Bush on Social Security reform in 2005, devoted considerable communications resources to strategies that eventually failed? If the president's efforts in speaking are centered on moving public opinion, then the contemporary presidency is replete with anecdotes signifying that presidents are unwise to attempt to directly lead public opinion, whether or not these failures are a product of hubris (Edwards 2003, 5) or arrogance within the White House (Jacobs and Shapiro 2000). Indeed, the cost of public relations may be too high, given the low level of payoff that has resulted.

Failure to lead the public has not deterred the contemporary White House in its public relations efforts, of course. The White House communications operation, buttressed by a staff of several hundred to assist with public relations, devotes substantial resources to impart the president's message, after all, including facilitating the delivery of hundreds of speeches, dozens of interviews, and formal and informal exchanges with reporters annually (Kumar 2007, 5). With all of this effort, surely the White House has achieved some return on its investment in public leadership, despite the lack of clear direct opinion leadership.

To be sure, President Obama's public efforts on health care reform are a clear illustration of the benefits of public leadership even in the absence of an increase in public support for top policy priorities. First, news coverage of health care reform was extensive, occupying a sizeable percentage of the weekly news hole through much of the second half of 2009.[7] Second, health care reform became a top priority of the American people, as a quarter of the public in September 2009 considered health care to be the most important problem facing the nation, up from just 9 percent in May (Jones 2009). Most importantly, the president scored a signature policy success when he signed health care reform into law on March 23, 2010.[8]

Our discussion contends that if presidential speeches do not affect public opinion, then going public should provide other important benefits for the president. Given the strong link between the media's and public's policy agendas (McCombs 2004)—and in light of the difficulties presidents encounter attempting to lead the public directly—our efforts to explore this topic center on presidential leadership of the news media. We argue that presidential leadership of the public occurs through increased news coverage of the president's policies. By affecting the news media's policy agenda, presidents may then influence the public's policy agenda. However, as presidents lament their inability to penetrate the "filter" or overcome the "noise" of contemporary presidential news coverage in the recent media age, it remains unclear whether presidents and their massive communications operation can indeed lead news coverage.

With this in mind, our study explores simultaneously presidential leadership of both the media and public agendas. Despite the common assumption that presidents can influence the public's agenda, there is only limited evidence to support this claim (Cohen 1995; but see Young and Perkins 2005). More importantly, prior research leaves uncovered the effects of the media in the president's relationship with the public despite the strong impact that media have on public concerns (but see Baum and Groeling 2010). Although there exists a larger body of literature on presidential agenda setting of news coverage (see Edwards and Wood 1999), this research does not simultaneously model the public's agenda and its impact on the president–media relationship, despite the working assumption that media are vital to reaching the public.[9] The media's importance

4

to the public presidency (see Cohen 2008) requires a study that accounts for both the media and public simultaneously in a model of presidential leadership.

Given this backdrop, we offer a fresh theoretical and empirical look at presidential leadership of the media and public. First, we argue that presidents may be using their institutional resources primarily to communicate their policy priorities through news coverage. If presidents can lead the media, then this presents a promising opportunity for indirect leadership of the public given the strong interrelationship between the public and news media. Second, we conceptualize leadership in a manner that reflects both leadership and responsiveness (Burns 1978; Geer 1996; Pitkin 1967). We then consider leadership in a way that accounts for the impact that presidents may have on the public and news media and how the public and media may also affect the president. Third, the presidents' efforts at public leadership are not geared so much at changing public preferences, that is, *moving* public opinion, but rather at influencing the issues the public considers important, that is, agenda setting. We test our claims across three strategies of presidential leadership most common to modern presidencies: focused attention, whereby presidents address the nation on television; sustained attention, whereby presidents discuss their priorities through a series of major and minor addresses; and going local, whereby presidents use domestic travel to affect local news coverage and local public opinion. In addition, we explore how presidential leadership differs across foreign and economic policy, two key policy responsibilities of modern presidents.

In this book, we ask the following questions: How successful are presidents as they attempt to lead the media and public agendas? Do presidents lead the media agenda, and does this leadership translate into indirect leadership of the public? Does simultaneously accounting for leadership and responsiveness alter our expectations and conclusions concerning presidential leadership of the public? How does this play out across different leadership strategies and policy areas? Although our focus is not on how presidential leadership affects legislation, presidents ultimately hope to make major changes in public policy, and their speeches are often geared to pressure Congress (Beckmann 2010; Kernell 1997). Thus, we

INTRODUCTION

conclude the book with a discussion of the implications of our results on
the prospects for going public and legislative victory.

THE PUZZLE OF PRESIDENTIAL LEADERSHIP

Presidents speak more today than they have at any time in the modern
presidency, an observation made by a number of scholars (including Hager
and Sullivan 1994; Lammers 1982; Powell 1999). According to Ragsdale
(2009), presidential speeches have increased noticeably since the Truman
administration. Despite some variation, including Gerald Ford's extraordinary speech making during his election campaign of 1976, there is a clear
upward trajectory in the number of presidential speeches over time, with
presidents delivering over 400 speeches per year throughout much of the
1980s and 1990s. This is up substantially from the 1950s and 1960s, when
presidents averaged 154 speeches per year. More recently, from 1974 to 2009,
presidents average 351 yearly speeches. Without question, presidents engage
frequently in public speaking to communicate their policy agendas to interested political actors and lead the national policy agenda (Barrett 2004;
Eshbaugh-Soha 2006b; Kernell 1997; Whitford and Yates 2003, 2009).

The president's greatest institutional means to lead the policy agenda is
through public relations. Behind these efforts at public leadership are considerable White House resources. Buttressed by a competent and flexible
staff, the White House Office of Communications and the Press Office assist
the president's efforts to communicate with the Washington media, regional
and local media, and the American public (Hult and Walcott 2004; Kumar
2003, 2007; Maltese 1994; Walcott and Hult 1995). As Kumar (2007) shows,
the president's communications operations are central to this development
and potential effectiveness of presidential speeches. The Office of Communications (OOC) has become an indispensable part of presidential public
relations strategy (Kumar 2007; Maltese 1994) and has grown along with
the increase in presidential speeches since the 1970s. According to Kumar's
(2007, 157–164) counts, the staff resources devoted specifically to the OOC
have risen alongside the president's tendency to deliver more speeches.

Establishing the policy agenda is one of the primary tasks of the contemporary White House and is of particular purview of the communications office (Kumar 2007; Maltese 1994). The OOC acts as a liaison with

6

non–Washington-based media, a coordinator of information flows from the White House, and a "political tool for generating public support for administration initiatives" (Maltese 1994, 118). Its staff advocates for the president, defends his actions, coordinates publicity, and explains the president's many decisions (Kumar 2007, 6–32). Not to be outdone, the Press Office provides the official record of the president and is geared toward influencing (or at least communicating with) the Washington press corps. Kumar (2007, 199) identifies three roles for the press secretary: information conduit, constituencies' representative, and manager of the Press Office. Each of these roles is crucial as presidents seek to manage press operations to lead not only the news media but also the public. Whereas presidents undoubtedly hope to do much more with these offices than simply begin a conversation on policy—presidents also desire to build public support and sign legislation that they prefer—affecting the priorities of others in and outside of government is a critical and necessary focus of presidential leadership.

In short, the White House communications operation provides the organizational resources to manage effectively and efficiently growing expectations about presidential public leadership. As a result, presidents are able to deliver hundreds of speeches every year. There is thus plenty of opportunity for the media to cover the presidency if they choose to or for the president to influence the media through a communications strategy. The modern presidential communications operation is well positioned to set the policy agenda, especially—as was the case for both Presidents Reagan and George W. Bush, who are seen as having successful, first-term communication organizations—when one issue takes clear priority. Most importantly, White House staffers clearly believe that correct application of these resources can generate the public support presidents need to govern successfully. Martha Kumar (2007, 5) summarizes, quoting from President Clinton's press secretary Mike McCurry:

I'd say 25 to 30 percent of the paid White House staff devotes at least two-thirds of its time to communicating and shaping the storyline. But the truth is, just about everybody who has any serious, consequential role at the White House, from the chief of staff on down, has to be mindful of, cognizant of playing a role in how are we going to communicate, how are we going to present our message, how are we going to put our best argument forward? [After all], the modern presidency revolves around this question of how you use or how you penetrate the filter of the press to go directly to the American people, which is your ultimate source of political strength.

The empirical reality appears starkly different, however. Even as we have witnessed an increase in presidential speech making and an expansion of the institutional resources devoted to public leadership, presidents are no more successful leading public opinion. Whether Reagan's efforts to change opinion on government spending or taxes, Clinton's leadership on NAFTA (Edwards 2003), George H. W. Bush's support for clean air, or even Obama's litany of domestic policy priorities, public opinion simply does not move in the president's favor (Edwards 2010). At worst, it trends against the president's position (Wood 2009a). Figure 1.1 illustrates this using a broad measure of public support, the president's job approval ratings. Even as presidential speeches and institutional resources devoted to public communication and leadership have trended upwards over time, the president's approval ratings have trended downward.

Perhaps the best case examples to illustrate this are George W. Bush's efforts to reform Social Security in 2005 and his numerous speeches to maintain support for the war in Iraq in 2003. In 2005, the Bush White House marshaled the full range of resources available to the president's communications office, including his top administration officials from the vice president to the secretary of the treasury, in an intensive sixty-day public relations tour to build public support for the president's plans to reform Social Security. Public opinion on Social Security did not move in the president's favor. Rather, public support for the president's handling of Social Security was highest, at 41 percent, *before* he announced his intentions during his 2005 State of the Union address and dropped precipitously during his sixty-day tour, plummeting to 29 percent by the end of July 2005 (Eshbaugh-Soha and Peake 2006, 701). President Bush also campaigned extensively for public support on Iraq in 2003. Although his efforts generated voluminous news coverage, the public's support of his handling of Iraq dropped from a high of 76 percent at the start of the invasion to a low of 45 percent in November.[10]

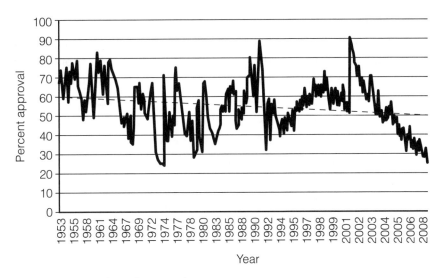

FIGURE I.I. Presidential approval ratings, 1953–2009.

Source: The Gallup Poll

These difficulties concern not just the relationships between the president and public opinion but also the president's relationship with the news media. As presidents have devoted more resources to cultivate media coverage, news coverage of the presidency has declined in its amount and tone. Cohen (2008) documents a clear decline in the amount of presidential news coverage on both network television (see Patterson 2000) and as printed in *New York Times* (see Ragsdale 1997). For example, although the Obama administration witnessed a honeymoon of extensive news coverage, higher than both Clinton and Bush's first fifty days combined, it declined soon after the honeymoon faded (Rieck 2009b). Cohen (2008, 91) illustrates increasing negativity in presidential news, despite the president's best efforts to influence news coverage. Even focusing public relations on local media does not guarantee positive coverage. For example, President Bush's extensive domestic travels to affect local media coverage of the Iraq War led to an increase in negative news stories in 2003 (Eshbaugh-Soha and Peake 2008).

This is the puzzle of public leadership. Presidents increase their speech making over time but have no demonstrable positive impact on public opinion. Even as they increase speech making and devote more resources to public leadership, most evidence shows that presidential news coverage has declined in amount and has become more negative. This could mean that presidents have to devote greater effort to public leadership even as they receive fewer payoffs. It also suggests that presidents may be waging a losing battle. Nevertheless, given the political and technological context of presidents in the era of twenty-four-hour news, presidents must penetrate the news to even think of reaching the public. Their efforts at speech making and communications, in general, are geared toward getting on the news. In an interview with George Stephanopoulos on January 20, 2010, President Obama reasoned that:

In this political environment, what I haven't always been successful at doing is breaking through the noise and speaking directly to the American people in a way that during the campaign you could do. You know I'd just get, I wouldn't be here and I wouldn't be bogged down with how are we negotiating this provision or that provision of a bill. I could speak directly to people and hear from them.

Whether Obama's difficulties in leading public opinion can be reduced to a failure of communication, as so many of his predecessors have also claimed (Edwards 2003), it is clear that presidents expend innumerable resources with little payoff. We tackle the idea of presidential public leadership from another perspective: that presidents may yet achieve a minimum payoff from their public efforts, even if their primary goal of opinion leadership falls short. That is, if presidents can set the news agenda, they may lead the public's agenda, both of which may assist the president in achieving his larger policy goals.

EXISTING EVIDENCE

Given presidents' monumental efforts at public leadership and the myriad resources presidents bring from their institutional base to succeed, one might expect presidents to successfully lead the public through speech making. As we have already suggested, this simplified view is unlikely to be supported by the empirical record. Moreover, the existing political science literature presents a mixed picture, at best, of the president's success in leading the public. At worst, it shows that presidential leadership of the public typically fails, even though public relations are at the core of the president's governing strategy. Because our theory hinges on the notion that responsiveness is an important component to studying presidential leadership, we review not only whether presidents successfully lead the public but also the extent to which presidents are responsive to the public.

Do Presidents Lead the Public?

The literature presents mixed evidence that presidents can lead the public, despite clear expectations that presidents should be capable leaders of public opinion. The reasoning behind an expectation for presidential leadership focuses on the president's institutional capacity to lead the public. As singular leader of the United States, with the "bully pulpit" at their disposal, presidents have the most frequent and consistent access to the media, and therefore the public, of any public official. By speaking often about a policy, presidents may be able to "expand the scope of conflict" (Schattschneider 1960), focus policy makers' attention on an issue (Baumgartner and Jones 1993), or increase an issue's salience (Druckman and Holmes 2004). In so doing, presidents may set the national agenda (Kingdon 1995) or prime the public to evaluate the president (Brace and Hinckley 1992) and his policies more favorably. Being able to lead the public is also central to "going public," with at least suggestive evidence that presidents can successfully lead the public through nationally televised addresses (Kernell 1997; Rottinghaus 2010).

Most scholarship is clear that presidents at least attempt to lead public opinion, whether or not it illustrates that presidents have been successful doing so. The people are the source of power for the "personal president" (Lowi 1985), and presidents are "active players in the game of public opinion" (Hart 1987). Increased resources available to the president buttress this claim. Moreover, technological advances have made public leadership more practical (Hager and Sullivan 1994; Lammers 1982). Although the goal of presidential communication is to generate political support (Stuckey 1991), its context and focus has undoubtedly changed over time with changing public expectations and media environments (Cohen 2010; Laracey 2002; Tulis 1987).

For the most part, scholarship that portrays presidents as successful leaders of public opinion does so in terms of agenda setting, whereby presidential attention affects public attention to a set of issues. Jeff Cohen's (1995) work was one of the first to demonstrate systematically that presidents can lead the public's agenda. For all three policy areas in his analysis—the economy, civil rights, and foreign policy—Cohen shows that increased attention in the State of the Union address leads to an increase in public concern for these policy areas, at least in the short term. Scholars have also demonstrated that presidents can influence their public approval ratings through priming. Through the State of the Union address, for example, a president can increase his own approval ratings by priming the people to evaluate his job performance based on issues favorable to him (Druckman and Holmes 2004). Presidents have also been effective using their public rhetoric, not to change public support for an issue but, for example, to change the public's intensity of support for the military's "don't ask, don't tell" policy (Bailey, Sigelman, and Wilcox 2003).

Dan Wood's (2007) recent study provides the most compelling evidence that presidential rhetoric has important effects on public opinion. He examines the impact that the level of presidential optimism on the economy has on the public's approval of job performance, the president's handling of the economy, and several indicators of economic growth. Wood finds that presidential optimism has a positive, indirect impact on the president's economic approval ratings (2007, 133). Wood also concludes that presidential optimism directly improves consumer behavior, at least in the short term, and has a long-term and positive impact on business investment (2007, 155). In an earlier article, Wood, Owens, and Durham (2005) illustrate that presidential optimism increases consumer confidence in the economy, leading to an indirect impact over broader economic indicators.

Despite these leadership effects, much research has raised doubts about the extent to which presidents can successfully lead public opinion. Most notably, George Edwards (2003) tackles the presidencies of Reagan and Clinton, two best cases given the accepted wisdom that they are both gifted orators and best able to lead public opinion if the assumptions that rhetoric matters are correct. Edwards illustrates convincingly that presidents are generally unable to move public opinion, even on their top priorities, despite noticeable communication skills and an arsenal of resources at their disposal. For example, public support for increases in defense spending actually declined after Reagan took office, and public support for Clinton's health care reform program decreased as he paid more attention to it (see Jacobs and Shapiro 2000). Wood (2009a) adds some nuance to the difficulties of presidential leadership when he reports that the public reacts against the president's publicly expressed liberalism, becoming more conservative as presidents are more liberal and vice versa.

A consistent theme in the literature is that the changing media environment has made it more difficult for presidential leadership of the public. Specifically, declining audiences for the president's nationally televised addresses and the rise of cable television and alternative media have ended the "golden age of presidential television." No longer can presidents go on television and speak to captive audiences (Baum and Kernell 1999). This plain fact has diminished the impact of the president's rhetoric on the public agenda. Young and Perkins (2005) find that since the mid-1980s, what the authors call the "post–golden age" of presidential television, the president's State of the Union address no longer influences the public's concern for issues as it once had (see Cohen 1995). Cohen (2008) furthers this general point by noting that presidents may face increasing difficulty leading public opinion given the complexities that the age of twenty-four-hour news presents for presidential leadership. While presidents engage in a greater number of public activities over time, it appears that their audiences have diminished considerably. Such realities have led presidents to alter their public leadership strategies to directly cultivate local media (Cohen 2010).

Ultimately, successful presidential leadership of the public may be conditional and strategic. A growing body of research maintains, indeed, that if presidents are to influence policy through speech making, they must be strategic and consider the larger political context and the existing public support for a policy initiative. Brandice Canes-Wrone's (2006, 6) work epitomizes this approach. She argues that presidential decisions to make public appeals are premised on the idea that presidents "avoid publicizing initiatives that face strong popular opposition," especially on domestic policy issues. Presidents usually prioritize issues that are already popular with the public and engage in pandering in a limited fashion—when they have average popularity and face reelection. Canes-Wrone holds that when presidents make public appeals strategically they will be more successful using them to affect legislation. Edwards (2003, 73) makes a similar argument, suggesting that Reagan's successes came when he was able to increase an issue's salience when public support for the president's favored policy was already widespread.

Other scholars recognize the conditional effectiveness of presidential speech making. Rottinghaus (2010) finds, for example, that the more uncertain the public is about its policy preferences, the greater the opportunity for presidential leadership of the public. Moreover, televised addresses and barnstorming for public support positively influence public support for the president's position, especially in the short term. Wood (2009a, 141) shows that political conditions, specifically the president's honeymoon period, contribute to successful public persuasion in comparison with the remainder of the president's tenure. The president's approval ratings also matter, as presidents with above-average approval ratings generate shifts toward the president's public liberalism. Wood (2009a) also notes that presidential efforts to lead the public are primarily a partisan enterprise, not one geared toward the median voter. In contrast, Jacobs and Shapiro (2000) suggest that presidents tailor their public speeches in an effort to alter opinion by transforming how the public evaluates the president's policy preferences. That is, presidents use polls to craft policy arguments in a way that will maximize support from the median voter rather than adjusting their own policy positions and priorities to coincide with what is popular. All in all, the state of political science research indicates that presidential leadership of the public is mixed, at best. This contrasts substantially with the picture painted by pundits and White House staffers alike.

Do Presidents Respond to the Public?

Responsiveness to public opinion is an important component of democratic theory (Dahl 1982). Although research illustrates a good deal of responsiveness by elected legislators to their constituents (Hill and Hurley

1999; Miller and Stokes 1963), only a few studies seek to explain presidential responsiveness. Of the few studies that focus on presidential responsiveness, several show substantial responsiveness to public opinion (Erikson, MacKuen, and Stimson 2002; Stimson, MacKuen, and Erikson 1995). Even Wood (2007, 51), in arguing that presidential rhetoric on the economy affects public opinion, found that the amount of presidential attention devoted to various aspects of the economy was highly responsive to public concerns. Geer (1996) holds that presidential responsiveness to public opinion has increased in recent decades because presidents are better able to gauge the desires of the public due to improvements in public opinion polling, thereby furthering democratic leadership. Heith (2004) and Towle (2004) make similar arguments.

Much like leadership of the public, presidential responsiveness may also be conditional and strategic. Presidents tend to respond to public opinion on issues familiar to the public, when they are modestly popular, during their first terms in office, and as election day nears (Canes-Wrone and Schotts 2004; Yates and Whitford 2005). For example, Rottinghaus (2006) shows that presidents' policy positions are typically congruent with majority opinion, even after reelection, as presidents remain responsive due to concern for their party's success in future elections.

Responsiveness does not mean that presidents pander to public opinion, however. Instead, existing public preferences provide important information that is helpful to presidents as they frame their policy priorities in an effort to lead the public. Jacobs and Shapiro (2000) conclude that presidents "do not pander" to public opinion but instead use information about the public's existing policy preferences to craft more effective messages. By more effectively framing their messages, presidents may be able to change opinion by altering the dimensions by which the public evaluates the president's policy preferences.

Additional evidence suggests that presidential responsiveness may be conditional. Canes-Wrone (2006) holds that strategic conditions, such as high popularity, may encourage presidents to be unresponsive, particularly when they disagree with majority opinion. Cohen (1997) finds no statistical relationship between the president's rhetorical liberalism and public opinion and suggests that, when presidents are responsive, it is usually symbolic rather than substantive. More recently, Wood (2009a) contends that presidents are partisan leaders and reports that presidential liberalism does not respond to changes in the public's liberalism. Although presidents have an incentive to remain congruent with public preferences because an increase in presidential approval ratings typically follows, Wood (2009a) concludes that presidential responsiveness to centrist public opinion is a "myth."

THE IMPORTANCE OF OUR STUDY

The bulk of the existing literature casts doubt on the president's ability to lead the public. This is in spite of the vast resources devoted to public leadership by recent presidents. Some research suggests, however, that the presidency's capacity for public leadership is substantial, at least under favorable conditions. Our approach takes the question of public leadership a step further, with the goal of shedding additional light on why presidents expend so much effort without the expected payoff of increasing public support. In the next section, we explore why the media matter to the president–public relationship and how the media environment may shape the prospects for leadership. Additionally, we examine the importance of responsiveness to presidential leadership and underscore why agenda setting is important to this exploration.

Why Media Are Important

As the central figure in American government, the president is the focal point of national news coverage. A content analysis of network television news reveals that the networks cover the president twice as much as Congress and nearly five times as much as the U.S. Supreme Court (Graber 2002, 273). The literature is also replete with expectations that presidents should be able to shape what media cover. Kumar (2007) provides detailed analysis of the efforts that recent presidential administrations have gone to in cultivating national and local news coverage, from timing the announcement of key policy initiatives to inviting local weather reporters to highlight President Clinton's global warming policy. Institutionally, the White House is structured to facilitate communication with the media, whether through the Press Office (Walcott and Hult 1995) or the Office of Communications (Maltese 1994). Although success may vary by regular cycles of presidential–press interactions (Grossman and Kumar 1981), the sense from the literature is that presidents have ample opportunity and resources to influence news coverage.

Research that quantifies and tests the relationship between the presidency and media reveals some support for this assessment. When it comes to leading local news coverage, presidents are particularly adept at using local visits to affect both the amount and tone of newspaper coverage (Barrett and Peake 2007; Cohen 2010; Eshbaugh-Soha and Peake 2006). In some areas of policy, in particular news on foreign policy crises, recent scholarship indicates that presidents tend to dictate coverage in general. This was especially the case with President George W. Bush and the Iraq War (Bennett, Lawrence, and Livingston 2007).

The media are crucial to the president's relationship with the public, given the strong link between the public and media. We see this manifested in several ways. First, the media influence what issues are important to the public (Iyengar, Peters, and Kinder 1982; McCombs 2004), with news stories being a primary determinant of the public's agenda (Iyengar 1991). Second, media attention to an issue affects public familiarity and knowledge with that issue (Bennett 2009; Page and Shapiro 1992). Third, media coverage of issues primes the public's evaluation of the president (Edwards, Mitchell, and Welch 1995; Iyengar 1991; Krosnick and Kinder 1990), such that when the media report extensively on an issue, the public is more likely to use that issue to evaluate presidential job performance. Fourth, media coverage shapes public support for U.S. foreign policy (Baum and Groeling 2010) and is theoretically important to presidential leadership of public opinion (Rottinghaus 2010).

Despite the clear linkages between the president and media, and media and the public, when presidential leadership of the public relies on the news media, it does so precariously. The media lack "staying power" to stick with policy issues over time (Downs 1972; Kingdon 1995, 62) and shift their focus to other stories besides the president's priorities. Today's media also tend to report "soft" rather than policy-related "hard" news, which may trivialize news about the presidency (Baum 2003; Bennett 2009; Cohen 2008). Moreover, presidents have difficulty affecting what the media cover in part because issues compete for limited agenda space (Jones and Baumgatner 2005, 20, 237; Wood and Peake 1998). As new issues arise on the media's agenda, they may supplant attention to the president's priorities. Each of these conditions limits the president's ability to sustain media attention to presidential priorities or count on consistent coverage of presidential policies on the news.

Edwards (2003, 173–183) notes several other difficulties for presidential leadership of the public that the structure of news coverage exacerbates. Coverage tends to be superficial and devoid of policy content but instead focuses on the person and on human interest stories. This varies little by president, as Edwards shows, and may even shape the conclusions we draw concerning the benefits of news coverage to the president's agenda. Early coverage of President Obama is a case in point. The amount of coverage given President Obama was greater and substantially more positive than his two immediate predecessors during his first 100 days in office. However, a large portion of the coverage was focused on his personal and leadership qualities rather than his policies. Coverage of Obama's policies was far more critical (Pew Research Center's Project for Excellence in Journalism 2009b; Rieck 2009a), and the positive coverage of Obama's personal and leadership qualities did not last much past his honeymoon (Rieck 2009b). Even though the media may cover the presidency more than any other political institution, much of the coverage fails to emphasize the president's policy priorities, and when it does it may underline negativity and conflict.

There is no guarantee that when presidents emphasize their policy priorities in their public speeches that the media will cover them. This is problematic for presidents as they seek to lead the agenda, whether through a national address (Peake and Eshbaugh-Soha 2008) or minor presidential speeches (Barrett 2007). Edwards and Wood (1999) present one of the most comprehensive treatments of the interaction between presidential and media agendas, while also accounting for congressional attention to policies. They find that presidential leadership of the media on foreign policy issues (U.S.–Soviet relations and the Arab–Israeli conflict) is virtually nonexistent, which echoes Wood and Peake's (1998) earlier analysis. Instead, presidents respond to media coverage on foreign policy issues and external events. Although presidents tend to lead media attention on some domestic issues, particularly health care and education, they respond to media attention to education and crime. At best, Edwards and Wood (1999) demonstrate a mixed assessment of presidential leadership of the news media's agenda on domestic policy issues and a responsive presidency on foreign policy issues.

Other studies confirm these findings across other policy areas. Eshbaugh-Soha and Peake (2005) reveal that presidents respond to media attention devoted to the economy, in general, and specific economic issues; for example, federal spending, inflation and unemployment, and international economic issues. Presidents tend to lead media attention only on inflation and unemployment and on international economic issues. These findings vary, as well, by president. Clinton led the media across most economic issues, while George H. W. Bush was largely responsive. They conclude that the objective state of the economy is important in that media tend to focus on negative stories and force presidents to respond to them. Conversely, when the economy is strong, positive stories are fewer, but those that exist are prompted by presidential credit claiming.

The bottom line is that the media play an important role in the relationship between the president and public for two reasons: (1) The president increasingly needs the media to reach the public, and (2) the media have important effects on the public. In other words, if presidents cannot affect news coverage of their top priorities, then they may be even less likely to influence the public's policy priorities. If this happens, and presidents still speak about a policy, then they may speak primarily about issues after public concern and media attention have already increased. Such responsiveness would further limit the prospects for presidential leadership of the public's and media's agendas. At the same time, presidents who can affect media attention to issues may increase their prospects for leading the public's agenda indirectly.

Despite these clear interrelationships among the president, the media, and public opinion, we know little about them. Measures of media attention are often excluded from analyses of presidents and public opinion (Cohen 1995, 1997; Edwards 2003; Geer 1996; Rottinghaus 2006), just as studies that analyze the dynamics of presidential and media agendas exclude measures of public opinion (for example, Edwards and Wood 1999; Eshbaugh-Soha and Peake 2005). Only recently has research begun to more thoroughly explore the complexities that media add to presidential leadership of the public. Cohen's (2008) book on recent developments in the news media and how they affect the presidency is the best example of such research. He notes, among other things, that presidential leadership styles have changed in response to the changing media environment. As public consumption of mass media has declined, presidents have shifted their focus from national efforts at public leadership to increasing efforts at going local and going narrow. It is the mobilization of specialized constituencies that changes the media–public–president relationship, according to Cohen's (2008) argument. More precisely, less national news coverage devoted to the president and his policies should limit the president's ability to lead public opinion.

In another study, Cohen (2010) tests more clearly the interrelationships among presidential speeches, news coverage, and public opinion. He concludes that presidential speeches increase the volume and tone of news coverage. Subsequently, the tone of news coverage correlates positively with the public's evaluations of the president. Although he does not examine these entities simultaneously, Cohen (2010) provides strong suggestive evidence that the president's ability to influence news coverage is vital to the president's effectiveness in leading public opinion. Cohen's innovative research prompts us to explore further how the president, media, and public interact and whether the media do indeed mitigate or expand opportunities for presidential leadership.

Why Reciprocal Causation Is Important

Just as much research focuses separately on the questions of presidential leadership (Edwards 2003) or responsiveness (Rottinghaus 2006), there is reason to believe that simultaneously accounting for both directions of the causal arrow will enrich our understanding of the public presidency. If only briefly stated for now (we tackle this in substantial detail in Chapter 2), Geer (1996) proves that presidents who respond to public opinion may have enormous difficulty when attempting to lead it. Moreover, Canes-Wrone (2006) illustrates that presidents' public leadership efforts are driven, in part, by the public's policy preferences. Presidents lead by determining which policies to emphasize in response to the public's set of preferred policies. Therefore, an examination of presidential leadership that does not consider responsiveness may conclude correctly that presidents do not lead the public. Such a study may not be able to say why this is so, however, and may understate the success presidents have had responding to the public.

Scholars have long been aware of the importance of responsiveness to leadership, as the need to examine both leadership and responsiveness to public opinion is central to theories of democratic leadership (Burns 1978; Geer 1996; Pitkin 1967; Wood 2009a). Hill (1998, 1333) rightly cautions researchers to test for both leadership and responsiveness to understand fully the relationships between elites and the public. Edwards (2009, 190) argues that there is a "critical independence between leaders and followers, which we miss when we focus on the pinnacle of power . . . We need to devote more attention to thinking about politics from the bottom up as well as the top down." Our integration of reciprocal causation is partially a response to Jacobs and Shapiro's (2000, 298) call for a study that examines "both political responsiveness to public opinion and efforts by political elites to move public opinion." Heeding this call, we focus on the reciprocal relationships among the president, the public, and the media as they pertain to agenda setting.

Why Agenda Setting Is Important

Agenda setting is of central importance to American politics (Schattsneider 1960), in particular, and the presidency more specifically. Recent presidents certainly understand the importance of agenda setting and have spent vast institutional resources on efforts to lead the agenda. A central function of the White House communications operations is agenda setting. According to Maltese (1994, 2), the following goals guide the Office of Communications: "to set the public agenda, to make sure that all parts of the presidential team . . . are adhering to that public agenda, and to aggressively promote that agenda through a form of mass marketing." Kumar (2007, 9) echoes this sentiment, writing: "From the perspective of the White House staff, the key to successful advocacy is controlling the public agenda." The OOC coordinates a number of media events and is responsible for organizing an effective public relations strategy geared to set the public's agenda. OOC staff use the calendar year to plan out the president's efforts to establish the policy agenda through predictable and regular events; for example, the State of the Union address, commencement appearances, and budget negotiations (Kumar 2007, 9). Efforts to coordinate public appearances by administration officials, including the president, are the purview of the OOC. For example, the OOC coordinated the Bush administration's Social Security reform tour in early 2005, a case study that we examine in detail in Chapter 6.

Agenda-setting scholars have largely concluded that presidents are effective agenda setters. For example, in his groundbreaking work on agenda setting, John Kingdon (1995, 25) maintains that presidents are well situated to lead the policy agenda if they choose to, noting that "there is little doubt that the president remains a powerful force in agenda setting, particularly when compared to other actors." The president has at his disposal formal tools, such as the veto, organizational resources, and public leadership capacity to set the policy agenda and should do so frequently or at least more frequently than any other political actor. In their seminal study on agenda setting, Baumgartner and Jones (1993, 241) similarly conclude that "no single actor can focus attention as clearly, or change the motivations of such a great number of other actors, as the president." While making claims to presidential leadership, neither of these important studies directly examines the impact presidents have on the agendas of the public or media.

Some research, however, has sought to directly assess the agenda-setting influence of presidential speeches, with mixed results. Scholarship demonstrates that presidents are able to focus the public's attention, yet the evidence tends to be limited to analysis of State of the Union addresses (e.g., Cohen 1995; Hill 1998) or single case studies (for example, Jones 1994). However, these effects appear to be time bound given the changing media context, in particular the advent of cable television, which has diminished presidential audiences (Young and Perkins 2005). A number of other studies that examine the effects of speeches by recent presidents report a limited capability of presidents to influence the media's agenda (Peake and Eshbaugh-Soha 2008; Wood and Peake 1998).

In spite of this mixed evidence, scholars often assume that presidents can set the public's agenda. Such an assumption underlies the model of public leadership employed by Canes-Wrone (2006). She argues that if presidents can increase the salience of an issue they can translate the public's support into legislative success in typical "going public" fashion. The agenda-setting assumption underlying this strategic theory of public leadership has only limited support, however, as we have already discussed.[11] Edwards (2009, 108) makes clear, nevertheless, that focusing attention is "the first step in the president's efforts to lead the public." As a result, success and failure in public leadership often flow from success and failure in agenda setting.

By explicitly testing the agenda-setting assumption, an assumption that undergirds both practical politics within the White House Office of Communications and research on the public presidency, we gain purchase on key explanations for why and when presidents are successful public leaders. Given the apparent capacity of the institution to influence agendas, agenda setting provides a best test for presidential leadership. Examining agenda setting may also help us solve the puzzle inherent in the study of the public presidency and which guides our research: Why do presidents have difficulty leading the public's policy preferences despite the great lengths they go to in order to lead the public? Our arguments and the results presented in this book amplify the importance of agenda setting as a precursor to opinion leadership.

PLAN OF THE BOOK

We develop our framework in Chapters 2 and 3. In Chapter 2, we closely examine the various conceptual definitions of leadership as applied to the presidency. We find that a systematic analysis of leadership would benefit from the reciprocal relationships between the public and president. A fuller understanding of presidential leadership requires examination of both causal arrows. Thus, we consider the influence that existing public opinion may have on presidential leadership efforts (see Geer 1996). We also conceptualize presidential leadership in a relatively straightforward manner—leadership as agenda setting—not only because we think this is theoretically acceptable but because it is also empirically viable given our reciprocal definition of leadership.

In Chapter 3, we develop our general theory and expectations. It is here that we establish the prospects for direct presidential leadership of the public's agenda and the possibility for indirect public leadership through the news media. This chapter presents the first of our two primary hypotheses, our indirect leadership hypothesis. We also explain why the existing policy agendas of the public and news media may constrain presidential leadership and promote presidential responsiveness, generating what we call our salience hypothesis. Finally, we frame each of these relationships as being conditional on the political context, the policy under debate, and the president's choice of leadership strategy. It is here that we justify selection of our two primary policy areas, the economy and Iraq.

In the empirical chapters, we use quantitative data and case studies to assess three presidential leadership strategies. In Chapter 4, we examine a focused strategy of agenda leadership, or presidential use of nationally televised addresses to set the media and public agendas. This strategy provides the president with the best opportunity to lead the public agenda, especially in the short term, as evidenced by limited research on the subject. Nevertheless, national addresses are not a guarantee of presidential leadership of the media (Peake and Eshbaugh-Soha 2008). In keeping with our assessment of both leadership and responsiveness, we examine both the impact of these speeches on media and public attention and the influence that media and public attention have on the likelihood of the president to deliver a national address on an issue. We examine the economy from 1969 to 2008 and Iraq from 1989 to 2008 and illustrate that, although a few specific presidential addresses clearly set the public's economic policy agenda, most do not. This is in part because the president tends to be highly responsive to the public's economic policy agenda. We find that presidents can lead the news media, and because the media influence the public's agenda presidents indirectly lead the public's economic agenda. We report similar results concerning Iraq.

In Chapter 5, we address the sustained leadership strategy, whereby the president seeks to influence the agenda through multiple minor and major addresses over time. Because presidents have increased their use of minor speeches in recent years, the strategy has grown in importance. There is good reason to believe that a sustained strategy may be effective in terms of influencing the agenda, despite limits shown by previous re-search (Eshbaugh-Soha and Peake 2005; Wood and Peake 1998). Using data on all presidential remarks, media coverage, and public concern on the economy and Iraq over several decades, we assess the strategy using vector autoregression (VAR) analysis. Our analysis of economic issues shows that presidential leadership of the public is premised on the public's agenda and the president's strategic position to act entrepreneurially: In the face of existing public concern, such as with unemployment issues, presidents are primarily responsive to the public's agenda. When the pub-lic displays little concern for issues, such as with spending and the budget deficit, presidents are well positioned to lead. Of course, the media also play a key intervening role, such that presidents indirectly lead the pub-lic's economic agenda by increasing news coverage of the economy. On Iraq, the president is best situated to set the public's agenda indirectly by first influencing news coverage but tends to be responsive when the issue permeates the news already. These findings serve to confirm the media's central role in presidential leadership of the public.

In Chapter 6, we assesses "going local" as a strategy of public leader-ship. We first examine the nature of domestic travel during the Clinton, George W. Bush, and Obama presidencies to show how going local has become an important governing strategy. Next, we assess the prospects for agenda leadership through a going local strategy using three case studies. These case studies include two going local efforts by President George W. Bush, who chose to circumvent the "filter" of the Washington press corps to influence both local media and public opinion on his tax cut policy during his first year in office and Social Security reform in early 2005. The other case study concerns President Obama's use of the strategy to influence media and the public on health care reform in 2009. All three case studies indicate that going local can be an effective means to influ-ence not only the news media but the public's agenda as well.

We conclude in Chapter 7 by summarizing the findings as they relate to our core research questions. The findings, on balance, provide broad support for our theoretical argument that the likelihood of presidential leadership is premised on the agendas of the public and news media. We assess the broader implications of our findings as they relate to going public as a governing strategy and the wisdom of pursing agenda leadership. Our conclusions indicate that responsiveness is an important and enduring feature of the public presidency. The implications of our findings extend beyond our analysis of the public and news media but ultimately to the achievement in Congress of presidential policy goals. This is the central puzzle of presidential leadership: How can presidents maximize their institutional resources and public responsibilities to translate their public speeches, and their impact over the public and news media, into a successful legislative agenda? Our answer is that leadership of the public agenda is a vital component to the president's larger governing strategy and that responsiveness is a central component of the president's public relations strategies.

CONCLUSION

Whether we call it the "permanent campaign" (Blumenthal 1982) or "going public" (Kernell 1997), public leadership is unquestionably at the core of the modern presidency. Edwards (2003, 4) suggests that three premises are fundamental to this view. First, public support is vital to presidential success. Second, presidents must actively appeal for public support throughout their terms in office. Third, presidents believe that they can successfully move public opinion and, as we have shown, the White House devotes vast institutional resources to cultivating public support. This is the conventional wisdom of modern presidential leadership, despite limited evidence of successful presidential leadership of public opinion. What remains is exploring whether this conventional wisdom is true as applied to agenda setting, while also accounting for the interrelationships among the president, public, and news media. The president is arguably the most relevant and certainly most visible individual in American politics. It is thus important that we know the extent to which presidents lead or respond to the public and media, whether media accentuate opportunities for presidential leadership, and what these relationships mean for democratic presidential governance.

CHAPTER 2

Presidential Leadership

PRESIDENTIAL LEADERSHIP IS A CORE CONCEPT in the presidency literature. However, its treatment by presidency scholars has been vague. We
often know it when we see it but fail to establish clearly what constitutes
leadership and how presidents lead. Nevertheless, the concept of leadership
is central to our understanding of the presidency and is at the foundation
of how political scientists, journalists, and historians evaluate presidential
performance. Given that the prevailing wisdom holds that skillful presidents
are "uncommonly" successful (Davidson 1984, 374; see Edwards 1989,
168), presidential success is promoted as being the product of leadership
skills, and estimations of presidential failure are often reduced to unskilled
leadership. Most notions of leadership, moreover, neglect the possibility
that presidents are leaders, even when they act in a responsive manner.

The general perception—reflected in numerous accounts of recent
presidencies—indicates that leadership is *the president's* willful effort to
influence others. Lyndon Johnson was successful pushing the Great Society through Congress because he possessed extraordinary individual skill
in influencing members of Congress to support him (Greenstein 2000).
Ronald Reagan employed his strong communication skills through the
medium of television to influence the American people and legislators to
support his policies, despite his party lacking majority control in the House
of Representatives (Kernell 1997). Barack Obama's success in reforming
health care will invariably be traced to his skillful handling of Congress
in the months after the surprise election of Republican Scott Brown to
the Senate, which broke the filibuster-proof Democratic majority that
left reform all but dead. A lack of leadership skill is a criticism of many
failed policy efforts, from Carter's failed energy policy (Light 1999) to
Clinton's unsuccessful efforts to reform health care. Even Clinton himself
lamented that his misfortune on health care was a product of *his* failure

to lead; specifically, that he was unable to communicate clearly the benefits of his health care policy to the American people (see Edwards 2003).

This line of thinking neglects two important elements of presidential success or failure. First, it tends to ignore context, or the idea that existing circumstances constrain or expand opportunities for presidential success. Although Neustadt (1990) observed that presidential leadership was the power of individual presidents to persuade others, research since has concluded quite forcefully that personal influence only marginally increases a president's success in Congress (see Bond and Fleisher 1990, Chapter 8; Edwards 1989, Chapter 9). Moreover, recent scholarship suggests that personal skills are unrelated to the effectiveness of presidential leadership of the public (Edwards 2003, 4). We contend that presidential leadership is most often a product of context.

Second, the focus on personal skills overlooks the reasons why and ways by which presidents may respond to the public, media, or Congress through their public actions. If we do not witness a presidential speech affecting a change in public opinion, for example, we may conclude that the president has failed to lead. But given the importance of responsiveness to a democratic leader, accounting for both the impact that presidents have on others and the impact that others have on the president paints a more complete picture of the public presidency. By considering leadership as a product of context and related to responsiveness, we are better able to theorize and then illustrate how a president's political environment conditions his or her propensity to lead. In short, political circumstances—and especially the priorities of the media and the public—shape the prospects for presidential leadership or democratic responsiveness.

Before we explore how context influences presidential leadership, we must first unpack leadership as a concept. In doing so, we present not only the conventional understanding of leadership as an individual attribute but also our favored conceptualization of leadership, one that it is born out of opportunity and circumstance. Thus, we are able to develop how responsiveness is relevant to leadership. Then, we illustrate why exploring leadership as agenda setting—not as direct opinion leadership—allows us to quantify and study the complexities of presidential leadership. Our assessment of the literature produces a definition of presidential leadership as it pertains to agenda setting. In short, presidential leadership consists of affecting the policy priorities of others. When policy priorities are already clear, public leadership involves speaking on those priorities.

DEFINING PRESIDENTIAL LEADERSHIP

Scholarship on the presidency devotes much attention to the concept of leadership, despite a lack of agreement on its meaning (see Edwards 2009, 3). Definitions of presidential leadership are varied and numerous, as myriad works attempt to describe and define it. Bert Rockman (1984, 6) conceives of leadership as "the capacity to impart and sustain direction" and Steven Shull (1993, 8) sees leadership as something that requires "ideological commitment and assertiveness." For Neustadt (1990), persuasion, which is central to leadership, involves bargaining with members of Congress (or the bureaucracy; see Waterman 1989). Kernell (1997) conceives of leadership as "going public,"[1] whereby presidents use the tools and stature of the public presidency to generate public support for the president's policies in an effort to achieve those goals in Congress. For others, "leading the public is at the core of the modern presidency" (Edwards 2003, 4) and "rhetorical leadership" is at the "heart" of modern presidential governance (Tulis 1987, 4).

It is our task in this chapter to grapple with several conceptions of leadership toward building our own. We first summarize several prominent treatments of leadership that are foundational to politics and the presidency. We differentiate between conceptions of leadership that are a function of individual presidential skill and those that see leadership as a by-product of the opportunities afforded to presidents. Second, we explore the importance of responsiveness to presidential leadership. It is not simply the president's ability to shape the actions of the news media and public that is of interest to us but also how the actions of the news media and public shape or constrain opportunities for the president's public leadership.

Leadership: Individuals and Context

The individual leader is central to many definitions of leadership. Most notably, James MacGregor Burns (1978) offers a foundational assessment of political leadership. For Burns, transactional leadership is the most basic form, whereby a leader approaches another—a follower—to exchange one thing for another. Similar to Neustadt's (1990) idea of bargaining, transactional leadership may be a presidential request of a legislator to support an increase in defense spending in exchange for presidential support of the legislator's request for a cut in the capital gains tax. Transformative leadership, on the other hand, requires the leader to "exploit" a follower's need and "motivate" him or her to "satisfy higher needs" (Burns 1978, 4). Burns's (1973) heroic leader, who leads the entire nation and may ignore his or her party and its preferences when deemed necessary, fits this category. The collegial leader, on the other hand, is constrained by the party and the majority that elected him or her and is generally "undramatic" in style (Burns 1973). Moral leadership is a "higher level" of leadership that "can produce social change" in which not only do leaders take responsibility for their actions, but followers also have a choice as to whom to follow (Burns 1978, 4). Here, transformative leadership becomes moral when the aspirations of both leaders and followers are elevated (1978, 20).

Instead of thoroughly developing the broad contours of leadership as Burns has done, presidential scholars have either offered frameworks within which to view presidential leadership or have attempted to define it more concisely or feasibly. Perhaps the most significant effort on behalf of presidential scholars to tackle the concept of leadership is Richard Neustadt's seminal work, *Presidential Power*. Power is, of course, central to Neustadt's (1990, 11) conception of leadership. His often-quoted summation, "presidential power is the power to persuade," launched presidency research in a new direction, where the focus became explaining presidential behavior and leadership rather than the constitutional powers of the executive branch (Corwin 1948). If power is synonymous with leadership, and for Burns (1978, 12) the two concepts are highly related, then surely Neustadt's (1990, 30) definition of power, that the president's central task is to persuade others that what the president wants is what they "ought to do for their sake and on their authority" is leadership.[2] That persuasion involves bargaining does not evoke Burns's transformative leader but rather Burns's more mundane transactional leader, for which, perhaps, the presidency is best situated.

Burns (1978) is clear that leadership is about change, influence, and power, and that there are different degrees of it. But even so, his assessment of political style and skill, which are central components of his conception of leadership, is problematic if one hopes to measure and evaluate leadership effects. This difficulty has been unearthed by political scientists who reject style and skill as necessary conditions for successful leadership of the public or Congress (see Bond and Fleisher 1990; Edwards 1989; 2003). In his examination of charisma, for example, Edwards (2003, Chapter 4) shows that it is difficult, if not impossible, to define, operationalize, and measure *charisma* because it is a subjective concept. In addition to the logical flaws that Edwards observes, he shows that charisma has proven ineffective in characterizing presidential leadership.[3] The public viewed Richard Nixon as more "charismatic" than John F. Kennedy in 1960, for example, despite the overwhelming conventional wisdom that would suggest otherwise (Edwards 2003, 87). Moreover, variations in presidential approval ratings appear unaffected by post hoc assessments of charisma.

Neustadt's understanding of leadership may be limited in its application to the complexities of the public presidency, as well. It is, like Burns's, premised on the individual skills of a president, which appear to be limited in affecting presidential–congressional relations (Bond and Fleisher 1990; Edwards 1989), the focus of Neustadt's treatise. Because presidential power is the power to persuade, moreover, and persuasion involves bargaining, it is not entirely clear how a president might bargain with the public in order to lead it. A further complication for presidential leadership of the public for Neustadt is that he sees the public as largely disengaged from politics. Neustadt (1990, 82) writes, "One should never underestimate the public's power to ignore, to acquiesce, and to forget." His notion of leadership, when applied to the public, involves "the President-as-teacher . . . a hard and risky job" (89). Neustadt (1990, 89) provides a bridge to the importance of circumstance, nevertheless, by holding that presidential leadership of the public requires presidents to capture and maintain the public's attention, something that is far from guaranteed, given that events "create his opportunities to teach."

Scholars have spent the last several decades moving beyond Neustadt's conception of leadership given that, like Burns's, it falls too close to the observation that individual attributes drive the capacity for leadership and that individual bargaining skills differentiate the successful president from the failure. Edwards (2009, 188) bluntly concludes that "presidential power is *not* the power to persuade." Even the most successful presidents analyzed by Edwards do not rely on persuasion to succeed. Central to this general evolution in the literature is recognition that the political context in which a president must govern is important. Because presidents are better positioned to succeed under some circumstances than others, failures of leadership are not necessarily due to the personal failings of presidents, such as that they were not charismatic enough. Instead, a president's inability to shape change may be a result of difficult circumstances, such as divided partisan control of government, heightened partisan polarization, an economic recession, or an unwillingness of the public to follow the president, especially among those who identify with the opposition.

Both George Edwards and Stephen Skowronek (1993) echo these themes in their treatments of presidential leadership. Both authors emphasize the president's political environment, which tends to shape opportunities for leadership, rather than the president's individual abilities to persuade.[4]

To this end, Edwards's (1989, 4–5; 2009, 10–14) framework of presidents as directors or facilitators of change proves instructive. Directors create opportunities for change or cause change more directly, much like Burns's transformational leader. The more realistic facilitator, however, takes advantage of opportunities present in the political environment in order to lead. For Edwards, presidential leadership occurs "at the margins" because modern presidents are ill equipped to structure their environment and thus are unable to direct change. As such, successful leaders act as facilitators in that they recognize and exploit "opportunities for change" (Edwards 2009, 11).

Among its other virtues, this framework challenges scholars to move beyond the apparently unattainable myths of Theodore and Franklin Roosevelt, who are assumed to have been able to incite the fires of the masses and elites through force of will and effective rhetoric. More critical assessment of these presidents, however, reveals leaders who exploited opportunities within the political environment rather than working to persuade others to follow (Edwards 2009, Chapter 2). According to Edwards's line of argument, these presidents were successful not because they persuaded the public and Congress but because they took advantage of opportunities afforded them to lead. Indeed, Edwards's primary contribution is to move beyond the acceptance that "unsuccessful leadership lies with the leader rather than opportunities for change in the leader's environment" (2009, 10).

In his treatment of presidential leadership, Stephen Skowronek (1993) emphasizes political context through a historical mesh of categories focused on political time. Presidential leadership, for Skowronek, is premised on the attempt by presidents to "resolve the disruptive consequences of executive action in the reproduction of legitimate political order" (19). Skowronek organizes political time based on presidential leadership in shattering, affirming, or creating political order, which produces four types of presidential politics: reconstruction, preemption, articulation, and disjunction. His typology of presidential politics relies on political context at the time of a president's ascendency, whether the dominant political regime is resilient or weakened, and the president's own relationship to the dominant regime. The best circumstances for presidential leadership involve the politics of reconstruction, where a new president challenges the dominant but vulnerable regime and supplants it with a new political order. The exemplar is Franklin Roosevelt, who successfully challenged the moribund Republican regime of the time, reordering the political landscape to a new dominant regime, that of the New Deal Democrats (Skowronek 1993, Chapter 7).

Both the Edwards and Skowronek frameworks are broad enough to explain presidential leadership in multiple arenas, but only if the context is favorable will presidents have opportunities to lead the public, media, or Congress. In recognition that context, not charisma, and opportunities, not individuals, drive presidential leadership, scholars who use quantitative techniques to study presidential leadership of the public have identified simple rules for identifying successful presidential leadership. Leadership of the public exists, for example, when presidential speeches have some demonstrable impact on public preferences, such as increasing public support for the president's policy positions (Rottinghaus 2009) or the issues the public considers to be most important (Cohen 1995; Hill 1998). We may also find leadership when presidents parlay existing public support for policies into success in Congress (Canes-Wrone 2001). These studies conceive of leadership success as not being based on the president's skill to motivate or raise public aspirations but to the extent it takes advantage of the political context to accomplish goals. To lead, successful presidents—whom Edwards would call facilitators—behave strategically. Their public leadership efforts coincide with a broad strategy of leadership designed to take advantage of existing circumstances.[5] To be sure, these studies advance our knowledge and understanding of presidential leadership of the public. What they do not do, however, is explore the reciprocal nature of presidential leadership and the importance of responsiveness to presidential leadership.

Leadership: Concerning Responsiveness

Having surveyed literature that conceptualizes presidential leadership as the impact that presidential activity has on the actions or opinions of others, we turn now to responsiveness. We do so because presidential leadership requires an understanding of those whom the president is trying to lead. After all, "great leadership requires great followership" (Burns 1978, as quoted in Rockman 1984, 8). In the words of Fiorina and Shepsle (1989, 36): "One cannot have leaders without followers, but going further, one cannot understand leadership without understanding followership." The attributes and willingness of followers may provide or restrict opportunities for presidential leadership. We extend the concept of followership and define it not simply as the willingness of the public and media to follow but include the notion that the public's own policy priorities matter to the prospects for presidential leadership. To fully assess presidential leadership, therefore, we argue that leadership not only concerns efforts to affect behavior in others; it also concerns responsiveness: the influence of others, such as the media and public, on the president.

Several scholars agree and inform the meaning of responsiveness as it relates to leadership. Geer (1996, 24) notes that democratic followership (or presidential responsiveness to the public) occurs when the president's policy positions are in line with public opinion. When presidents engage in democratic followership, through Geer's (1996) reasoning, they assess the public's positions on policy and adjust their own positions to reflect the public's preferences. In other words, the president responds to public opinion.[6] The essence of Canes-Wrone's (2006, 105) understanding of leadership relies on knowledge of public support for an issue, so much so that presidents are apt to speak about issues that are already popular with the public. Thus, leadership is predicated on existing public opinion or, in effect, presidential responsiveness to public preferences. Edwards (2009, 61) echoes this claim that presidents "are unlikely to *change* opinion," but a successful facilitator may "exploit *existing* opinion" (emphasis in original) by leading. Without question, the president ignores the public at his peril in a democracy, and responsiveness is an integral part of the strategic president's leadership efforts.

That leadership and responsiveness are not mutually exclusive activities is uncontroversial, as a number of scholars have already made this claim (see Geer 1996; Jones 1989; Key 1961; Stimson 1999). Burns (1978, 5) recognizes that a significant failure "in the study of leadership has been the bifurcation between the literature on leadership and the literature on followership." Thus, responsiveness is essential to Burns's (1978, 19) definition of leadership when he writes,

. . . leaders inducing followers to act for certain goals that represent the values and motivations—the wants and needs, the aspirations and expectations—*of both leaders and followers.* And the genius of leadership lies in the manner in which leaders see and act on their own and their followers' values and motivations . . . leadership is thus inseparable from followers' needs and goals. (emphasis in original)

In her seminal work on representation, Hannah Pitkin (1967, 232–233) matches leadership with responsiveness in two ways. First, representative governments "must not merely be in control, not merely promote the public interest, but must also be responsive to the people." Second, although she notes that representation and leadership are distinct concepts, Pitkin recognizes that leadership and representation are compatible, whereas manipulation (what we might call blind following by the public) is not attuned to representation. Moreover, "leadership is, in a sense, at the mercy of the led. It succeeds only so long as they are willing to follow" (233). In other words, leadership is parcel to representation, and because responsiveness also involves representation then leadership and representation are compatible concepts. Stimson (1999, 10) echoes this by noting that leadership and responsiveness are not mutually exclusive concepts. Instead, "Politicians engage in representative behavior because they wish to lead."

The idea that presidential leadership is compatible with responsiveness is also driven by the public's own expectations of the president. These expectations are exceedingly high and are often contradictory (Cohen 1997, Chapter 1; Wayne 1982), providing another reason why presidential leadership in the modern era is most clearly a public and responsive effort. On the one hand, the public expects the president to lead. There exists a clear perception among the American people that the presidency is at the center of government and, thus, capable of solving problems over which the president is constrained constitutionally (Lowi 1985). On the other hand, the public expects presidents to respond to the public's preferences for policy change or stability. It goes without saying that presidents are wise to respond to public preferences in a democracy to assist in their policy and reelection goals. As the essence of responsiveness is grounded in the nature of representative democracy, following public opinion is central to being an effective facilitator (Edwards 2003, 245).

It is these expectations that ultimately encourage presidents to engage in a permanent public campaign or to otherwise lead publicly. Presidents speak frequently in the modern era for many reasons. Clearly, presidents hope to speak to influence public opinion or set the public's agenda, despite their difficulties in doing so (Edwards 2003). Presidents also speak to meet public expectations, which may be an important benefit of speaking hundreds of times in a year when the public rarely moves in response to the president. As we have already shown, presidents devote enormous institutional resources to reach out to the public, primarily through efforts at influencing the media. Presidents have also cultivated an extensive polling apparatus to be able to respond to public preferences or to use the public's opinion to help them craft more effective policy messages (Jacobs and Shapiro 2000).

Conceptually, we have shown how scholars have treated presidential leadership and responsiveness. Practically, however, it is difficult to disentangle or even account simultaneously for the two concepts, as evidenced by the unidirectional focus of the public presidency literature. Canes-Wrone (2006) discusses presidential leadership and its successful application but only after public opinion is accounted for. Indeed, the title of her book, *Who Leads Whom?*, is indicative of the prominence of responsiveness to presidential leadership. Much of her quantitative and formal analysis of leadership concerns pandering, which is a form of political responsiveness, as opposed to leadership conceived of conventionally whereby the president changes public preferences. Although she does not explicate this reciprocal argument, she clearly accounts for responsiveness in her definition and application of leadership. Geer (1996) explores both ends of the spectrum and emphasizes how public opinion polls—a way for leaders to know existing public opinion and then respond to it—have altered modern political leadership. He also observes that leadership effects may be muted when the public salience of an issue is already high. Stimson (1999) concurs when he implies that politicians are attuned to public opinion and that they "lay low" on issues when they are not supported by the public and emphasize issues instead when they match public preferences. As much research shows actual responsiveness on the part of leaders (Stimson, MacKuen, and Erikson 1995), we are on firm ground in holding that presidential responsiveness is likely due to the structure of the modern presidency, which facilitates engaging the public through a variety of leadership activities.[7] Considering both leadership and responsiveness quantitatively means that we can measure leadership when we see a response to presidential actions and measure responsiveness when presidents react to others' behavior.

APPLICATIONS OF LEADERSHIP

Facing numerous possible ways to examine presidential leadership of the public,[8] we detail two primary outcomes of the president's public leadership efforts. One concerns opinion leadership, or the tendency for the public to accept the president's policy preferences—his support or opposition for policy solutions or issue positions—as their own. A second, referred to as agenda setting, considers presidential leadership as the president's ability to affect the importance others, especially the public and news media, attach to policy priorities. Simply stated, agenda leadership requires that presidents focus and maintain public attention on presidential priorities. For reasons we detail in the following pages, we study leadership as agenda setting in this book.

Opinion Leadership

Given the centrality of public preferences to democratic governance, a good deal of scholarship has focused extensively on opinion leadership. Presidents attempt to lead public opinion when they attempt to influence, change, or convert public opinion on issues (see Burns 1978, 274–286). This is consistent with Edwards's (2003) examination and synonymous with Geer's (1996) definition of democratic leadership. For example, if a president discusses the benefits of increasing defense spending, opinion leadership exists if the president convinces those who otherwise do not support an increase in defense spending (or who are undecided) to subsequently support an increase. For Geer (1996, 23), more specifically, "democratic leadership [or Periclean leadership] occurs when politicians move the median point of the distribution of public opinion toward their stated position." Alternatively, Wilsonian leadership happens when the public does not have clear preferences on a policy issue, so that presidents can also "create a distribution of opinion favoring their stated position" (Geer 1996, 47). In either case, opinion leadership requires that the president affect public preferences in favor of presidential preferences.

A variation on this is conditional opinion leadership, whereby presidents may attempt to lead on issues that are already viewed favorably by the public (Canes-Wrone 2006). This does not require changing the public's mind but allows presidents to strategically target issues in such a way that existing public support may help them achieve their goals. If presidents can increase the salience of these issues, they should be able to parlay existing public support into legislative success. In this vein, Rottinghaus (2006) examines policy congruence, or the level of policy agreement, between presidential rhetoric and public opinion. In later work, Rottinghaus (2010) tests whether presidential speeches increase public support for the president's position. Both approaches require an understanding, operationalization, and examination of public preferences for specific policy issues.

Whether through opinion leadership or conditional opinion leadership, assessing the complexities of leadership under these constructs is difficult due to data limitations. To systematically examine the relationships among presidents, media, and the public, we need a relatively stable set of public opinion questions over a long time frame. The variability in question wording and inconsistency of topics asked over time make it difficult to examine opinion leadership in the manner we aspire to (see Monroe 1998; Page and Shapiro 1983). It is not surprising, then, that scholarship that examines the public's policy preferences tends to examine one direction of the causal arrow at a time, whether responsiveness (Jacobs and Shapiro 2000; Rottinghaus 2006), leadership (Edwards 2003; Rottinghaus 2010), or some variation of one or the other (Canes-Wrone 2006). Previous scholarship has simply been unclear about how to examine systematically the interrelationships among the president, public, and media and do so while accounting for the reciprocal causality of leadership in an examination of the public's preferences on specific policies.[9]

Stimson (1999) offers a possible solution to these data limitations by combining a number of public opinion questions into a measure of public mood liberalism (see Wood 2009a), but using this approach presents its own problems. Although we recognize the benefits to the policy liberalism and mood approach, we think that it is not ideal for several reasons. First, this approach may be predisposed to finding a link. We know from a vast body of research that the public tends to act rationally in the collective. Composite measures of public opinion consistently relate with other measures of elite preferences (Page and Shapiro 1992; Stimson, MacKuen, and Erikson 1995). This is in spite of the evidence that shows a lack of consistency between public opinion on individual policies (Monroe 1998) and that responsiveness between the public and government has declined over time (Page and Shapiro 1983). Second, presidents simply do not make decisions at this macrolevel; presidents make decisions about specific policies rather than a general liberal or conservative direction for their policy agenda. So even though policy liberalism presents a useful aggregate measure with which to examine complex causal relationships, it is far from how presidents actually make decisions while in office. Therefore, we think that focusing on specific policies is a stronger test of the interrelationships among the public, media, and the president. Thus, we shift our attention away from opinion leadership to a more manageable definition, one that will allow us to examine complex reciprocal relationships in a causal fashion.

Agenda Leadership

Another type of leadership is agenda-setting. Kingdon (1995, 3) defines the agenda as "the list of subjects or problems to which governmental officials, and people outside of government closely associated with those officials, are paying some serious attention at any given time." Edwards and Wood (1999, 327) consider it "the set of issues that receives serious attention from policymakers." Jones (1994, 17) sees the policy agenda as "how a political system comes to treat an idea as a serious matter for policy action." Agendas may more precisely apply to an institution or set of political actors. Agendas are the motions to be voted on before Congress or "a general set of topics that a policymaking body considers for formal action during a specific period of time" (Jones 1994, 17). They include issues that are considered important by elites in general or those in government (Cobb and Elder 1972). They thus include the formal policy agenda and also the systemic agenda, as identified by Cobb and Elder (1972, 85). The systemic agenda includes those "issues that are commonly perceived by members of the political community as meriting public attention and as involving matters within the legitimate jurisdiction of existing governmental authority."

Thus, agendas not only concern policy issues; they are also defined by the amount of attention devoted to issues. Moreover, the institutions and political actors that are the focus of this study necessarily shape our definition of the agenda. So, the president's agenda consists of those issues to which the president attends, the media's agenda consists of those issues that the media cover on the news, and the public's agenda includes those issues with which they are primarily concerned. Just as any agenda may change over time, our concern is whether one agenda affects another and whether these relationships are reciprocal.

Like Kingdon (1995, 4), we differentiate between agendas and alternatives and focus on the former. Although we will analyze specific aspects of a broader policy area (that is, the economy), we do not examine whether the policy alternatives or the president's specific policy positions affect media attention to those specific positions or influence the public's support for those policies. Furthermore, we are not interested in how issues rise on and fall off the agenda, which is the focus of Kingdon (1995). Rather, we are interested in whether the president leads or responds to the media and public agendas. We contend that the agenda is of central importance because, if presidents cannot influence what the media and public consider important in the first place, this complicates their ability to influence the nature of the stories media cover or the public's opinions on policy specifics.

Through agenda setting, presidential attention, signified in this study through the president's public speech making, may increase media attention to an issue, thereby affecting the media's agenda. Whether directly or indirectly through increased news coverage, speeches may also increase the public's awareness of an issue, thereby affecting the public's agenda. When presidents speak about an issue, in other words, they may increase the importance of a policy problem to the media or the American people. Naturally, if presidents increase public concern for an issue strategically, on issues where the president's policy preferences are consistent with those of the public, the president may be able to use existing public support to achieve other goals, such as increased legislative success (Canes-Wrone 2006; see Edwards 2009). For our purposes, we stop short of this extension and instead examine whether the president can use speech making to increase public attention to issues, regardless of the public's support or opposition for the president's specific policy preferences.

Agenda setting offers an alternative perspective of presidential leadership that may present a greater opportunity for success, especially when compared with the more difficult task of moving public opinion. Prior accounts of presidential agenda setting cite the significance of the "bully pulpit" as a tool of presidential governance. Indeed, presidents are well positioned to affect the public and media agendas, according to numerous accounts of agenda setting (Baumgartner and Jones 1993; Kingdon 1995). Of the national political institutions, the presidency is most frequently covered by the press (Graber 2006). Presidential pronouncements are newsworthy because the president is recognized as the singular leader of the executive branch. Being newsworthy is an important necessity to effective agenda leadership.

Understanding the degree to which presidents affect the public and media agendas through speech making is integral to understanding presidential leadership more broadly. It follows that if presidents are unable to directly affect the public's agenda—those issues Americans consider most important—then the prospects for direct leadership of public opinion (such as influencing policy preferences) are diminished. Focusing attention is necessary for effective opinion leadership, even when placed in the more circumscribed perspective of Edwards's facilitator: "Increasing the salience of an issue, clarifying, framing, or channeling opinion, and taking advantage of fluid views require that the president focus the public's attention on issues of his choosing" (Edwards 2009, 95). Our claim that agenda setting is critical to the president's public leadership also coincides with Neustadt's (1990, 89) view of the president-as-teacher, where presidential leadership requires that the public first "become attentive" to learn from the president.

Indeed, agenda setting is a necessary first step in the president's public leadership efforts. Even theories of opinion leadership note that presidents cannot be expected to lead public opinion if they cannot first set the public agenda or, in other words, increase the salience of issues to the public or media. That presidents can set the public's agenda through speech making is a central assumption of Canes-Wrone's (2006) contributions, after all. Presidents who follow the public's agenda and attempt to lead on issues that are already salient with the public have greater difficulty increasing public support for their policy positions (Rottinghaus 2010). Jones (1994, 125) argues that there is a clear distinction between attention and preferences and that "attentiveness to situations that activate those preferences is also critical" to understanding the policy process. Jones (1994, 127) concludes, furthermore, that "preferences only become relevant when a policy area becomes salient. For preferences to become important citizens must attend to them; so preferences are not likely to influence policy on their own." In other words, agenda setting is necessary to lead or influence opinion, much as it is a necessary first step in other aspects of information processing by the public, such as priming (Miller and Krosnick 2000, 311). It is thus justifiable that we have selected agenda setting as the focus of our analysis.

Cohen (1997, Chapter 2) echoes our claim in his examination of presidential leadership of the public's agenda. For presidents to know whether something is on the public's agenda—whether the public thinks the issue is important enough to identify as a "most important problem" or not—underlies public leadership. Our contribution is also similar to Cohen's (1997) in that we are interested in whether presidential leadership—the president's agenda on policies—affects the public's agenda or vice versa. Even so, we move beyond Cohen's analysis not by assessing the correlation between these two factors—"public concern with a policy area increases as presidential emphasis with the policy area increases" (Cohen 1997, 55)—but by examining more precisely the causal and reciprocal dynamics of this relationship. By doing so, we are able to account for the reciprocal nature of the relationship, identified by Hill (1998) in his replication of Cohen's study. We also consider indirect opportunities for leading the public's agenda, so long as the president can first affect the media's agenda.

Defining leadership as agenda setting allows us to study a concept central to American politics. Schattsneider (1960, 66) notes that agenda setting "is the supreme instrument of power . . . he who determines what politics is about runs the country." By expanding public interest in an issue, a president can bring other groups into a supportive coalition by making the issue more relevant and by altering the dimensions that shape the debate (Edwards 2009, 80; Jones and Baumgartner 2005). This should benefit the president in multiple arenas and help achieve a variety of policy and other goals. Often, public support will change, even without altering the fundamental components of policy, in response to an alternatively framed debate. According to Jones (1994, Chapter 4), this occurred during the early 1990s on the superconducting supercollider debate, as opponents were able to shift the debate away from scientific discovery (a supportive dimension) and toward one related to exploding government deficits (a negative dimension). Even though we do not assess outcomes in this way, much research holds that successful agenda setting biases outcomes in the agenda setter's favor (Fiorina and Shepsle 1989), yet another reason why agenda setting is a central topic worth additional exploration.

SUMMARY

Leadership is central to political science. It has proven to be a difficult concept to define and apply to systematic analysis of presidential politics. Just as scholarship has correctly identified presidential success as a by-product of contextual circumstances, conceptual studies of leadership identify another way that political scientists' applications of leadership will evolve. That is, leadership entails not only presidential influence of the public or some other entity but also responsiveness, or the impact that others have on presidential efforts to lead. Part of the reason responsiveness is absent in previous research lies in the dearth of good data available for studies of opinion leadership, especially, as we argue, given the role that media play in the likelihood for presidential leadership or responsiveness. By focusing on only one or the other, previous research provides an opportunity to develop further the complexities of presidential leadership.

We apply a reciprocal definition of leadership to agenda setting in an effort to systematically analyze presidential leadership—and its impact on the public and media—at the agenda-setting stage of the policy process. At the risk of oversimplifying, we contend that presidential leadership occurs when the president influences the policy priorities of the public and media. When the president acts on existing public priorities, we call this responsiveness. Our remaining task is to develop a theory and use a methodological technique that allows us to account simultaneously for both directions of the leadership arrow. In doing so, we may find out precisely whether presidents can lead while being responsive or whether leadership is evident only absent presidential responsiveness.

CHAPTER 3

Theoretical Framework and Organization

IN THIS CHAPTER, we develop a theory to address the following questions. What impact does presidential attention to issues have on public and media attention to issues? How does public and media attention affect the president's level of attention to issues? How might the media provide an opportunity for indirect presidential leadership of the public's policy agenda? In addition, how does presidential leadership vary by strategy, policy area, and the larger political context? To organize our argument, we examine first the relationship between the president and the public and then that between the president and the media. Here, we recognize that existing public opinion is a key factor that influences the president's propensity to lead or respond. Next, we consider how the media may facilitate the president's indirect leadership of the public's agenda, given the unequivocal link between the media and the public. Moreover, variation in policy and the political context will likely condition presidential leadership. To account for these factors, we examine economic and foreign policies in subsequent chapters and outline several political conditions that may hinder or expand opportunities for presidential leadership. But first we explore why presidents attempt to lead the public's agenda.

WHY PRESIDENTS ATTEMPT TO
LEAD THE PUBLIC'S AGENDA

There are a number of reasons that presidents attempt to lead the public through agenda setting. Indeed, we assume that presidents are purposive individuals who act to achieve a set of goals. Although the specific policy goals and strategies used by individual presidents undoubtedly vary with each president's leadership style (Greenstein 2000) and world view (Barber 1972) and the events that slide on and off the national policy agenda (Kingdon 1995), each president desires three things: good policy, reelection, and historical achievement (Pfiffner 1988). As Paul Light (1999, 64–69) notes, these goals are at the forefront when presidents decide where to focus their policy agendas and are instrumental in the president's efforts at public leadership. It is our contention that setting the agenda is central to the president's goal achievement.

Presidents want to set the agenda for short-term, political benefits. They seek to dictate the news and publicize the issues that are on their agendas to increase the chances that their policies may pass Congress. Presidents also want to highlight issues, especially when presidential and public preferences agree, as a way to maintain public and media focus on issues that benefit the president. For example, by prioritizing foreign policy during the first two years of his presidency, President George H. W. Bush maintained high approval ratings. Once Bush lost control of the agenda in late 1991, however, his popularity plummeted, setting the stage for a very difficult reelection campaign (see Edwards, Mitchell, and Welch 1995).[1] Maintaining attention to issues, especially those that the president's party "owns" and through which the public views the president favorably, is important to achieving short-term political goals (Holian 2006).

First-term presidents also desire reelection. Presidents want to prioritize issues that will help them achieve reelection, whether in response to public concern or to influence the public's agenda so that it matches their own priorities. Especially in the context of a reelection campaign, presidents will emphasize those issues on which the public views them most favorably (Jacobs and Shapiro 1994). Presidents who can set the policy agenda during their reelection campaigns are more likely to win. Light (1999, 65) even claims that reelection is the preeminent goal of presidents, trumping good public policy, such that the policies that presidents pursue are predicated on the electoral benefits they may receive from pursuing them.

Although the reelection goal is immaterial to second-term presidents due to the Twenty-Second Amendment, presidents still pursue public leadership to achieve their three primary goals throughout their tenure. First, presidents still desire good public policy during their second term in office. Light (1999) suggests that the beginning of a president's second term is the best time to achieve monumental legislative victories. Setting the agenda early in the second term is therefore imperative if presidents hope to translate their political capital into legislative success. Second, presidents continue to benefit from high job approval ratings during their second term because popularity may help achieve policy goals. Presidents are in a better position to influence their approval ratings, as we have already mentioned, if they control the policy agenda. Third, presidents might consider the prospects of their party in the intervening midterm congressional elections. If the president is successful in shaping even a handful of midterm congressional races, the president's prospects for policy success during the remainder of the second term increase (Cohen, Krassa, and Hamman 1991).

Presidents, particularly second-term presidents, do not simply consider the short-term benefits of public leadership; they also contemplate how their efforts may influence their place in history. When Congress is unresponsive and the public does not approve, for example, presidents can always hang their hat on the mantle of history's judgment (see Light 1999, 66). Setting the agenda is one way for presidents to do this. For example, as conditions worsened in Iraq and the public soured on his administration, President George W. Bush urged patience in judging his decisions. He believed his 2003 decision to invade Iraq would be vindicated and history would judge him favorably if Iraq were to become a stable democracy. If presidents cannot encourage the public to think about or the media to cover their top priorities, it is unlikely that presidents will be able to frame an issue in a way that favors their historical legacy.

Along with achieving reelection, what they perceive as good public policy, and a favorable historical legacy, presidents also attempt to lead the public agenda to meet public expectations. The public has high expectations for what presidents can accomplish. Whether they are successful or even capable of meeting these expectations, it is imperative that presidents communicate their efforts to the American people. It is often a failure of communication, presidents lament, that undermines their policy triumphs (Edward 2003, 4). Even though presidents may not generate additional political capital by going public, at least they can "do no harm" or please the converted (Edwards 2003, 244–246). Speaking to meet expectations, while reminding supporters why they elected the president in the first place, may be an effective way for presidents to emphasize their priorities and achieve their goals in the face of much difficulty.

Presidents enter office with a set of policies that they intend to pursue. It is these priorities that are the cornerstone of presidents' reelection chances and historical significance. The president's policy priorities are the focus of public leadership efforts. To be sure, these priorities are driven by a combination of the president's ideological predispositions, election campaign promises, and existing issues on the national agenda. Regardless of the origin of their policy priorities, presidents devote numerous resources to achieve these goals. By attempting to set the agenda, presidents try to raise awareness of policy issues that they think are important. If successful in setting the agenda, the president has met a vital criterion of policy change, despite much work that remains, including issue framing and coalition building in Congress.[2] Ultimately, however, agenda setting is important to presidents because it sets the stage for them to achieve their goals.

PRESIDENTIAL LEADERSHIP OF THE PUBLIC'S AGENDA

Although public leadership is a central governing strategy of modern presidents, one that is grounded in and consistent with most democratic theories, the prospects for presidential leadership of the public's agenda are inauspicious according to much of the research we have already reviewed. Additionally, our theory projects that the public's agenda itself is vital to understanding leadership and that responsiveness is conceptually tied to leadership. We conclude this section with our expectations for the likelihood of presidential leadership of the public's agenda.

The Prospects for Presidential Leadership of the Public's Agenda

Presidents are in a strong position to lead the public. Kernell (1997) argues that changing structural incentives for presidential leadership, including increasing instances of divided government and legislative gridlock, provide presidents with the motivation to speak directly to the American people—not legislators—to achieve their legislative goals. Surely, technological advances in communicating with the public (Lammers 1982); the prospects of speaking to large television audiences, especially in the

1970s (Baum and Kernell 1999); and organizational expertise in the White House (Kumar 2007; Maltese 1994) also motivate presidents to speak frequently. Whether or not presidents typically lead public support for policy issues, speaking more frequently in public has positioned presidents to be the primary agenda setters in American politics. Tying this to Theodore Roosevelt's notion of the "bully pulpit," presidents should be able to encourage others to take action, especially at the agenda-setting stage of the policy process (see Edwards and Barrett 2000).

Theoretically, we expect presidents to lead the public's agenda given the nature of human cognition. People look to process information in a relatively costless fashion. As such, they will use mental shortcuts to assess politics. Accessibility is a central feature of the public's decision making on policy (see Jones 1994, 72–73). Thus, people are most likely to use information that is easily accessible in determining the issues they think are most important, that is, their issue priorities. It follows that so long as a president can capture the attention of the American people through public rhetoric, influence over the issues the public finds most important should follow.

Zaller (1992) holds that opinion effects flow from elite to mass opinion. If true, then presidential leadership of mass opinion requires presidents to maintain the focus of the public on their own political message. Moreover, if the public responds to surveys in an off-the-top-of-one's-head fashion, as some scholars argue (Zaller and Feldman 1992), then presidents may find leadership of the public's agenda to be rather easy, at least in the short term. The president simply has to influence what the public is thinking about to engender short-term congruence between presidential and public agendas. Using an "aggressive foreign policy marketing strategy," for example, Ronald Reagan was able to parlay national addresses into increased public support for Grenada and Lebanon in the short term (Rosenblatt 1998). Generating a long-term impact should prove more difficult, however, because to do so presidents would need to maintain not only their own attention to an issue in the face of numerous responsibilities and unexpected developments but also deliver their messages in a way that will sustain the public's focus on presidential policy priorities. Moreover, the president may be forced to respond to public concerns over the long term.

Others confirm that the president can lead public opinion. B. Dan Wood (2007) argues that, by speaking frequently about the economy, presidents make their points of view more accessible to the public, resulting in a public response to presidential rhetoric on the economy. Bryan Jones (1994, 107) shows that a public response is a likely outcome for a national address. President George H. W. Bush's "War on Drugs" speech in 1989 significantly increased both media attention and public concern for the drug problem, prompting Jones to conclude that "a peak in awareness of the drug problem was caused primarily by presidential attention to it." In other words, Jones demonstrates that presidential attention can influence the public's agenda based in part on the malleability of public perceptions. Perceptions change based on the public's access to political information, and a presidential address is a primary way to increase access to the president's agenda. A limited body of research also illustrates that presidents lead the public's agenda, primarily using the State of the Union address (Cohen 1995; Hill 1998) or other major televised addresses (Behr and Iyengar 1985; Iyengar and Kinder 1987).

Despite the prospects for agenda leadership, there are numerous impediments. A long line of research documents the public's general disinterest in politics (Campbell et al. 1960). Neuman (1986) confirms that most Americans are, at best, only marginally interested in politics. Political disinterest matters when a president attempts to highlight a policy issue. If the president cannot count on the public to pay attention to the policies that *the president* thinks are important, then influence over what *the public* thinks is important is unlikely. Indeed, the public's lack of interest in politics may be the fundamental obstacle to successful leadership of the public's agenda.

The prospects for presidential leadership are further limited by the notion that presidential speeches are much less accessible to the public today than they used to be. According to Edwards (2003) the national audiences for Presidents Reagan, Bush, and Clinton were small and, among those who did tune in, substantial percentages often missed the main points of the message. Moreover, agenda-setting effects of State of the Union addresses have decayed over time (Young and Perkins 2005), and the end of the "golden age of presidential television" means that a much smaller audience watches televised addresses (Baum and Kernell 1999). Additionally, negative coverage of the presidency and an overall emphasis on soft news stories—which by definition do not address important public policies—epitomize the recent presidential news era (Cohen 2008). Even if presidents have a sizeable national audience, political predispositions make it difficult to ensure that the public takes the president's priorities as its own. After all, "people tend to resist arguments that are inconsistent with their political predispositions" (Zaller 1992, 44). Given that a significant percentage of the public is predisposed to disagree with the president, whether due to their partisanship or their disapproval of the president, the prospects for public leadership are diminished. Edwards (2003, 187) summarizes the difficulty of presidential leadership in the recent era when he writes, "Given the problems the president has in disseminating his message, the public's low interest in politics, and the easy access that cable television provides a large array of alternatives to news programs, we should expect that a large percentage of the public will not be aware of the president's messages." In short, although the tools available for presidential leadership of the public agenda are plentiful, the prospects for effective leadership are quite mixed.

How the Public Affects the President's Agenda

Whereas most research focuses on the president's ability to affect the public (defining that unidirectional relationship as leadership), we take care to emphasize the prominent role the public plays in this relationship. As we discussed in Chapter 2, presidents might be responsive to the public, a fundamental feature of democratic leadership (Burns 1978; Geer 1996). More pointedly, presidents have good reason to address issues of public concern in their speeches, whether to bolster reelection chances or to increase their ability to persuade legislators to support the administration's policy priorities (see Canes-Wrone 2006). As Geer (1996) suggests, such responsiveness by presidents is rational, and presidents are even more likely to be responsive in recent years as they can more reliably calculate public opinion through improved polling technology.

We agree with Geer (1996) that the existing distribution of public opinion may constrain or provide opportunities for presidential leadership. If the public's current priorities are unclear, the president is better situated to act entrepreneurially and set the public's agenda. Under such a context, the president has greater flexibility to choose which policies to prioritize, providing greater opportunity for leadership. In other words, when the public salience of an issue is low or when public priorities are unclear, the president is less constrained by the political environment. If public concern for an issue is high, however, the president is likely to respond to the public through speech making. Existing public concern for an issue limits the impact that presidential speeches may have on the public's concern for the issue, virtually eliminating the observation of presidential agenda leadership. This exposes a difficult condition for presidents to dictate the public's agenda: If the public is already attentive to an issue, the public may expect presidents to act, which may force presidents to prioritize responsiveness as a way to meet these expectations.[3]

This is not to say that presidents who respond to the public are ignoring democratic governance. Rather, presidents have a strong incentive to respond to public concerns in their public speeches given their goals. Presidents can still achieve policy success, reelection, and even an historical legacy by being responsive. When presidents are responsive, they may look to the public for what is important to them and use the public agenda as a guide for determining what policies to prioritize. This is at odds with being out in front of the public's agenda, which is what we typically conceive of when we think of agenda leadership. In the main, however, the president who chooses to follow—to pursue a policy that is already on the public agenda—may be severely limited in leading the public (Geer 1996, 24).

The Likelihood of Presidential Leadership of the Public's Agenda

Based on our theory and as expressed in the previous literature, we identify three possible expectations for presidential leadership of the public agenda. First, presidents are primary agenda setters in the American system of government (Kingdon 1995) and fulfill this role successfully vis-à-vis their influence over the public's agenda (Cohen 1995; Hill 1998). Second, presidents have much difficulty leading the public's agenda given a lack of public interest in politics and the public's tendency to be unresponsive to most presidential efforts to build public support (Edwards 2003). Third, the relationship between the president and the public may be reciprocal. The dynamics of leadership in the modern age suggest that the president and the public may continually adjust their agendas in response to each other. That is, the president who speaks about issues not currently on the public's agenda stands a greater chance of influencing public concern; yet the president may be inclined to respond to the public's agenda when the public register concern with an issue. Thus, presidents may increase their attention to an issue so that they may demonstrate resolve and responsiveness.

Consistent with this third expectation, we theorize that the public's agenda—specifically the level of importance the public gives to an issue—is a primary determinant of the likelihood of presidential attention to issues in public speeches, the president's agenda. Presidents simply have more capacity to affect the public on issues that are not already on their agenda because presidents can increase public attention to issues that have not yet registered as a problem with the public. When the public is already cognizant of a policy problem—when an issue is already salient to the public—then presidential responsiveness to the public's agenda is more likely. Further, the third expectation is more consistent with our reciprocal definition of the president's public leadership efforts and the causal mechanisms that we intend to illustrate. We qualify and refine these expectations in subsequent chapters because presidential leadership of public opinion should vary by leadership strategy and policy area. The media should play an important role as well.

PRESIDENTIAL LEADERSHIP OF
THE MEDIA'S AGENDA

We have argued so far that presidents have clear incentives and potential to influence the public's agenda. It is likely, nevertheless, that presidential leadership of the public's agenda is constrained by the public's agenda itself so that we cannot predict presidential leadership of the public's agenda without considering existing sentiment. This picture remains incomplete, nevertheless. Just as technological advances have increased the opportunities for presidential leadership of the public, so too have they increased presidents' reliance on news media. Given the absence of consistent presidential leadership of the public, especially after the golden age of presidential television, we contend that accounting for the media is essential to further comprehending the president's relationship with the public. In this section, we first identify whether presidents can lead the news media's agenda. Next, we explore the relevance of presidential responsiveness to the news media and how this shapes the potential for presidential leadership of the news agenda. Before we tackle the question of indirect presidential leadership of the public through the news media in the next section, we conclude this section with expectations about the one-to-one relationship between presidents and news media.

The Prospects for Presidential Leadership of the Media

Presidents are well positioned to lead the news media. The president is the focal point of news coverage in American politics (Graber 2006), and the White House is loaded with the institutional capacity to manage news routines (Kumar 2007; Maltese 1994). The White House provides the major source of information on politics for the news media (Ansolabehere, Behr, and Iyengar 1993), and public interest in presidential news is high when compared to demand for news on others in government (Gans 1979; Graber 2006). Without a doubt, other institutions, whether at the federal or state levels, cannot compete with the president's centrality to political news.

The structure of news production, including beats and the concept of gatekeeping, encourages presidential news. Each network has a White House correspondent to cover the president at need. Gatekeeping decisions—what gets into the news and what does not—are influenced by economic pressures and audience considerations (Hamilton 2004). It is economical for news organizations to report stories emanating from regular news beats, especially on a subject in which public interest is high. Moreover, news organizations are prone to reporting the official line, which increases the likelihood that the president's perspective will be reported more heavily than a legitimate criticism from an alternative governmental source.[4] Clearly, the structure of news routines can benefit a president as he attempts to influence what the news media cover.

A prominent view of political news coverage, which reflects this president-centered perspective of national news coverage, is that news is rather similar from day to day (Cook 1998) and the president provides media with a constant source of predictable and credible news. Indeed, the indexing theory of the press, offered by Bennett, Lawrence, and Livingston (2007, 49), suggests we should find a dependable relationship between the president and news media because

mainstream news generally stays within the official consensus and conflict displayed in the public statements of the key government officials who manage the policy areas and decision-making process that make the news. . . . The process is simplified by focusing on key policies that are in play . . . This ongoing, implicit calibration process conducted by the press corps creates a weighting system for what gets into the news (and) how long it gets covered.

Indexing by journalists tends to benefit the White House when its perspective dominates and goes unchallenged among other legitimate news sources (Bennett 1990). Problems might arise, however, for a president when others in power (including members of the opposition party in Congress) give voice to strong opposition. Nevertheless, indexing is driven "by the pervasive and direct dependence of journalists on sources for everything they report" (Zaller and Chiu 2000), and administration sources tend to dominate, given the significance of the White House beat. Indexing was quite prominent during the lead-up to the Iraq War in late 2002. Howell and Pevehouse (2007, 188) conclude that, overall, "journalists merely reflected the views expressed within Washington." Additionally, given the routines and sourcing that structure modern journalism, issues that are already on the agenda and are part of the debate are likely to stay there and be covered by the news. This adumbrates that if presidents can influence initially what is on the news, they should have a sustaining impact on the issues media cover. Extending this out in time, nevertheless, implies that the relationship may be reciprocal, such that the media's continued attention to what is on the agenda may encourage presidents to continue to prioritize the issue.

Furthermore, much is made of the idea that the profit- and government-driven media do not act adequately as watchdogs. Sparrow (1998, 133) describes the media instead as a "fourth corner" in the proverbial iron triangle (or square) of policy making, a compliant partner in the Washington power structure. This perspective predicts, we think, that the president, being the dominant political player in Washington, should drive news attention. The alternative to presidential leadership of the news is that other leaders in government, such as congressional leaders, might diverge from the president's message, thus creating mixed messages in the news. Yet because Congress plays a limited role in media agenda setting (Edwards and Wood 1999; Eshbaugh-Soha and Peake 2005; but see Howell and Pevehouse 2007) and tends to be mostly responsive to news coverage (Baumgartner and Jones 1993), this line of reasoning suggests substantial presidential influence over the news.

Given the demand for presidential news, presidents actively seek to cultivate news coverage (Grossman and Kumar 1981; Rozell 1996; Smoller 1990). Presidents attempt to manage the news media in a number of ways (Maltese 1994). They may do so indirectly, such as putting out the line of the day, coordinating news within the executive branch, conducting opinion polling and market research, and providing services for the press as mundane as travel arrangements and as critical as interview opportunities (Bennett 2003, 146–149). More directly, presidents routinely hold press conferences (Eshbaugh-Soha 2003; Hager and Sullivan 1994), travel abroad and domestically (Brace and Hinckley 1992; Cohen 2010), and deliver minor addresses to influence the news (Cohen 2008). The president's best opportunity to affect news coverage may be the national address, given the spectacle that accompanies televised speeches (Miroff 1990). Here, presidents typically gain a sizable, although diminishing, prime-time audience and the attention of the national media.

A president-driven event may present an opportunity for presidential leadership of the media. The president who creates (or is at least out in front of) the event, such as a missile strike, invasion, or White House–staged tours around the nation is in a good position to influence news coverage. President George W. Bush successfully influenced news coverage in the early days of his Social Security reform tour in 2005 (Eshbaugh-Soha and Peake 2006). To be sure, when presidents send American troops into harm's way, the media respond with heavy coverage (Peake 1999; Peake and Eshbaugh-Soha 2008). Such events may not only generate news coverage of the president's agenda but may also distract the public and decrease public concern for other issues, most notably the economy (DeRouen and Peake 2002).

It is clear that presidential activity and speech making attract media attention (Cohen 2010). What is not clear is whether presidential efforts at setting the media's agenda have a substantial long-term influence on the media's coverage of the issues. For example, analysis of the impact of State of the Union addresses on subsequent media attention to issues proves mixed. Although Lawrence (2004) finds a modest impact on media attention, Wanta and his coauthors (1989) report mixed results in their analysis of several addresses across two decades. Peake and Eshbaugh-Soha (2008) report that only a third of the forty nationally televised policy-specific addresses they examined had a statistically significant impact on nightly television news coverage of related issues.

The current literature is uncertain as to whether we should expect to find presidential influence over the media, as most examinations of the president's public speeches do not examine media but analyze influence over public opinion or Congress. The studies that do examine presidential speeches and media attention find substantial limits in presidential leadership of media. Analyses of event-driven foreign policy issues (Peake 2001; Wood and Peake 1998) and the economy (Eshbaugh-Soha and Peake 2005) indicate that, generally, presidents are responsive to media attention. Conversely, Canes-Wrone (2006, 73) finds only a marginal impact of media attention on the propensity for public appeals by the president on budgetary proposals; an impact that disappears once the public's approval of the president's policy is taken into consideration. Although Wood and his colleagues (2005) illustrate the importance of media to presidential leadership of the economy, their study includes a measure only of the public's perception of news—whether or not the public heard negative news—not a direct measure of news coverage. As Wood (2007, 168) himself points out, his study cannot comment on the complexities of the relationship between presidential rhetoric and the media due in part to the absence of a measure of the media's agenda in his models of the presidency, public opinion, and the economy.

It is likely that the prospects for leadership of the media have dimmed considerably in recent years. Previously, presidents expected mostly positive and hard (or policy-driven) news coverage delivered to a sizeable portion of the American public. Grossman and Kumar (1981) show that between 1953 and 1978 (and especially before 1965), presidents could expect more positive than negative news. Since the rise of cable television and other forms of "new media" (such as talk radio and the Internet), however, presidential news has focused less on policy and become more negative, just as the audience for presidential news and public trust of the news media have declined substantially. Cohen (2008) illustrates, indeed, that television coverage of the presidency has declined since 1980, negative coverage of the presidency in newspapers has increased dramatically since 1949, and the policy content of presidential news has summarily declined. A substantial body of work reveals severe limitations to presidential leadership of the media. Even so, the existing evidence is incomplete because it does not simultaneously account for public pressures on media to respond to presidential leadership.

How Media Affect the President's Agenda

Just as the current public agenda constrains or provides opportunities for presidential leadership of the public, so too does the news media agenda condition presidential leadership of the media. Thus, accounting for the power of news media is vital to a complete assessment of the probabilities for successful presidential agenda setting. If the media influence presidential agendas, much as we have argued the public does, then the prominence of an issue on the media's agenda may preclude presidential leadership and promote responsiveness. Linsky (1986) illustrates that government elites are highly responsive to the media's agenda. He surveyed dozens of political officials and journalists and concluded that the media have a large, identifiable impact in setting the policy agenda:

Policymakers generally share the view that among the most significant impacts of the press occur early on in the policymaking process, when it is not yet clear which issues will be addressed and what questions will be decided. Officials believe that the media do a lot to set the policy agenda and to influence how an issue is understood by policymakers, interest groups, and the public. (Linsky 1986, 87)

Linksy also finds that, even though officials often try to influence what the press covers, "there was an overall sense that in general the press, or perhaps the public through the press, was the dominant force in controlling the agenda" (Linsky 1986, 92). Rogers and Dearing (2000, 82), in their review of the literature, confirm that media "have a direct, sometimes strong, influence upon the policy agenda of elite decision makers." They suggest an indirect agenda-setting link, as well, such that the media influence the mass public's agenda, which in turn affects the policy agenda of elites in government. Jacobs and Shapiro (2000) support a similar relationship in their work.

Part of the effectiveness of media-to-elite agenda setting relates to media coverage of events that arise independent of presidential action. Acting as gatekeepers, reporters, producers, and editors can "choose from among myriad events . . . which to describe, which to ignore" (Cater 1959, 7). Focusing events and subsequent media attention may force a presidential response. According to accounts by Secretary of State Lawrence Eagleburger, for example, television coverage of starving children in Somalia encouraged President George H. W. Bush to send troops to Mogadishu in 1992. Eagleburger stated, "Somalia, yes—television made a big difference because of the daily drumbeat of pictures of starving children" (quoted in Hess and Kalb 2003). Foreign policy icon George F. Kennon (1993), in an op-ed in the *New York Times*, similarly concluded that media images influenced Bush's policy response in the case of Somalia (Kennon 1993).[5] Major domestic events can also force a presidential response. For example, on May 1, 1992, President George H. W. Bush delivered a national address in response to the Los Angeles riots that followed the trial and acquittal of police accused of beating Rodney King. More recently, President Barack Obama used a national address to demonstrate his commitment to cleaning up BP's massive oil spill in the Gulf of Mexico. Extensive news coverage of an event may undermine presidential leadership, however, by forcing responsiveness to these issues not previously on the president's agenda. The president may be seen as late to the game, as was the case with Obama and the oil spill. What is more, the public tends to be least interested in news about international events and foreign policy,[6] augmenting the media's agenda-setting role over this policy area.

In the absence of a hard news event that must be covered, the news media may diverge from their coverage of politics and the presidency altogether. Presidential efforts to generate news of their policies compete with Americans' preferences for infotainment and soft news coverage of celebrities and scandal. Thus, an event surrounding a Hollywood celebrity may supersede coverage of even a major presidential event or policy announcement, as profit-seeking news media try to satisfy audience preferences. For example, the PEW Research Center for the People and the Press reports that even three weeks after the death of pop icon Michael Jackson on June 25, 2009, news coverage and reported interest by viewers in Michael Jackson was substantially higher than President Obama's first state visit to Russia, the poor state of the economy, and health care reform under consideration in Congress.[7] This situation does not entirely preclude presidential leadership of the news media, nevertheless, so long as the president can compete with such infotainment by addressing policies that are timely and novel and do so in a way that will generate news coverage.

The Likelihood of Presidential Leadership of the Media's Agenda

Media are not beholden to the presidency for news. There is limited space in newspapers and magazines and limited time on network news broadcasts and cable news channels. Accordingly, news gatekeepers have significant influence over what becomes a story and what does not. Even though the president is especially newsworthy, media are driven more by profit than presidents, so newscasts and newspapers must appeal to the breadth of society, many of whom share little interest in politics (Prior 2007). Entertainment, infotainment, and pseudocrises may drive news coverage irrespective of the president's policy agenda. Soft news coverage of important international events may also ignore the substantive policy issues in favor of episodic frames and personal interest stories (Baum 2003). Because decisions that news organizations make will reflect audience preferences and ownership's demand for profits and cost cutting, the president may be left off the air, so to speak.

According to the profit-seeker model of news, news making is a business, so media will appeal to their readers, viewers, or listeners, much as any business will respond to its customers (Leighley 2004). Consequently, the news audience may influence the media's agenda. Indeed, it is this customer-to-business relationship that leads us to believe that the public should have a significant impact over whether media cover a set of stories. The president is likely to be a part of this equation, but not always. This presents an obstacle to presidents who hope to generate news of their policies when the American people—and media's profits, therefore—are tied more directly to soft news coverage of celebrities and scandal, or the president's personality, than they are to policies.

In light of the quantitative evidence and our theory, we expect presidents to have some difficulty leading the media. Yet this is a reciprocal and dynamic relationship, so the presence of media attention invariably influences the likelihood of presidential leadership of the media. Therefore, presidential leadership of the news media tends to be most likely on issues where presidents may act as entrepreneurs, prioritizing issues not previously on the agenda. If the president gets ahead of the news media, acting as a policy entrepreneur, he should be in a stronger position to lead news coverage (Edwards and Wood 1999; Peake 2001). This is especially important when it comes to presidential strategies, as national addresses, themselves, should be especially newsworthy and most likely to affect media attention. Naturally, events play an important role, as they mitigate or expand opportunities for presidential leadership, particularly on foreign policy issues (Andrade and Young 1996; Peake 2001).

Our discussion suggests the following proposition: Presidents are uniquely situated to lead the news media and will have some success doing so, despite numerous impediments. We expect that, as long as presidents can act entrepreneurially and focus on policies that are not currently on the media's agenda, they will be successful leaders. As with the public's agenda, however, presidents will be responsive to news coverage when media are consumed by an issue before the president emphasizes it. Moreover, policy variation matters to the prospects for presidential leadership of the media and different strategies of leadership present different possibilities for influence over the media. Because the president's ultimate goal in speaking publicly is affecting the public, leading the media may be a means to that end, promoting indirect leadership of the public's agenda.

NEWS MEDIA AND PRESIDENTIAL
LEADERSHIP OF THE PUBLIC

The news media present a vital intervening link between the president and public in American democracy. From Cohen (1963) to McCombs (2004), a long tradition of scholarship recognizes the central role that the news media play in affecting the public's policy agenda. Given that the media can emphasize any number of events to the exclusion of others, issues that the media focus on tend to remain on the public agenda. Conversely, but equally important, those issues that the media ignore are likely to fade from the public agenda. Presidential leadership of the public's agenda could therefore be indirect and occur through leadership of the news media. Given that the news media have an impact on the public's agenda, if presidents can affect media attention to issues, the potential exists for indirect presidential leadership of the public's agenda through news coverage.

This view of news media influence over the public has been supported in numerous studies by a generation of scholars interested in media effects. News media influence what issues are important to the public (Iyengar and Kinder 1987; Iyengar et al. 1982; McCombs 2004); media attention to an issue affects public familiarity with that issue (Page and Shapiro 1992); and media coverage of issues primes the public's evaluation of the president (Edwards et al. 1995; Iyengar 1991; Krosnick and Kinder 1990). Not only do media have a positive influence on the public's agenda, but some argue that media are so important that, without media attention, issues simply will not reach the public agenda. Maxwell McCombs (1976, 3) contends, "This basic, primitive notion of agenda-setting is a truism. If the media tell us nothing about a topic or event, then in most cases it simply will not exist on our personal agenda or in our life space."

The theoretical underpinnings of these media effects are similar to those we outline in the preceding pages regarding possible direct influence of presidential attention on public opinion. Much as presidential speeches increase accessibility of information to public evaluation, so too does media coverage of certain issues make those issues more accessible to individuals when forming their opinions (Leighley 2004; Scheufele 2000). Moreover, coverage in the news means that an issue is more likely to be considered an important national problem by individuals given their use of social cues when making political evaluations (Miller and Krosnick 2000). Thus, a potential pathway for presidents to influence the public is through their influence over the media. This is especially pronounced given the fewer opportunities afforded presidents today to directly set the public's agenda since the rise of cable television news has seriously diminished audiences for presidents' speeches (Cohen 2008).

Ostensibly, the president is in a relatively favorable position to affect the public's agenda through increased news coverage. The president's routine activities are newsworthy, after all, as he is the single most covered individual in the news (Gans, 1979, 9; see Graber 2006). Moreover, 67 percent of readers of local newspapers have at least some interest in stories devoted to the U.S. government (Bogart 1989, 301–302), and, according to the Pew Research Center (2008, 39), 21 percent of Americans follow politics and Washington news "very closely." Given that media cover the president more than any other national politician, these studies indicate not only that presidents should influence what is on the news but also that the news audience prefers these stories. What is more, media agenda-setting effects over the public tend to persist for some time (Iyenger and Kinder 1987, 25), suggesting the possibility that presidents can sustain the public's attention if they can first influence the news media.

There may be a supporting effect, too. Although the literature reports limited presidential leadership of public opinion, it has yet to consider the tendency for media to cover some presidential stories more or less than others. If these same studies included measures of media attention—a necessary component to the public presidency, we argue—presidential speeches may become magnified in the context of presidential leadership efforts. Consequently, models that exclude media attention may underestimate the impact that presidential speeches have on the public's agenda. For example, Hayes (2008) shows that political candidates are most effective influencing the public's campaign agenda when candidates and media focus on the same issues.

In practice, however, indirect leadership through the media is not a given. Jacobs and Shapiro (2000, 64–65) recognize the importance of media to presidential efforts at public leadership. They argue that politicians influence the media because the media report on the content of the very proposals politicians put forth. Such logic recognizes how politicians may affect public opinion indirectly through media coverage. Nevertheless, Jacobs and Shapiro find that President Clinton was ultimately unable to shape media coverage in a way that would secure his health care reform goals, and media coverage ultimately drove the public to oppose Clinton's proposal. Baum and Groeling (2010) illustrate the central importance of media to public support for U.S. policy in Iraq. Contrary to indexing theory, which holds that news coverage simply mirrors a policy reality proffered by government officials, these authors show that media are vital intermediaries that shape the public's support for the war in Iraq. Mainly, the media's influence over the public varies by the perceived credibility (or partisan leaning) of a news organization, and the way in which the media cover the war, including the range of supportive or opposition rhetoric by elites in the news, strongly affects public support for the war effort. Given the driving negativity of news, this study also implies that presidential leadership of the public is confounded by an independent and often countervailing news media.

A counterargument to our contention that media are central to presidential leadership of the public is that the media matter less today to the president–public relationship than they used to. This is Cohen's (2008, 1) argument: "News coverage of the presidency no longer resonates so strongly with the mass public." The implication is that the current state of presidential–media relations should confound presidential efforts at leading the public. If Cohen is correct, then even if presidents can set the media's agenda, this is no guarantee—indeed, it is highly unlikely—that presidents can lead the public indirectly through the news media. The current media environment, therefore, may present presidents with the proverbial double whammy: Presidents have less direct influence over the public through focused events, such as the nationally televised address (Baum and Kernell 1999) or the State of the Union (Young and Perkins 2005) and, according to Cohen (2008), cannot expect to see their leadership of the media translate into leadership of the public.

Such a pessimistic view of presidential leadership in the new media age suggests that we should find no indirect link between the president and public, facilitated by the news media. Conversely, media may be even more important now to presidential leadership of the pubic given presidents' more limited ability to reach the public through national addresses. Whether our analysis supports or rejects Cohen's assertion, his expectations are valuable because no scholarship has tested them by modeling simultaneously the president, public, and media agendas.[8] In short, if there is no relationship between presidential attention and the public agenda, then we can explain why presidents are unable to lead the public. Such an inability would rest with their difficulty in leading the news media in the first place.

The Likelihood of Indirect Leadership

There is a strong and unequivocal link between the news media and the public. For over a half-century, scholars have marshaled firm evidence that the media directly influence the public's agenda. Presidents who can affect news coverage, therefore, may be able to lead the public's agenda in a fashion that previous research may have missed. This possibility presents great difficulty, but substantial opportunity, for presidential leadership of the public. On the one hand, and as we have already reviewed, the likelihood for direct presidential leadership of the media is not guaranteed. On the other hand, the president can expect numerous opportunities to lead the media. If the president can influence the media's agenda, given the link between the public and news media, the president may be able to indirectly lead the public. This is perhaps even more likely than direct presidential leadership of the public. Theoretically, agenda setting is about the president providing information shortcuts, not only to the public but also to the news media. If the media cover the presidency, then it is the media that provide short-cuts to the public and increase the people's accessibility to the president's agenda.

Our expectation of indirect presidential leadership of the public through news media is a by-product of our theoretical argument about public cognition and the media's profit incentive. The profit incentive drives the relationship between the public and the news media such that media make money the more viewers and readers they have. Undoubtedly, the news media can ignore the president but, especially for political news, the public expects and prefers coverage of the presidency over any other political institution. The media are, therefore, likely to cover the president when he is newsworthy, and a correlation between what is on the news and what the public thinks about should be positive and relatively strong. The reason the public will respond to the news media rests considerably on the nature of public cognition: The public looks for mental shortcuts to discern vast amounts of relevant (and sometimes inconsequential) bits of information. The news media simplify this process for the public, making it easy for them to know what is important in society and also to the president. So long as the media also cover what the president speaks about (having established several reasons why this should occur regularly), then the president should be able to lead the public's agenda indirectly through increased news coverage of the president's policy agenda.

APPLYING THE THEORY

Thus far, we have argued several key points. First, presidential leadership of the media and public is reciprocal, and its full treatment requires consideration of both presidential influence over the media and public and *their* impact on presidential speech making. Second, presidential leadership of the public agenda is steeped with complications, ranging from a lack of public interest in presidential rhetoric to the immovability of ingrained opinions held by the American people. Third, media are profit seekers, which may undermine the president's ability to set the media's agenda. Fourth, because presidents need the media to influence public opinion, any difficulties presidents may face leading the media may also undercut presidents' ability to reach the public and thus influence their agenda. Each of these points has led to broad expectations about presidential leadership of the public and the media, and the important role that media may play in the prospects for successful presidential leadership through agenda setting.

Taken together, these expectations suggest the following causal diagrams. The first set of diagrams, shown in Figure 3.1, illustrates both leadership and responsiveness. As our theory contends, considering the public and media dictates either leadership or responsiveness. On the one hand, when an issue is of little concern to the public or news media, the president is in a strong position to lead the agenda. On the other hand, if

FIGURE 3.1. Expectations for presidential leadership or responsiveness.

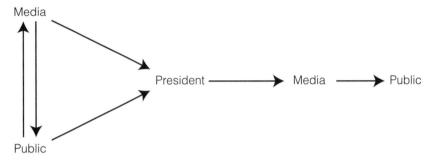

FIGURE 3.2. A causal diagram of indirect presidential leadership of the public.

an issue is already of high public concern or heavily covered by the news media, then the president is likely to be responsive to the public or media. This constitutes our *salience hypothesis*.

We illustrate a more complete model of presidential agenda-setting leadership, taking into account the various interrelationships we described above, in Figure 3.2. Just as we expect media influence over the public, so too do we think that this will be reciprocal, as public preferences may also influence news coverage. Just as the media and public agendas should influence the president's agenda, we only expect this, as illustrated in Figure 3.1, when public concern and news coverage are already high. Absent this, presidents are in a better position to lead directly the media and public agendas (as in Figure 3.1) but also are well positioned to indirectly lead the public's agenda through increased news coverage, our *indirect leadership hypothesis*. As also illustrated in Figure 3.2, the prospects for indirect leadership of the public's agenda are not necessarily precluded if the president is also responsive to the public's high level of concern to a policy problem.

Presidential leadership does not, however, occur in a vacuum. This is illustrated in three ways. First, as Edwards (2009) makes clear, the larger contextual environment should condition successful public leadership. Just as some opportunities may facilitate leadership, other conditions may restrict the prospects for leadership of the public and news media. Second, the policy area in which the president attempts to lead matters. Some policy domains are more amenable to presidential leadership than others, as is commonly put forth by the notion of "two presidencies," one for foreign and defense policy and one for domestic and economic policy (Canes-Wrone, Howell, and Lewis 2007; Wildavsky 1966; but see Bond and Fleisher 1988; 1990; Edwards 1989). Third, the president's choice of leadership strategy is likely to matter. We have identified three strategies—focused attention, sustained attention, and going local—that we discuss in the following pages and apply in our three empirical chapters.

Conditional Leadership

The president's propensity to speak about policy issues should be conditioned by the larger political context, in addition to any impact that the public and media may have on presidential leadership. The news media's decision to cover the president or a policy should be conditioned by the larger political environment, as well. Finally, the public's tendency to pay attention to the news media or president will also vary. Theoretically, several factors should condition presidential leadership of the public and media. The factors include presidential approval ratings, reelection years, the president's term in office, and real-world cues as indicated by important international and domestic events and the objective economy.

Presidential Approval   Presidential approval ratings should condition presidential agenda setting. The president's public approval ratings act as an informational cue to others in the political system. This has worked most notably with the president's relationship with Congress, as high approval ratings increase presidential success in Congress (Rivers and Rose 1985). Presidential approval ratings provide legislators with information about how the public views the president and, inferentially, the president's policies. As long as partisanship does not impinge on this relationship and undermine the cue's relevance to legislators (see Bond, Fleisher, and Wood

2003), high approval ratings should increase the president's legislative success rate. The converse, that presidents will be less successful when their public support is low, should also hold true (Neustadt 1990).

The president's approval ratings should affect the likelihood that presidents influence either the public or the media agendas for similar reasons. Higher approval ratings prime the public to be more responsive to the president by making the public more receptive to the president's message. The public should be more receptive to popular presidents, according to cue theory, because higher approval ratings equal more credibility. In short, a message sent by a credible source is more likely to be believed and accepted (Matthews and Stimson 1976; Mondak 1993). This is similar, in an aggregate sense, to Zaller's (1992, 44) resistance axiom, whereby individuals resist messages that counter their political predispositions. One way to measure current disposition is public approval. If the public approves of the president, they should be less resistant and thus more receptive of the president's message. Thus, high presidential approval creates a more favorable environment for presidential leadership. Unpopular presidents are often marginalized and less relevant, providing additional evidence for the importance of presidential approval ratings to presidential leadership of the public (see Wood 2009a, 143).

Limited research supports the idea that higher approval ratings lead to an increase in public support for the president's policies (Page and Shapiro 1985). Yet, unpopular presidents can be the "kiss of death" to a public policy, as the public is likely to oppose a policy if an unpopular president's name is attached to the proposal (Sigelman 1980). Although Cohen (1995) finds little impact of approval ratings on presidential influence over the public agenda, Wood's (2009a, 145) results may be most telling: Although the public tends to react negatively to the president's efforts at persuasion, the exception appears to be when the president's approval ratings are above average.

Additionally, presidents may be less responsive to public concerns when they are highly popular, increasing the chances that they will act in an entrepreneurial fashion to set the agenda. When their public standing is high, presidents may choose to tackle difficult issues and spend some of their political capital to achieve a legislative victory. Although presidential selection of which issues to prioritize may be strategic even when presidents are popular (Canes-Wrone 2006), presidents may be more likely to focus on issues irrespective of public opinion when their approval ratings are above average (Rottinghaus 2006). Conversely, presidents with below-average approval ratings may be similarly unresponsive to public opinion. It is those presidents who have near-average support, with a bare majority perhaps, who are most likely to be responsive to public opinion (Canes-Wrone and Shotts 2004).

The media also use public approval as a cue to decide whether to cover the president. Yet, the extent of the relationship is unclear. If the public supports the president, news organizations can glean that the public wants more news about the president and thus provide more news coverage on the White House. Indeed, local areas that support the president cover him more in amount and in a more positive tone than those areas that do not support him (Barrett and Peake 2007; Eshbaugh-Soha 2010b; Eshbaugh-Soha and Peake 2006). Extended television news coverage of a president's national addresses on the economy is also more likely when he has high approval ratings (Peake and Eshbaugh-Soha 2008). Surely, presidents tend to receive more positive coverage during their honeymoon period (Grossman and Kumar 1981), which is also when they are likely to be most popular. Conversely, the profit-seeker model indicates that negative news coverage of the presidency is more interesting to viewers and, therefore, is more prominent (Farnsworth and Lichter 2006). Negative stories about the president are also more attractive to news media. Groeling and Kernell (1998), for example, demonstrate how the television networks are more likely to cover declining rather than increasing presidential approval ratings (see also Groeling 2008). Even so, Cohen (2010, 116) reports that approval ratings matter little to national news coverage of the presidency, though it appears to influence the tone of local newspaper coverage (165).

Finally, the president's own decision to speak in the first place may be conditioned by approval ratings. If the president thinks that he will be more effective leading the public or influencing news coverage when he is popular, then it makes sense for him to speak more often when approval ratings are high. Yet, once again, the evidence is mixed. Studies that examine annual presidential speech making find no link between approval ratings and the number of yearly speeches (Hager and Sullivan 1994; Powell 1999; but see Eshbaugh-Soha 2010a). Others show that changes in approval ratings lead to an increased likelihood of a national address (Ragsdale 1984), even though the scholarly record is mixed. Canes-Wrone (2001) finds no such link between presidential approval and her measure of public appeals delivered through national addresses.

Reelection Years and Term in Office   Timing matters to presidential leadership. Presidents should be most cognizant of the public's issue concerns during their first term in office and especially while they are up for reelection. Although this suggests that presidents are conditionally responsive (Canes-Wrone and Shotts 2004), it also implies that presidential leadership is conditional. Presidents who choose to be responsive and cater to public concerns during their first term in office and especially during reelection years will then be less able to lead the public. Reelection is a primary goal of sitting presidents, after all, and so the president's agenda should align with the public's more so during reelection years when compared to all other years because a president wishes to appear most responsive to public concerns when voters are about to decide whether to support him for another term in office. Accordingly, presidential attention to issues should increase as the president campaigns for reelection. Without the specter of reelection, conversely, presidents presumably could prioritize issues unrelated to public concern. This may mean tackling large and complicated issues during the second term in office, contributing to a less pronounced link between the public's and president's agendas during a second term. In short, the theory of conditional leadership suggests that first-term presidents and presidents during reelection years should increase their public attention to issues of public concern.

Events and Real-World Cues   Events should condition the likelihood of presidential leadership in three ways. First, events focus attention on related issues, causing the president, the media, and presumably the public to take on the issue as part of their respective agendas. Second, events related to one issue can disrupt what Wood and Peake (1998) term the "economy of attention" by causing the president or media to shift focus away from other issues in their efforts to respond to the event. For instance, a dramatic event that leads to a presidential response, like the Iraqi invasion of Kuwait in August 1990, necessarily diminishes presidential and media attention to other foreign policy issues. Third, focusing events driven by the president's own actions, such as an invasion order or other use of force, may promote agenda leadership by attracting media and public attention (DeRouen and Peake 2002). Events are especially important to control for given that "news accounts remain fairly stable after policy decisions are taken . . . , until the next decisive moment occurs, in which case the Washington consensus and news accounts may shift again" (Bennett et al. 2007, 50). Any new event may be crucial to shifting the attention of the president, public, or news media.

Real-world cues, in particular objective economic conditions, can dictate media coverage and public concern for a variety of issues in several ways. Real-world cues may condition the receptivity of the public to media messages. For example, as economic conditions worsen, individuals may be concerned about the economy and thus more likely to pay attention to news coverage about it. This, in turn, could reinforce public concern about economic issues (Erbring, Goldenberg, and Miller 1980),[9] perhaps leading to additional media or presidential attention. Although real-world cues do not always accurately predict the public's agenda (see, as an example, Iyengar and McGrady 2007, 211), ignoring them may overstate the impact that media have on the public's agenda (Behr and Iyengar 1985).

Policy Differences

Public policy matters to political processes in many ways (Lowi 1972). Some policies encourage public involvement, whereas others are best suited for action outside of the public's eye (Gormley 1986). Policy conditions the impact that presidential approval ratings have on the president's legislative success rate (Canes-Wrone and de Marchi 2002), the effectiveness of presidential speeches over bureaucratic and congressional policy decisions (Eshbaugh-Soha 2006a), and the extent of policy learning and diffusion in the America states (Nicholson-Crotty 2009). Eshbaugh-Soha and Peake (2004) found that presidents are more influential over media attention to salient and uncomplicated policies (such as civil rights) than highly complex and low salience policies (such as farm policy). Given these findings, it is plausible that variation by policy area will shape our findings.

One of the most enduring applications of policy differences and their impact on presidential leadership is the two presidencies thesis (Wildavsky 1966; also see Canes-Wrone et al. 2007). The two presidencies thesis contends that presidents, having greater constitutional authority on national security policy than Congress, are better situated to lead on foreign and defense policy than on domestic or economic policy. The president is on firm constitutional ground when leading in foreign policy given his clear roles as commander in chief and chief negotiator of international agreements. The president also has ample institutional resources devoted to monitoring and pursuing foreign policies. The unilateral tools presidents use to make foreign policy are numerous, including national security directives and findings, uses of force and movement of troops, and executive agreements (Cooper 2002; Crenson and Ginsberg 2007; Howell and Pevehouse 2007; Krutz and Peake 2009). It is these tools that undergird what some have termed the "imperial presidency" (Rudalevige 2005; Schlesinger 1973).

Although Congress is also important to foreign policy making (Lindsay 1994) and presidential leadership in foreign policy varies by the political context (McCormick and Wittkopf 1990; 1992), the White House maintains advantages over foreign and defense policy that it does not have over the domestic and economic policy arenas. This is so even though Wildavsky's (1966) basis for declaring a two presidencies thesis, as it relates to legislative success, has proven to be time bound (Bond and Fleisher 1988; Edwards 1989; Fleisher et al. 2000; Meernik 1993). Indeed, much recent scholarship finds important differences between presidential leadership capabilities over foreign and defense policies than economic and domestic policies (Canes-Wrone et al. 2007; Marshall and Pacelle 2005; Prins and Marshall 2001). This mixed evidence concerns presidential–congressional relations, however, leaving open the possibility that differences may correspond more clearly to the president's interactions with the public and news media. In some cases, it is the president's own words that dictate U.S. foreign policy. For example, a presidential statement may become a "doctrine" and form the basis for future foreign policy (Crabb 1982).

This alone justifies additional exploration of the two presidencies as applied to the president's public leadership capabilities.

Analysis of public opinion and media reveals some variation by foreign and domestic policy that may affect presidential leadership. First, although the public is uninterested in politics generally, it is least interested in foreign policy issues (Wittkopf 1990). A majority of the public follows international news "only when something is happening," and just 26 percent of Americans follow foreign policy issues "very closely." [10] Holsti (2004, 55) also finds that the American public is "poorly informed" about international affairs, suggesting that one has to be interested in international affairs to be informed about it. Moreover, the public tends to defer to leaders on foreign policy issues. These conditions suggest a greater propensity for presidential leadership of the public's agenda on foreign policy than other policy areas.

Second, presidents may be more likely to lead the media on foreign than other policy issues. Indexing theory posits (Bennett 1990) and Zaller and Chiu (1996) demonstrate that elites generally lead the news media on foreign policy issues. The profit incentive of media also ensures that if the public is less interested in an issue, then the media will be less likely to cover it. Moreover, news coverage of foreign policy issues is less common given the institutional constraints against producing it, as many news organizations, including network television news, lack international news bureaus with which to cover extensively international events (Graber 2006). Consistent with our theory that presidents are more likely to lead on issues that are not of high news coverage, this evidence suggests that the news media should be more likely to follow the president's policy agenda on foreign policy than other issues and that presidents should find it easier to influence the public's agenda as a result. These differences should be more pronounced in recent decades as the amount of attention given to international issues in American news publications and programs has declined precipitously. During the 1970s, the share of television news stories devoted to international news was 45 percent. But by 1995, this plummeted to 14 percent (Hoge 1997). Besides, only if something is happening, such as the Persian Gulf War or war in Iraq, do news organizations send numerous reporters on location to cover it (see Bennett 2009, 22–23).

Combined, the evidence for policy differences strongly suggests that presidential leadership should be greater in foreign policy than in other policy areas. First, lower public interest in foreign policy increases the likelihood that presidents will be out in front of the public's agenda. Second, media indexing and business constraints on foreign policy news production imply that presidents are more likely to dictate the media's agenda on foreign policy issues. By contrast, domestic and economic issues may promote presidential responsiveness given the public's greater interest in these policies and the media's desire to cover what interests the public.

Policy Selection

Of the myriad domestic and foreign policy issues available to analyze, we selected the economy and Iraq, two of the most important issues addressed by recent presidents. There is little debate that the economy is important to the American presidency. The state of the economy is vital not only to presidential approval ratings (Brody 1991; Kernell 1978; Zaller 1998) but also to electoral success (Campbell 2000; Erikson 1989; Tufte 1978). The public typically holds presidents responsible for the state of the economy (Rudolph 2003), which encourages presidents to devote substantial resources to improving it (Wood 2007). If the president can affect the economic agendas of the public and media, he may benefit both politically and electorally. Next in importance for presidents is foreign policy. Presidents are typically held responsible for foreign policy, making it important electorally (Hurwitz and Peffley 1987). Like economic policy, foreign policy often structures presidential approval ratings (Kernell 1978; Mueller 1973; Zaller 1998), especially when it is salient (Edwards et al. 1995).[11] Of the myriad foreign policy issues that have affected the presidency over the past several decades, Iraq proves to be the issue most relevant to presidential and American politics, as two wars with Iraq and intermittent conflict have kept the issue on the agenda for presidents since 1990.[12] Therefore, we selected the economy for its obvious importance to the presidency and Iraq because it is an important foreign policy issue that has garnered substantial attention over the past twenty years.

Examining the economy and Iraq ensures that we can quantify both the reciprocal nature of leadership and test for indirect presidential effects through news coverage. It goes without saying that the economy is highly salient to the American public.[13] Foreign policy is also of great concern to the American people, especially during wartime (Smith 1980).[14] Iraq has been of particular concern to presidents, the public, and media for most of the past twenty years. Examining only a broad policy category, such as the economy, provides less variation than we need to properly test our salience hypothesis, however. For this reason, in our analysis in Chapter 5, we also disaggregate the economy into two subsets, unemployment and spending and deficits. The two subsets tend to vary a priori by public salience, with unemployment being of relatively high salience and spending and deficits being of relatively low salience.[15] In Chapter 6, we add another dimension to the generalizability of our findings by testing our hypotheses according to three very specific policies—tax cuts, Social Security, and health care reform.[16] This policy variation allows us to account for whether evidence of presidential leadership or responsiveness is an artifact of broad policy categories or the specific public policies we have selected.

Ideally, we would examine an even wider range of policy areas derived from a broad policy schema to ensure the generalizability of our findings and provide even greater variation in issue salience over time. Doing so would be impractical for a number of reasons. Primarily, exploring the dynamics of presidential leadership of the media and public requires a lengthy time series to ensure that inferences drawn are reliable. Data availability is a central requirement for examining time series dynamics in general and for us to be able to test our indirect leadership hypothesis, in particular. Public opinion data is particularly sparse over time (see Monroe 1998). Thus, we select the economy and Iraq as best test cases for assessing the propensity for presidential leadership of and responsiveness to the public and media. Doing so ensures that we have sufficient data to test our hypotheses and provides modest variability by policy area within a two presidencies framework.

Given that the economy may not be representative of other domestic policy areas and that Iraq may not be representative of other foreign policies, our results may not be reflected in an examination of a wider range of policies. Our issue selection, in other words, may reveal the propensity for presidents to lead or respond regarding the economy and Iraq alone. We hope to minimize some of these concerns by examining more specific subsets of economic issues, for example, unemployment and deficits in Chapter 5 and the more specific policies of tax cuts, Social Security, and health care reform in Chapter 6. Because our hypotheses center on an issue's salience, moreover, they are broad enough for future scholarship to test them according to a different set of policies. We comment further on the generalizability of our findings—and what we expect future scholarship to find—in the concluding chapter.

Three Strategies of Leadership

Unlike the "golden age of presidential television" of the 1970s when a president could count on high television ratings when he delivered a national address, presidents now must cultivate media coverage to even reach the public's ear. This means that the White House communications operation creates media events—such as joint press conferences with foreign leaders or staged speeches—to generate news coverage while the president is in Washington. Additionally, presidents engage in travel across the country to cultivate local news coverage. Although presidents also use national addresses to reach the public, successfully affecting the public's priorities through national addresses may be tied to the president's efforts to sustain media attention after the speech. Whether presidents lead using a sustained, focused, or going local strategy, each is an effort by presidents to influence public opinion, either directly or indirectly through the news media. As we will treat each strategy separately in the following chapters, with an eye toward refining our expectations based on these strategies of communication, we only summarize them as part of our theoretical framework here.

Focused leadership entails using a nationally televised address to lead the media and public. This is arguably the best strategy for presidential leadership, at least in the short term, as media are predisposed to cover the president's national addresses. The public is likely to pay some attention to a national address or at least news coverage of it. What is more, a novel and innovative policy proposal announced during a national address should stimulate significant news coverage (Cohen 2008, 75). Nationally televised addresses also provide the president with a visible opportunity to respond to the public or media, an important responsibility of democratically elected leaders. Therefore, we expect that, if presidents are to be responsive to public opinion, they are likely to use a national address to underscore their commitment to issues important to the public. Even so, the best the president can expect from national addresses is a short-term impact over the public's agenda. This is likely to come indirectly through increased news coverage.

The strategy of sustained attention involves repeated and consistent attention to an issue by the president. This strategy includes local or national addresses, speeches to specialized groups, press conferences, and radio addresses. Simply, if the president speaks publicly about an issue multiple times, this is considered part of a continuous and sustained strategy to influence attention to that issue. In part because only presidential priorities are likely to affect the agendas of others, presidents who engage in this strategy meet a necessary condition of presidential agenda setting, that of making it clear that the policy to which a president devotes continuous attention is a top policy priority. By focusing on an issue to the exclusion of others, the president encourages the media to report on that issue. The more a president repeats an issue in speeches, the more likely it will affect news coverage and the public's agenda. Unlike a focused strategy of attention, a strategy of sustained attention, if successful, is likely to generate a longer-term impact on the policy agenda.

Going local is a specialized and purposive effort used by recent presidents to lead the news media and public. This strategy relies on two things: local, targeted speeches aimed at communities throughout the United States as part of the president's domestic travel and cultivating local news coverage to affect not only news coverage but also the public's perception of the president and administration policies (Cohen 2010). Limited research on the strategy shows that presidents generate a large amount of news coverage by going local (Barrett and Peake 2007; Cohen 2010; Eshbaugh-Soha 2010b; Eshbaugh-Soha and Peake 2006; 2008). Although we think that presidents should be able to affect the media's agenda by going local, illustrating that this strategy also affects the public's agenda, particularly the local public's agenda, is a much more difficult undertaking.

CONCLUSION

Presidential public leadership is not a unidirectional relationship, nor is it geared toward a single set of actors. Instead, presidential public relations involve both leadership and responsiveness, and accounting for the public and media shape opportunities for the direction and extent of presidential public relations. Public leadership by the president necessarily incorporates the media, as they provide an important linkage between the public and the president. To examine the reciprocal relationships among these three entities, as well as the possibility of indirect presidential leadership through the news media, we examine agenda setting in this book.

Previous research presents conflicting expectations for presidential leadership of the public's agenda. On the one hand, the president's speeches are accessible to the public, making it possible that the public will adopt the president's priorities as their own. On the other hand, the public's lack of interest in American politics erects a significant barrier to presidential leadership of the public, even with repeated presidential attention to a policy priority. Considering the public simultaneously with presidential speech making also insinuates that heightened public concern will promote presidential responsiveness, rather than leadership on important issues facing the nation.

The news media similarly provide opportunities for presidential leadership, though limitations abound. The news media do more than interpret and report on government activity and newsworthy events. They are a central force in agenda setting, so much so that the news agenda may affect both the public's and president's agendas. The former link is especially important for presidential leadership of the public. If the president can influence the news media's agenda, then given the strong link between the media and public agendas presidents may be best situated to lead the public through news coverage. Not only may media affect the president's agenda, they also provide another avenue for indirect presidential leadership of the public.

Let us summarize our expectations even further. First, we contend, as our salience hypothesis explicates, that current agendas matter greatly to the propensity for presidential leadership or responsiveness. That is, when an issue is currently off the public's agenda, the president is afforded an opportunity to be out in front, to act as a policy entrepreneur and use speech making strategically to target a policy priority. When an issue is not previously salient to the public, in other words, we are most likely to uncover presidential leadership of the public's agenda. If, however, the public expresses heightened concern for a policy area, presidents may be forced to respond to this concern, rather than lead on it or another policy area. Second, our indirect leadership hypothesis holds that presidential speech making may not elicit a direct response from the public. Instead, presidents are wise to tap the unambiguous relationship between the media and the public. If presidents can influence news coverage, therefore, they should be able to indirectly lead the public's agenda. As we detail in subsequent chapters, the prospects for presidential leadership or responsiveness should also vary by the strategy presidents employ and the policy being considered.

CHAPTER 4

A Focused Strategy of Presidential Leadership

DURING HIS FIRST TELEVISED PRESIDENTIAL ADDRESS from the Oval Office on September 5, 1989, President George H. W. Bush announced a war on drugs, arguing that "the gravest domestic threat facing our nation today is drugs." As Jones (1994, 108) illustrates, the address had a clear impact on the level of concern the public expressed about illegal drugs. The Gallup Poll before the speech registered 27 percent who identified drugs as the most important problem facing the United States. After Bush's address, this increased to 63 percent, remaining higher than prespeech levels through April 1990. What is more, this national address had a clear and sizeable impact on media coverage of drugs, as the number of network news stories increased by seventy-seven for one month after the address (Peake and Eshbaugh-Soha 2008, 125). President Bush clearly used this national address to focus the public's and media's agenda on illegal drugs.[1]

This example illustrates President Bush's strategy of focused attention to lead public and media attention to the problem of illegal drugs. Yet, there may be other instances in which national addresses fail to lead either agenda or when presidents deliver them in response to heightened news coverage and public concern for an issue. As argued in earlier chapters, it is the reciprocal nature of leadership that may explain whether presidents lead or respond to the public or media, and the larger political system—especially the public's and media's policy agendas—should weigh heavily on the prospects for presidential leadership. In this case, Bush acted in an entrepreneurial fashion and led the public and media on the drug issue before it was a top issue. Other efforts to lead may prove ineffective, depending on the president's political context.

In this chapter, we systematically test the effectiveness of a focused strategy of presidential leadership. Conceiving the president's focused agenda as an issue-specific nationally televised address, the public agenda as public concern for an issue, and the media agenda as the amount of network news coverage on an issue, we maintain that the national address provides the president with the best opportunity to lead the public and media agendas, especially in the short term. The numerous environmental and reciprocal constraints on leading the nation through television suggests, however, that leadership success will be conditional and strategic and that responsiveness may be the likely outcome of this highly visible rhetorical opportunity.

FOCUSED LEADERSHIP

A focused strategy of presidential leadership, as we define it, is where the president appears on national television, typically during prime time, and delivers a policy-specific speech directly to the nation or Congress. Televised presidential addresses are dramatic events that give the president the undivided attention of the viewing audience, irrespective of any journalistic analysis of the speech. Although the speeches are targeted strategically, used sparingly (Kernell 1997), and subject to numerous limitations from an uninterested viewing public and superficial news media (Edwards 2003), presidents may be best positioned to affect the policy agenda with these speeches, as our opening vignette denotes. Such presidential drama, moreover, is significantly more costly, and thus rarer, than the more mundane presidential speeches delivered before local or Washington audiences. Because of this, we expect them to have a high payoff in terms of agenda-setting influence.

One of the difficulties presidents have leading the public is that doing so often requires influencing news coverage. It is likely that national news coverage of the presidency, which tends to be negative and decreasingly prominent (Cohen 2008), may undermine the president's ability to affect media coverage in a sustained fashion, as we explore in Chapter 5. National addresses are an opportunity for presidents to communicate directly to the American people and bypass the tendency for national media to filter the president's message through either negative or infrequent news coverage.[2] To be sure, presidents must request airtime for their addresses, a request that networks may reject when they deem the address not to be timely or novel (see Edwards 2003). Furthermore, the public has to watch the president for national addresses to influence the public directly, yet research is clear that the ratings for presidential addresses have declined

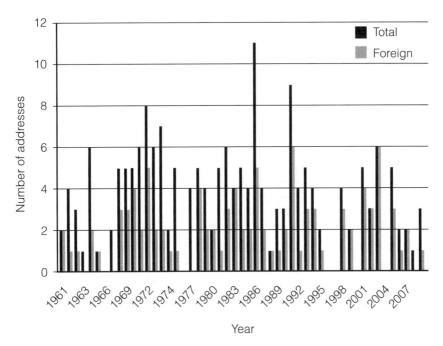

FIGURE 4.1. Number of total and foreign policy national addresses, 1961–2009.

Source: American presidency project—blank search for: "Oral: Addresses—major to the nation" and "Oral Address—to Congress (non SOTU); does not include Bush, Clinton, and Bush Administration Goals Speeches." Excludes addresses to the nation not identified as having been broadcast on television, most prominent during the George H. W. Bush Administration.

over time, perhaps limiting the effectiveness of a focused strategy (Baum and Kernell 1999; Young and Perkins 2005).

If these conditions deter presidential decisions to deliver nationally televised addresses, then at first glance they do so relatively equally across time. Graphing policy-specific national addresses from 1961 through 2009 in Figure 4.1 illustrates that presidents have used this strategy sparingly but with some consistency over time. The mode is five speeches per year, with an average of 3.65. The maximum is eleven national addresses for Reagan in 1986 and a minimum of zero for several years, including three years during the mid-1990s. There are also differences in the number of domestic and foreign policy-themed speeches. Foreign policy addresses tend to be more common, especially for the two most recent administrations.

For example, all of George W. Bush's national addresses in 2003 were on foreign policy. And just as Clinton did not deliver a national address in 1996, 1997, or 2000, he gave only one address on domestic policy in all but two of his years in office: 1993, when he gave two; and 1999, when he did not deliver a domestic address. Moreover, some of these non–foreign policy addresses related to scandal, including Watergate, Iran-Contra, and the Monica Lewinsky scandal, further differentiating foreign policy as the dominant policy choice in national addresses. The differences in the numbers of national addresses over time may be a function of not only the opportunities afforded to presidents and the discretion they have to use them but also a president's individual style and governing strategy (see Kumar 2007).

Of course, these data do not illustrate what we are most interested in: the effectiveness of the national address as a tool for agenda leadership, which we will examine in greater detail and with more policy-specific data. The data do illustrate, nevertheless, that the national address is a relatively rare event, something that should encourage public and media attention to televised addresses. The novelty of televised addresses almost guarantees their news coverage, satisfying an important condition of indirect presidential leadership of the public. The public, moreover, which may not be especially keen on watching a nationally televised address, at least will not experience viewing fatigue from watching too many addresses. This does not mean a focused strategy is an assurance of leadership, of course, given the numerous disadvantages to a strategy of focused attention that we discuss in the following pages.

Advantages of a Focused Strategy

The focused strategy of presidential leadership, in which presidents speak directly to the American people on national television, has been a staple of effective presidential leadership in several ways. National addresses may increase presidential approval ratings in the short term (Brace and Hinckley 1993; Ragsdale 1984; but see Edwards 2003; Simon and Ostrom 1989) or the public's support for the president's policy preferences (Rottinghaus 2010; but see Edwards 2003). National addresses may also affect the policy agenda. For example, major presidential addresses on energy and inflation have affected the public's concern for these issues, while controlling for media attention (Iyengar and Kinder 1987, 30–31). A type of national address, the State of the Union, has also increased public concern for foreign policy issues (Cohen 1995; Hill 1998; Young and Perkins 2005). Presidents have succeeded in increasing news attention to some policy priorities through policy-specific nationally televised addresses (Peake and Eshbaugh-Soha 2008).

A focused strategy of presidential agenda leadership is likely to generate a short-term response if presidents can increase accessibility of their agendas by enticing news coverage and attracting viewers. There is reason to believe that both happen. Although ratings for national addresses have declined over time (Baum and Kernell 1999), a considerable portion of the public still watches the president on television. As an example, an average of approximately 46 percent of Americans watched at least part of Reagan's nationally televised addresses during his first term in office (Welch 2000, 44), a sizeable audience, and a higher percentage of individuals than those who read or heard nothing about the speech afterwards (40 percent). Across all of their national addresses, President Carter averaged about 69 million viewers and Reagan averaged 55 million (Foote 1990, 153, from Edwards 2003, 189). President Obama's addresses have also produced sizeable television ratings. Approximately 50 million viewers watched Barack Obama's first national address in February 2009, even though his address before a joint session of Congress on health care reform in September 2009 drew a much smaller audience, approximately 32 million viewers. A foreign policy speech regarding his decision to increase American troops in Afghanistan in December drew a somewhat larger audience of 41 million (NielsenWire 2009a).

Although Edwards (2003, 189–190) is correct to infer that the White House would rather have much larger audiences given the 100.8 million American households (comprised of 260 million people) that own televisions,[3] these audiences are still much larger than any single minor address the president may give to local audiences or those broadcast on cable television given that a typical cable news prime-time audience has ranged between 1 and 4 million viewers during the last decade.[4] Nationally televised addresses provide the best opportunity to reach the most citizens at one time, to be sure, although not all of the public will be watching.

The presidency is well equipped to maximize viewing audiences. As we described in Chapter 1, the president has an extensive communications operation designed to facilitate public relations. One way that presidents have used these resources strategically is to target times when viewership is already high, taking advantage of any accidental viewers (see Baum 2003). President George W. Bush accomplished this on at least two occasions. First, he delivered his May 1, 2003, "Mission Accomplished" in Iraq speech aboard the USS *Lincoln* during sweeps—a time of high ratings for network evening programming—and actually bumped top-ranked network shows off the air.[5] Second, his April 2004 speech on Iraq preempted the phenomenally popular *American Idol*, moving it from Tuesday (the night of the president's speech) to Wednesday night. President Obama received similar treatment when he requested and received airtime from the networks (all except Fox) for his third prime-time press conference in the middle of sweeps week, April 29, 2009.

Targeting messages through a nationally televised address can be beneficial to presidential leadership, as well. Unlike the State of the Union address, which typically consists of a laundry list of proposals that range across policy areas, the nationally televised address focuses on a specific policy, such as the economy or illegal drug use.[6] Research shows that the public were more likely to remember a major point from one of Reagan's addresses the more the president focused on that point in his speech (Welch 2003). The media are also more likely to cover the president's priorities the more his speech addresses one topic (Barrett 2007). Thus, presidents may be advantaged in setting the agenda when using a focused, policy-specific address rather than through the obligatory and wide-ranging State of the Union address.

Even if the public does not watch the address live, media coverage of national addresses is all but guaranteed (Iyengar and Kinder 1987, 124). Surely, the media do not want to give airtime at every request, as evidenced by the rarity of the addresses. Yet, if the networks do grant airtime, then they will cover the speech because the decision to air the speech in the first place speaks to its importance and newsworthiness. While short-term coverage of the actual speech is assured, this does not mean that news coverage of the president's agenda will increase substantially beyond the immediate aftermath of the address. A recent study that examined the agenda-setting effects of televised addresses found that only slightly more than a third of the forty addresses examined led to statistically significantly increases in media attention during the month of the speech. Only 10 percent of the addresses examined had a sustained and significant impact on coverage of the president's issue in the months after the speech was delivered (Peake and Eshbaugh-Soha 2008).

The news media are likely to cover national addresses, at least in the short term, because they tend to be about relatively novel topics and are central to the president's policy agenda. An innovative policy agenda, indeed, is likely to stimulate news coverage (Cohen 2008, 75). Additionally, presidents who act as entrepreneurs and take it on themselves to push an issue onto the national agenda are more likely to drive coverage by the news media (see Edwards and Wood 1999; Peake 2001). As leadership is most visible in the absence of previous concern by the public or attention by the media, delivering new ideas through a national address means that the president is less likely to be constrained by existing media or public attention. This, in turn, increases the prospects for presidential leadership of the media and public. To not only receive airtime but to also maximize news coverage and the potential impact on the media and public agendas, it behooves the president to present a novel program or idea through a focused strategy, not use it to repeat old policy proposals.

This does not mean that presidents will be unable to lead through national addresses that repeat policy priorities. On the contrary, presidents may be able to deliver multiple addresses within a short time frame, so long as a window of opportunity exists. As Kingdon (1995) illustrates, these opportunities arise when the public, media, and Congress agree that a policy problem is ripe for a governmental response. When a window opens, presidents may be in a strong position to reinforce their message through repeated national addresses and sustain the public's and media's attention on their own policy agendas. We infer that a window of opportunity exists when the networks grant presidents airtime for multiple addresses on the same topic. After all, the networks may be reluctant to grant airtime when they think the topic is of little importance or offers nothing new, but, as profit-maximizing institutions, they will grant airtime when the public is highly attuned to a policy issue. Much as presidents are unable to rely on the national address frequently, they are also unlikely frequently to deliver multiple addresses in the same month. When it does happen, this reinforcement hypothesis suggests that presidents who are able to deliver multiple speeches in a month will have more influence over the public and media.

Presidents may also benefit from a honeymoon effect of presidential speeches. The public and media are simply more interested in presidential politics shortly after the president's inauguration, as much research has illustrated in a presidential-congressional context (Dominguez 2005). Initial addresses on a policy may thus be most effective as leadership tools. Even if presidents cannot deviate from their policy agenda, the national address itself may be newsworthy, given the view by some that the news is actually rather similar from day to day (Cook 1998). An effort by the president to focus the media's attention on a policy priority through a national address may, in itself, be enough to generate news coverage about the president's agenda, especially early on in the president's tenure, when media coverage tends to be heavier and more positive.

Presidents have much discretion to choose when to deliver a national address and on what topic (Ragsdale 1984).[7] Presidents are wise to use this discretion strategically, delivering national addresses primarily when the policy proposal to be delivered in the address is popular with the public (Canes-Wrone 2001, 323). Therefore, a strategic president should deliver a national address when it is likely to have the largest impact. This may allow presidents to attempt to target airtime when viewers are already likely to be watching (such as during sweeps week) or discuss an innovative and novel policy idea. Such decisions may affect the likelihood that the addresses will affect the public's and media's agendas and suggests the possibility that presidents should be effective using the strategy, however infrequently it may be used.

A final advantage of a focused strategy is the benefit to presidents not when they are leading—as the foregoing discussion examines—but when they deliver a national address to respond to the public and news media. Responsiveness is expected of democratically elected leaders. As presidents display their commitment to public concerns through public speeches, one way to maximize the benefits of being responsive is through a strategically timed national address. It is the national address, after all, that entices the most viewers and carries with it the greatest likelihood of news coverage. If the economy is a top concern, for example, then presidents may be best able to demonstrate their congruence with the public on economic issues by delivering a national address on the economy. In short, even if a nationally televised address does not influence the public or media, it may serve to meet the democratically driven expectation that presidents respond to the public's policy concerns by adjusting their own agendas. Moreover, it would do so in a very high-profile fashion.

Disadvantages of a Focused Strategy

For a focused strategy to be an effective means for agenda leadership, several conditions must be met. A national address must draw a sizeable audience. The more viewers, the more the address is accessible to viewers, and the more potential the president has for leading the public's agenda. The audience, moreover, must pay attention to and remember the president's main points. Only if viewers remember the main points of the president's speech will they be able to translate the president's message into their own, thereby affecting their agendas. The media, in addition, would have to be compliant partners, providing the president with airtime and covering his agenda in news broadcasts for some time after the speech. Unfortunately for the president, these conditions are often not met.

Audience makeup is extremely important to strategic leadership of the public's agenda. Research demonstrates that the least-educated viewers are the most likely to be influenced by news coverage. The lower one's education level, the more likely television news will influence one's determination of the most important problem facing the nation (Iyengar and Kinder 1987, Chapter 6). This presumably extends to the president's ability to influence the public through the same medium. If this assumption is valid, and if the president's audiences are primarily comprised of those with low levels of education, then he has a golden opportunity to affect the public's agenda through a national address. It is clear, however, that it is the lower educated who are *least* likely to watch (Welch 2000, 55) or to hear about the address afterwards (Edwards 2003, 203). Therefore, the makeup of the audience may actually undermine the president's leadership because those who are the least likely to have their agendas influenced by more information are most likely to watch the president speak or watch news about the president's address afterwards.[8]

Receptivity of the audience matters to the effectiveness of the president's addresses. On this question, Welch (2003) illustrates that the audience does not usually embrace the president's message, which is consistent with the bulk of public opinion literature on the limits of processing information (see Zaller 1992, among others). Although it should be much easier for the audience to remember the general topic of the president's speech rather than specific policy proposals, limited public receptivity to the president's message severely limits his ability to lead the public agenda through a national address. This suggests several impediments to the public being responsive to national addresses: Citizens are simply not that receptive to the president's message, do not typically remember what the president discussed, and therefore may not accept the president's agenda as their own.[9]

To lead, the president needs viewers. And, despite the sizeable audience the president still receives, the aggregate audience of presidential speeches is simply not as large as it once was. Whereas Presidents Nixon, Ford, and Carter experienced audience shares approaching 50 percent, recent presidents have not fared as well (Baum and Kernell 1999, 100). Presidents since Reagan are unlikely to approach a 50 percent audience share, given the growth of other viewing options for the public with cable and satellite television. Only the occasional speech for more recent presidents, such as Clinton's economic address at the beginning of his first term in office or his speech following grand jury testimony during the Lewinsky scandal, registered over a 60 percent share (Edwards 2003, 198). The average presidential speech since 1985, according to the Nielsen ratings examined by Baum and Kernell (1999) and Edwards (2003), reached about a third of households watching television. As already discussed, while Obama reached nearly 50 million Americans in February 2009 (a respectable 47 percent share), only about 32 million watched his health care address in September (a much smaller 35 percent share). For presidents to influence directly what a significant segment of the public thinks is important they must first attract a large television audience. That viewership has decreased over time suggests that addresses delivered since the early 1980s should be much less influential over the public's agenda than addresses delivered during the 1970s (Young and Perkins 2005).

Audiences have not only declined over time, they also appear to decline during the president's term in office. During the first few months of the president's first year in office, the novelty of a new administration is high, and the public expects presidents to deliver a national address on their top priorities. As the president's honeymoon period fades, audiences tend to fade as well. This happened with Reagan's economic addresses when he received a fairly high percentage of viewers for his early first-term speeches, yet his audiences declined precipitously throughout his two terms in office (Edwards 2003, 197; Foote 1988; Welch 2003). Presidents George H. W. Bush and Bill Clinton experienced similar difficulties (Edwards 2003, 198), just as President Obama has more recently. With smaller audiences due to waning interest and other viewing options, more recent presidents are simply less likely to focus the public's agenda on their top priorities through a strategy of focused attention.

For a president to even have an audience, media must grant airtime, and, as gatekeepers of their broadcast content, there are numerous incentives for networks to deny presidents access to the airwaves. As businesses, the networks look to their bottom lines. Because they must forgo advertising revenue from top-rated prime time shows should they grant the president access, networks may deny presidents airtime. Even when some networks grant airtime, not all may grant access. Despite its being an address on the prospects for war in Iraq and the president having selected a relatively nonpartisan location from which to deliver the speech, the major networks refused to cover President George W. Bush's October 2002 address to the nation from Cincinnati, Ohio.[10] The Fox network declined to cover President Obama's September 9, 2009, address on health care reform, moreover, although it was aired on their cable news channel (NielsenWire 2009b). Of course, even when the president has the attention of the networks, other events, specifically significant soft news events, can compete for attention. Bill Clinton actually shared the television screen with the O. J. Simpson's not-guilty verdict during his February 4, 1997, State of the Union address, via split-screen coverage (Clines 1997).[11]

Limited effectiveness of subsequent addresses could also be a function of the success of previous addresses. Earlier addresses in a sequence may be most effective because this is when presidents can act in an entrepreneurial fashion and set the public's agenda. Once he leads the public's agenda, however, the president's ability to continue to be able to do so should diminish. If the public is initially not interested in a policy area, presidents can use a national address to raise interest in the policy, a theoretical expectation we developed in Chapter 3. But when the president has already succeeded in setting the public's agenda, a subsequent address is unlikely to further heighten public awareness of his policies.

Presidents who are unable to lead the public's agenda directly through a national address may be able to generate news coverage through a national address and indirectly lead the public. This allows for the public to watch and be influenced by the president through subsequent news coverage of his agenda without necessarily having watched the address. Yet, the president may fare no better leading the public indirectly through news coverage. If presidential leadership of the public lies with the media, it does so precariously. Presidential leadership is most likely to be effective when the president can sustain the attention of the public and media. But media do not stick with policy issues over time (Downs 1972; Kingdon 1995, 62) as events and other stories distract media from reporting on the president. Moreover, issues compete for very limited agenda space (Jones and Baumgartner 2005, 20, 237; Wood and Peake 1998), leaving presidents struggling, at times, to generate news coverage of their policies. That media tend to report on soft, entertainment-driven news, rather than policy-related hard news (Bennett 2009; Cohen 2008) further compounds the difficulties presidents have leading the public indirectly through news coverage, or leading the media's agenda at all.

Even if a strategy of focused attention affects the public or media, it may have only a fleeting impact. As we argued in earlier chapters, presidents must sustain the focus of the public and media to affect their agendas over the long term. Yet the media may be unlikely to cover the president's agenda after the excitement of the national address fades. Moreover, the media can either ignore the president's policies in the subsequent weeks or months or offer postspeech news coverage that does not reinforce the president's message.

Indeed, research on the State of the Union address illustrates that presidential influence on the public's economic and foreign policy agendas through this medium faces substantial limits (Cohen 1995; Young and Perkins 2005), just as presidents have only modest success affecting new coverage of the policies they discuss in other national addresses (Peake and Eshbaugh-Soha 2008).

At the same time, presidents may be constrained by public expectations for delivering national addresses. There are situations, such as national crises, to which the president must respond with a national address. Examples include addresses delivered in response to civil unrest during the 1960s, the 1992 Los Angeles riots, Hurricane Katrina in 2005, and the massive Gulf of Mexico oil spill in 2010. In each of these instances, the president had less discretion in using the national address strategically to lead the public or media. Rather, the president chose to speak on national television to demonstrate responsiveness and meet public expectations that he address the nation at times of national crisis. Certainly, discretion allows presidents to pick and choose when to deliver a national address. One must consider, however, that the president's decision to deliver a national address could be swayed by the existing media or public agendas, forcing presidential responsiveness. Such decisions may also be conditioned by the broader political context.

Summary

A strategy of focused attention affords presidents important advantages for successful leadership. However, there exist many disadvantages. After all, media may not grant airtime, they may not cover the president's speeches, and viewers may not watch or even comprehend the president's message. Nevertheless, the viewing audience for a national address is the largest the president will receive, giving presidents a substantial opportunity to lead the public's agenda directly or to demonstrate democratic responsiveness. Even if the viewing audience is smaller than it once was, presidents may still lead the public's agenda indirectly through coverage of the address and subsequent news coverage of the president's agenda. The opportunities for leadership are constrained by the existing agendas of the media and public, of course, and presidents are rarely afforded the opportunity to reinforce their message through multiple national addresses.

Having reviewed the advantages and disadvantages of a focused strategy of agenda setting, in this section we discuss briefly our theoretical expectations for whether national addresses will influence the public and media agendas on the economy and Iraq. In addition to the prospects for indirect or direct leadership, the national address is a rare event subject to the president's strategic use. Because of this, political conditions should be especially important to whether presidents deliver national addresses to lead or to respond to the public and media agendas. Having specified more extensively their importance in Chapter 3, we discuss them briefly in this section as they pertain specifically to national addresses. Policy is an important theoretical component of agenda setting and so factors that condition presidential leadership through a strategy of focused attention may also vary by policy area.

Policy Variation

That policy affects politics is a long-standing claim in political science. Our understanding of how policy areas should affect presidential leadership is limited, however. Because the most common and theoretically developed way to differentiate across policy areas—given the massive literature that argues for divergent effects—is by foreign and domestic policy areas, we have chosen to analyze one of each. As we discussed in Chapter 3, much research has questioned Wildavsky's (1966) original observation that presidential success in Congress differs between foreign and domestic policy. Much less has been written on how the two presidencies thesis might relate to presidential leadership of the media and public. That the public and media register more interest in economic than foreign policy issues suggests an enhanced opportunity for presidential leadership over foreign than over domestic policy issues. This is because entrepreneurial leadership is more likely on issues in which the public has less interest initially and media are therefore less likely to cover without a corresponding event. Foreign policy, therefore, presents greater opportunities for presidential agenda leadership than domestic policy.

Specific to a focused strategy, the media appear predisposed to give presidents more opportunity to address the nation on foreign policy than on other policy areas. Although we do not have data as to when requests were rejected, presidents have delivered more addresses on foreign policy than other policies over our entire time frame (look again at Figure 4.1). This has been especially so since the 1990s, even though domestic policies and economic growth were central to the Clinton years. If the media are more likely to grant airtime for foreign policy issues, then they may also be more likely to cover the president's agenda in the wake of a foreign policy speech. Indeed, media coverage of recent military conflicts tends to defer heavily to the White House, even though news coverage of international affairs has declined sharply in recent decades (Hoge 1997). Increased news coverage of the president's foreign policy agenda in response to an address should subsequently increase the probability of indirect presidential leadership of the public's foreign policy agenda, as well.

Conditional Leadership

The effectiveness of a focused strategy of leadership should vary by the larger political environment. Therefore, we include several control variables in our quantitative models to account for context. First, presidential approval ratings are important to presidential leadership. As we have already discussed in Chapter 3, the public and media may take cues from popular presidents and be more likely to receive the president's message. Indeed, Peake and Eshbaugh-Soha (2008, 128–129) estimate that a speech delivered by a popular president (60 percent approval) was 40 percent more likely to significantly increase media coverage of the economy than a speech delivered by a president with only average popularity. Thus, a higher approval rating indicates a more favorable context for presidential leadership and is a variable controlled for by prior research on presidential speeches (Canes-Wrone 2001; Rottinghaus 2010). Presidential approval ratings are taken from the Gallup Poll. When there are multiple surveys in a month, we use the average monthly rating.[12]

Second, reelection years matter to agenda leadership, such that the election season may structure presidential decisions to use a focused strategy. Presidents could use a nationally televised address during their own reelection campaign to appear responsive to the public and even to claim credit for successes.[13] Alternatively, presidents may wish to avoid speaking on national television during reelection years if doing so may undermine their prospects for reelection. Presidential responsiveness on the economy should be particularly conditioned on reelection years given the impact that the state of the economy has on presidential elections (Alvarez and Nagler 1998; Erikson 1989; Holbrook 1994; Nadeau and Lewis-Beck 2001). Given that poor economic news is more likely to be newsworthy than positive news,[14] the media are more likely to cover—and the public are more likely to be interested in—the economy when it is not doing well. Irrespective of their impact on the tendency for presidents to deliver a national address, the economy and foreign policy are significant electoral issues, and media coverage of and public interest in each may increase during reelection years. We code reelection years as a one during the first ten months of a presidential reelection year and zero otherwise.

Third, presidents should be more responsive to the public in their first rather than second term given their reelection goals (Rottinghaus 2006). This increased responsiveness might structure their proclivity to deliver a national address. Thus, we control for first-term presidents in our models, coding the first term as a one when the month occurs in the president's first term and zero otherwise.

Fourth, international events are important to the president's agenda as they can force presidents to address issues they may not have otherwise felt compelled to prioritize. Certainly, the events on September 11, 2001, pushed international terrorism onto President George W. Bush's agenda. For obvious reasons, events should affect the foreign policy model, but they are relevant to the public's economic considerations, as well (Wood 2009b), as they might distract from attention to the economy (DeRouen and Peake 2002). To account for a selection of important international events in our analysis, we include Wood's (2007) political drama measure in our models, coded one in a month in which an event occurred and zero otherwise.[15]

Finally, real-world cues, in general, and the objective economy, in particular, matter to presidential agenda setting on economic and foreign policies.[16] We model the objective economy in our analysis of the economy because it should be a strong predictor of presidential, media, and public attention to the economy. Indeed, the misery index, an additive measure of the inflation rate and unemployment, correlates highly with news media coverage of the economy (Pearson's r = 0.52). Similarly, public concern for the economy increases as objective indicators worsen, as evidenced by the strong relationship between the misery index and the percentage of the public who deem the economy to be the nation's most important problem (Pearson's r = 0.68). The state of the economy is important to agenda setting for additional reasons beyond its direct impact on the media and public agendas. Because we know little about when and why presidents deliver national addresses, the following two scenarios may be equally plausible. A poor economy may force presidents to deliver a national address given that a poor economy is more salient than a good one. Alternatively, presidents may wish to avoid advertising a recession through a national address, and so a poor economy may decrease the tendency for presidents to deliver a national address on the economy.

We also model the objective economy in our examination of Iraq. Howell and Pevehouse (2007) argue convincingly that the economy is relevant to decisions on military action. Specifically, presidents move faster and are more likely to engage in a military response when the unemployment rate, for example, ratchets upwards (106–107). Fordham (2005) finds that nations tend to be strategic and will wait for the U.S. economy to decline before acting in ways that might provoke an American response. Because a poor economy is often highly salient to the president, public, and media, it may push other policies, such as Iraq, off the national policy agenda. We use the monthly misery index,[17] which is provided by the Bureau of Labor Statistics.

Summary Expectations

A strategy of focused attention affords presidents the best opportunity to increase public and media accessibility to their policy agendas in the short term given that media are most likely to cover and the public is most likely to watch a televised presidential address. We expect not only differences in the dynamics of presidential leadership across policies but also that the impact of the political environment on presidential leadership and responsiveness should vary by policy area. Presidents may be in a stronger position to lead on Iraq, regardless of the political context, because it is not typically on the public's agenda until after presidential actions place it there. Furthermore, presidential responsiveness is more likely on economic than foreign policy issues given the economy's consistent importance to the American people and its relevance to the president's reelection prospects.

DEPENDENT VARIABLES

We operationalize our dependent variables, the policy agendas of the president, public, and news media, in three ways. First, we conceive of the president's agenda as attention devoted to issues through a nationally televised address. Our national addresses dependent variables are simply whether the president delivered a national address on the economy or Iraq in a month (coded one) or not (coded zero). Each national address we use is listed in the impact assessment tables. Our range of data is from January 1969 through December 2008 for the economy and from January 1989 through June 2008 for Iraq. We do not differentiate by specific economic topic in these analyses but instead identify only whether or not the national address concerned the economy. We do this to maximize the number of national addresses that we can analyze over a lengthy time series. After all, presidents are often very specific in their national addresses. For example, Ford focused on inflation in 1975, and Bush focused on spending and budget issues in 1990.

Second, we measure media attention, or the media's agenda, as the number of stories per month that the television networks (ABC, CBS, and NBC) devoted to economic policy and Iraq.[18] We use key word searches on the TV News Archive at Vanderbilt University, http://tvnews.vanderbilt .edu/.[19] A list of key words is provided in the Appendix.[20] Our measures of media attention are similar to those adopted by Eshbaugh-Soha and Peake (2005) and Edwards and Wood (1999).[21] In this chapter, we analyze the number of stories related to the economy and Iraq instead of the number of seconds or minutes, which is an alternative measure used in the literature. We do this for reasons of efficiency: Counting stories rather than seconds over a time series as long as we analyze for the economy proved a more effective use of our time.[22]

Actual news coverage is an appropriate measure of media attention and its impact on the public for two reasons. First, by studying agendas, we rely on what is on the news, similar to other studies that assess the media's agenda (for example, Edwards and Wood 1999). Second, an objective measure of media attention is superior to a survey response given the tendency for survey respondents to overestimate their news exposure. Prior (2009) notes that survey estimates of nightly news audiences are substantially inflated when compared to the more objective Nielsen ratings of network news audiences. Because survey responses concerning media consumption may be more guesswork than an accurate reflection of the public's news exposure, we think a count of news stories reflects a best measure of the media's agenda and its relationship to the president's and public's agendas.[23]

Third, we use one primary measure to represent the public's agenda concerning the economy and Iraq. The Gallup polling organization asks respondents, "What do you think is the most important problem (MIP) facing this country today?" Each respondent lists up to three problems that he or she deems most important, and we then categorize them as percentages of respondents who think economic issues are most important. We aggregate the percentages of respondents who cite any specific economic issue to create a total MIP category for the economy. We build a monthly time series over the time period we examine for the economy consistent with Wood's (2007) techniques for doing so.[24] Our measure of Iraq is constructed similarly and covers a period before the Persian Gulf War toward the end of the George W. Bush administration.[25]

Cohen (1997) uses MIP data for his measure of the public's agenda and Geer (1996, 97n3) conceives of a salient issue as one that "the electorate finds some problem to be of concern or worry." Other analysts question whether public "problems" are synonymous with an issue's salience and by extension the public's agenda (Edwards et al. 1995; see Wooley 2000 for an extensive list of salience measures). We think that they are. But even if scholars claim that we are not examining salience, we are still measuring the public's agenda based on the literature's standard, which is Gallup's measure of the nation's most important problem. Of course, theoretically and quantitatively, we move beyond previous analyses of presidential influence over the public's agenda by not just assessing the correlation between these two factors—"public concern with a policy area increases as presidential emphasis with the policy area increases" (Cohen 1997, 55)—but by also examining more precisely the causal and reciprocal dynamics of this relationship, including media and a broader treatment of the president's agenda.[26]

METHODS

To develop the direct, indirect, and reciprocal relationships between national addresses, the media's agenda, and the public's agenda, we analyze our data in two steps. In our first step, we assess the impact of all individual national addresses related to the economy or Iraq on the public's policy agendas using Box-Tiao impact assessment methods (Box and Tiao 1975), similar to Peake and Eshbaugh-Soha (2008). Impact assessment models allow us to isolate the impact that specific national addresses have on the public and media agendas.[27] They are parsimonious and very conservative, and the interventions can be influential only after controlling for the history or noise components of the time series. Moreover, spuriousness in a statistically significant relationship is unlikely in this quasi-experimental design (Campbell and Stanley 1963). If we conclude that a speech in a month, for example, has an independent impact on media attention or public concern, it is highly improbable that another factor would have caused an identical shift (see McLeary and Hay 1980). Finally, we have tested for nonstationarity (all series are stationary) and include autoregressive and moving average parameters to address any autocorrelation in the models.

In the second step of our analysis, we model a series of simultaneous equations to account for the reciprocal effects between national addresses, the public, and media. Because our national addresses variable is dichotomous, we cannot employ either vector autoregression (VAR) or three-stage least squares. Instead, we use a simultaneous equations generalized probit model as explained by Amemiya (1978) and implemented by Canes-Wrone (2001). The logic of this technique is the same as any other simultaneous equations model with one exception: It allows one to analyze simultaneity or reciprocal causation in the presence of one continuous and one dichotomous dependent variable (see Keshk 2003). Identifying each equation requires two instrumental variables: one that is correlated with the dependent variable it predicts, but not the other; and another that is correlated with the dependent variable it predicts, but not the other. For the economy, divided government proves to be a useful instrumental variable in the national address equation, and the misery index is a viable instrument in the media and public agendas equations. For Iraq, we use the number of Iraq War deaths[28] as an instrument in the media and public agendas models and job approval in the national address equations. Because we cannot run three equations simultaneously with this technique, we interpret each interrelationship in these models, which approximates the reciprocal relationships between national addresses and public opinion, national addresses and media attention, and public opinion and media attention. When we find consistent effects across the model, we conclude that a relationship is robust.[29]

FINDINGS

Economy

Presidents deliver national addresses on the economy infrequently but at a much higher rate than for all other domestic policy areas combined. According to Ragsdale's (2009, 192) counts, presidents since Calvin Coolidge have delivered sixty-four national addresses on the economy but only fifty-three on all other domestic policy issues combined. From 1969 through 2008, presidents delivered thirty nationally televised addresses on the economy, most of these during prime-time television hours. Reagan spoke most frequently on the economy, delivering ten addresses, and all but two were delivered during his first two years in office. Both Clinton and Nixon delivered five economic addresses, while Ford gave four during his two years as president. President Carter gave two economic addresses, and President George H. W. Bush delivered three (Eshbaugh-Soha and Peake 2008, 135–136). In a departure from his predecessors, President George W. Bush delivered only one national address on the economy during his eight years as president, and then only during the waning months of his final year in office in response to the collapse of the economy in 2008.

To explore the impact of these addresses on both the public and media economic agendas, we present several quantitative models that cover January 1969 through December 2008. The first set of impact assessment models illustrates some variability in presidential influence over the public through national addresses. These results, presented in Table 4.1, indicate that presidential addresses typically do not directly affect the public's agenda on economic issues, as only six of the twenty-eight addresses do so. Of these addresses, three—Nixon's July 1974, Carter's March 1980, and Bush's October 1990 speeches—are negatively associated with public concern. Even though one might infer that these were credit-claiming successes for the president, assuring the public that the economy was improving and should no longer be of public concern, a closer examination reveals that this conclusion is unwarranted. The economy continued to worsen throughout 1980 and was a reason for Carter's defeat in his re-election contest, along with the ongoing Iran hostage crisis that captured media and public attention. Nixon's speech was delivered days before his resignation (perhaps as an attempt to distract rather than lead), and Bush's address actually covered two topics: the economy, yes, but more importantly the crisis in the Persian Gulf. In each of these instances, it is feasible that the public was simply interested in the other more prominent issue on the national agenda.

Of the remaining speeches, only three had statistically significant and positive effects on the public's agenda: Nixon's September 1971 speech and Reagan's two February 1981 speeches, which are counted as a single intervention in the analysis because they were given in the same month. The Nixon speech is estimated to have increased public concern by 12 percent, a substantial increase. The Reagan addresses are estimated to have increased public concern by 9 percent, also a substantial increase, especially considering that public concern for the economy was already elevated before the addresses. That Reagan delivered two national addresses in the same month, at a time when the nation was fixated on the economy, conforms to our argument that presidents are most likely to lead within a window of opportunity in which the public and media are engaged in the same issues. Under these rare circumstances in a presidency, the effectiveness of one speech can be reinforced by another. The Nixon speech is peculiar because it did not occur early in his tenure, nor was it his first speech on the economy. It was, in fact, his third national address on economic issues, one sandwiched in between two other national

TABLE 4.1.

Impact of nationally televised presidential speeches on the public's and media's economic agendas, January 1969–December 2008.

	Public agenda		Media agenda	
	Parameter estimates	*Standard error*	*Parameter estimates*	*Standard error*
Nixon 6/70	−5.08	4.84	6.27	16.82
Nixon 8/71	−7.45	5.91	15.89	17.94
Nixon 9/71	11.91*	6.81	−9.67	18.79
Nixon 10/71	7.60	5.93	41.83*	17.99
Nixon 7/74	−17.16*	5.24	8.41	17.43
Ford 10/74	−0.56	5.15	−2.07	17.16
Ford 1/75	−2.33	4.91	29.96*	16.91
Ford 3/75	−0.11	4.85	−22.26	16.95
Ford 10/75	3.57	4.84	66.96*	16.81
Carter 10/78	−4.44	5.03	42.57*	17.04
Carter 3/80	−14.94*	4.94	80.60*	18.35
Carter 3/80, δ_{11}			0.69*	0.14
Reagan 2/81	9.12*	4.96	49.44*	11.10
Reagan 2/81, δ_{12}			0.98*	0.01
Reagan 4/81	0.80	5.08	0.78	17.05
Reagan 7/81	1.52	4.93	−41.18*	16.98
Reagan 9/81	−1.93	5.00	9.25	16.93
Reagan 4/82	6.58	4.91	9.54	16.84
Reagan 8/82	2.63	4.99	26.06	16.86
Reagan 10/82	−0.01	4.92	34.21*	16.88
Reagan 4/85	0.22	5.58	14.91	17.65
Reagan 5/85	−4.03	5.58	−28.69	17.64
G. H. W. Bush 9/90	−2.80	5.68	51.43*	11.95
G. H. W. Bush 9/90, δ_{21}			0.98*	0.01
G. H. W. Bush 10/90	−12.09*	5.97	−36.31*	17.67
G. H. W. Bush 6/92	−4.77	4.84	−13.04	16.97
Clinton 2/93	1.23	4.85	34.35*	16.83
Clinton 8/93	−1.67	4.85	−14.07	11.93
Clinton 12/94	0.94	3.42	−14.79	11.93
Clinton 6/95	−0.66	4.95	9.34	16.82
G. W. Bush 9/08	−3.10	5.04	4.97	17.07
Media agenda$_{t-1}$	0.05*	0.02		
Public agenda$_{t-1}$			0.02	0.10
Approval	−0.11	0.07	−0.20	0.15
First term	1.03	2.89	6.94	4.40
Reelection year	−1.48	2.04	−4.93	4.05
Events	1.46	1.17	−3.65	3.94
Misery index	2.06*	0.67	2.50*	0.87
Constant	29.23*	9.91	12.00	13.12
AR1	0.94*	0.02	0.65*	0.08
MA1			−0.26*	0.10
MA |4|	−0.18*	0.05		
MA |18|	0.19*	0.05	0.12*	0.05
R-squared	0.92		0.68	
Mean of Dependent	46.20		45.9	
Box-Ljung Q	37.34		27.43	
N	480		480	

* $p < .05$, one-tailed

Note: All speeches are pulse functions, indicating the short-term (same month) effect of the president's speech, with the parameter estimate reflecting the estimated number of stories or percent public concern increased in the month of the speech. δ indicates the decay or long-term effect of a speech on media attention or public concern. Reagan delivered two addresses in February 1981.

addresses on the economy delivered during the previous and subsequent months. This speech was also an afternoon address to Congress, not a prime-time speech to the nation. In any event, the direct effects for both sets of speeches on the public agenda were short term.

This analysis paints a picture of limited and mixed presidential leadership of the public through a strategy of focused attention. Although we present some support for our reinforcement hypothesis, there is other evidence that suggests limits to even this tactic. Neither Reagan's April nor his May speeches in 1985 has a reinforcing impact; Clinton's two speeches in February 1993—given only two days apart—proved similarly incapable of leading the public's economic policy agenda. The time frame appears relevant, too, as Reagan's 1981 addresses are the most recent to positively affect the public's economic agenda. Nevertheless, we cannot conclude definitively that the golden age of presidential television (pre-1985) benefited the president in terms of agenda leadership. Although presidents had higher television ratings during the 1970s, this does not translate strongly into presidential agenda leadership, despite the reasons for expecting greater influence before the rise of cable television news. Presidents in neither era were particularly effective directly leading the public's agenda on the economy, according to our analysis. We cannot even conclude that the effectiveness of individual speeches is based on ratings: Gerald Ford averaged the highest ratings during 1975, when he delivered three addresses on the economy, at 61 percent of homes watching (see Edwards 2003, 190), but none of his speeches was influential. Arguably, a smaller audience may lead to less opportunity for presidential leadership of the public's agenda, but we find no evidence that a larger audience guarantees it. In sum, of the twenty-eight nationally televised speeches delivered over our time frame, only three significantly and positively affected the public's agenda. Because some individual addresses increase media attention and the media's agenda also increases public concern for the economy (first-column results in Table 4.1), there exists the potential for indirect leadership, nevertheless.

Even though we find no direct impact of presidential leadership over the public's economic agenda, our analysis of the media's agenda, presented in second column in Table 4.1, supports limited direct presidential leadership over the media's economic policy agenda. Ten of the twenty-eight national economic addresses analyzed (again, counting Reagan's February 1981 success as two speeches) led to a significant increase in the media's attention to economic issues.[30] Two additional speeches, Reagan's July 1981 speech and Bush's October 1990 speech, significantly depressed media coverage. The media were likely distracted by other, more newsworthy topics after these addresses, such as the Iraq War in late 1990. A typical impediment to leadership of media is that other issues compete for media attention (Wood and Peake 1998). Overall, the findings corroborate those reported by Peake and Eshbaugh-Soha (2008), though some slight differences emerge due to the lengthier time frame and additional control variables presented here.[31]

Because only a handful of individual addresses directly affect the public's economic agenda, it is unlikely that a collapsed variable of national addresses would directly predict the public's agenda. Yet, one of the only parsimonious ways to examine any reciprocal effects between national addresses, the media, and public is to model a single variable that indicates whether the president delivered a national address in a month. To this end, we report a simultaneous equations generalized probit model in Table 4.2 (model 1). Whether the president gave an address in a month and the percentage of the public that finds all economic issues to be most important are the dependent variables. The results reveal two important findings.

First, a national address on the economy produces no positive impact on the public's agenda. This is unsurprising given the results of the impact assessment analyses already presented. In fact, the results indicate a statistically significant negative impact, the opposite results of what is typical for presidential leadership of the public agenda through televised addresses. This is a substantial blow to the effectiveness of a focused strategy of presidential leadership. Each president in our sample faced economic duress, but a strategy of focused attention proves ineffective in convincing the American people of the urgency of economic concerns. It is possible that presidents used their national addresses to claim credit for economic successes, helping to push the economy off the public's agenda, but presidents have not tended to use addresses in this way, as the individual analysis demonstrated.

TABLE 4.2.
The interrelationships among national addresses, the public, and media
on the economy.

Model 1		*Parameter estimates*		*Parameter estimates*
Dependent variable	Public agenda		National address	
Independent variables	National address	−7.36* (3.62)	Public agenda	0.03* (0.01)
	Media agenda	0.29* (0.06)	Approval	−0.01 (0.01)
			Reelection year	−0.91* (0.38)
	Approval	−0.29* (0.09)	First term	0.48 (0.31)
	Events	2.30 (4.94)	Events	−0.38 (0.49)
	Misery index	3.59* (0.39)	Divided government	0.58* (0.27)
	Constant	−4.70 (11.61)	Constant	−3.37* (0.73)
	R-squared 0.53	N = 478	Pseudo R-squared 0.19	N = 478
Model 2				
Dependent variable	Media agenda		National address	
Independent variables	National address	18.39* (6.16)	Media agenda	0.02* (0.01)
	Public agenda	0.48* (0.11)	Approval	−0.01 (0.01)
			Reelection year	−0.56 (0.35)
	Approval	0.36* (0.18)	First term	0.44 (0.33)
	Events	2.24 (9.39)	Events	−0.27 (0.45)
	Misery index	0.56 (0.96)	Divided government	0.32 (0.26)
	Constant	33.22 (21.91)	Constant	−2.19* (0.59)
	R-squared 0.38	N = 478	Pseudo R-squared 0.15	N = 478

* $p < 0.05$, one-tailed test
Note: Models 1 and 2 are generalized probit models. Standard errors are in parentheses.

Take, for example, perhaps one of the most unusual, albeit ineffective, instances of failed focused leadership: Gerald Ford's October 1974
national address on the economy. Not only did the president champion
a colorful campaign to "Whip Inflation Now," or WIN, as expressed
by myriad red and white lapel buttons distributed by the White House;
President Ford was adamant that the American people, "our constituents," he said, "want leadership, our constituents want action." Neither
the impeding threat of higher than 7 percent inflation nor the president's
address had a demonstrable impact on public concern for the economy.

This failure of leadership speaks again to the difficulty the president faces leading a public distracted by other issues (perhaps Watergate) or generally uninterested in politics. This negligible public response to Ford's October 1974 address occurred even with a relatively high 47 percent share on network television (Baum and Kernell 1999). More problematic for presidents who are unable to lead the public's economic agenda is that they may also be incapable of being able to parlay public speech making into a greater likelihood of success in Congress (see Canes-Wrone 2001).

Second, a heightened priority for the economy on the public's agenda encourages a presidential response, as a boost in public concern for the economy increases the likelihood that presidents will deliver a national address in a month.[32] It should be no surprise to the reader, therefore, that the vast majority of national addresses presidents have delivered on the economy occur during periods of high public concern for the economy. This includes Reagan's five addresses in 1981, Bush's address in June 1992, and Clinton's three addresses in 1993. Of course, President George W. Bush's September 2008 national address may be the most telling example of presidential responsiveness to the public's agenda. Facing an economic collapse and increasing public dismay over a lingering recession—with public concern rising from 38 percent of the American people identifying the economy as the most important problem facing the nation in January 2008 to 69 percent viewing it as such in the month before the president's speech—Bush delivered his first national address on the economy. Even though Bush's efforts did not calm an anxious public or help an economy that declined further, we do not conclude that Bush's inability to lead the public's agenda was an abject failure. Unlike much of the literature that bemoans the president's inability to lead the public, we interpret these findings of responsiveness as potentially beneficial to a democratically elected leader. At the least, these examples reveal that the president spoke to meet the public's expectations that he address the economy amid economic distress.

Ultimately, even a lack of leadership but the occurrence of responsiveness through a strategy of focused attention on the economy supports our primary theoretical expectations. Taking our two primary findings together, that presidents do not directly lead the public but that the public influences presidential attention to the economy, supports our salience hypothesis.

When an issue is important to the public, as we theorized, presidents are unlikely to be able to lead the public's agenda on that issue. Instead, presidents will respond through their national addresses to meet the public's expectations that they tackle issues already on the public's agenda. Existing public concern not only limits the prospects for presidents to lead the public's agenda, therefore, it also induces presidential responsiveness.

Does the president's responsiveness to the public preclude indirect presidential leadership through increased news coverage? The results presented in Table 4.2 (model 2) uncover possible indirect effects presidential addresses have had on the public's agenda through their impact on news coverage. Here, the dependent variables are the media's agenda and our national address dichotomy. The results illustrate that, even after accounting for simultaneity, national addresses increase media attention. A national address on the economy in a month increases network news stories on the economy by over eighteen in that month. The reverse is also true. Increased media attention increases the likelihood that the president will deliver a national address. In addition, model 1 illustrates that media influence the public's agenda, an important consideration for our indirect leadership hypothesis. Given this relationship, along with the impact that national addresses have on media coverage, presidents tend to lead the public indirectly through increased news coverage. In other words, national addresses affect the media's agenda, the media's agenda affects the public's agenda, and, therefore, the president's national addresses indirectly lead the public's economic agenda.

Although encouraging, this evidence is not definitive. We simply know of no way to model all three dependent variables in a single equation, given the difficulties presented by the dichotomous national address variable. As such, we concede that a more sophisticated statistical technique may reject our findings, however unlikely this may be. We also underscore that this relationship is contemporaneous, such that a national address in a month affects media attention in that month, and note that a lagged national address variable has no discernable impact on the media's agenda. For this reason, we could be witnessing, in part, news coverage of the lead-up to the national address, not solely the news coverage that occurs after the speech. Nevertheless, this should not be indicative of a lack of presidential influence over the news media. After all, our model in Table 4.1 addresses individual lags and still reveals that about a third of individual speeches positively influence media attention to the economy, even when controlling for economic conditions. Even if media coverage is generated before the president actually delivers the speech, the coverage may still be a function of the president's speech.

Examining our control variables, we find that reelection years negatively predict national addresses. Presidents are less likely to deliver a national address on the economy during a reelection year. It appears that if the economy is doing poorly in a reelection year, then presidents are not going to publicize this through a national address. Obviously, presidents have delivered national addresses on the economy during reelection years, as evidenced by President Carter's 1980 address and Bush's 1992 speech. Perhaps these speeches were designed to advertise their concern about the economy to an anxious public. Responsiveness proved ineffective for both presidents, however, as each president's approval ratings continued to decline after his address, and neither Carter nor Bush won reelection.

Three other controls offer additional perspective to our understanding of the effectiveness of a focused strategy of presidential leadership on the public's and media's economic agendas. First, the president's approval ratings act as informational cues for both the news media and public. On the one hand, approval ratings positively condition the media's economic agenda, such that the more popular the president is, the more frequently the media will cover the economy. This finding provides some clarification to the mixed expectations we presented in Chapter 3 and reveals that higher approval ratings represent a favorable context for presidential leadership, at least in terms of more media coverage of the economy. On the other hand, higher approval ratings suppress the public's concerns about the economy. This could be beneficial to presidents, nevertheless, and suggests the reverse, that a public who are less concerned about the economy are more likely to approve of the president's job performance. This may help the president achieve policy or electoral goals. Although this finding reinforces the conventional wisdom that high approval ratings are associated with positive economic growth, approval has no impact on the likelihood of presidents' delivering a national address. Second, conditions of divided government increase the likelihood of a national address, consistent with Kernell's (1997) theoretical reasoning that presidents are more likely to go public when bargaining with Congress is more difficult. Finally, a poor economy, measured using the misery index, increases public concern for the economy, as expected.

In sum, presidential leadership of the economic policy agenda is quite restricted for presidents who choose a strategy of focused attention. National addresses on the whole do not directly affect the public's agenda, in part because the public drives the president's decision to deliver an address on the economy in the first place. In other words, presidents respond to the public's economic agenda through national addresses. Even given these apparent weaknesses to the president's direct leadership of the public's agenda, televised national addresses have a larger impact on media attention to the economy. Because the news media also influence the public's agenda, we conclude that presidents indirectly lead the public's economic agenda through a strategy of focused attention. However, the primary focus of the strategy appears to be demonstrating responsiveness by speaking on national television about the economy.

Iraq

We analyze Iraq from 1989 to 2008, as this was the time period in which the issue was of primary relevance to American politics. Although U.S. relations with Iraq became strategically important during the Iran–Iraq war of the 1980s, in which the United States sided with Iraq, U.S. antagonism toward Iraq did not commence until early in the first Bush administration, in August 1990, after the Iraqi military invaded Kuwait.[33] After the Persian Gulf War expelled Saddam Hussein from Kuwait and imposed sanctions crippling to the Iraqi military, Iraq was the subject of periodic attention by the news media and public, even though it had indisputably been on each president's national security agenda since August 1990. President Clinton contended with an assassination attempt of former President Bush and authorized missile strikes in response to Iraq's refusal to cooperate with weapons inspectors inside Iraq. The Iraq War consumed the George W. Bush administration, an issue he passed along to his successor, Barack Obama. From 1989 through 2008, over all, presidents delivered sixteen nationally televised addresses on Iraq in their efforts to focus and lead the media and public agendas on Iraq.

Significant public attention to Iraq was absent prior to Iraq's invasion of Kuwait on August 2, 1990. President George H. W. Bush delivered the first national address on Iraq shortly after, on August 8, 1990, in which he explained to the public his reasons for sending American troops to Saudi Arabia as part of Operation Desert Shield. He delivered several more televised addresses, keeping the American people informed of efforts to encourage Saddam Hussein to leave Kuwait and surrender under conditions devised by the United States and its allies. The administration also spent considerable time cultivating alliances, from Great Britain to Egypt, in an effort to persuade Saddam Hussein that the world was against him and only unconditional withdrawal was acceptable. The threat of military action increased throughout the remaining months of 1990, and President Bush announced the invasion of Kuwait by allied forces on January 16, 1991. His remaining addresses were short and informative, with three delivered throughout the month of February, culminating in a declaration of victory speech to a joint session of Congress in March 1991.

President George H. W. Bush's national addresses proved modestly successful in leading the public's and media's agendas, as presented in Table 4.3. Of the seven national addresses delivered by President Bush in 1990 and 1991, only two effectively increased public attention to Iraq policy, the January and February speeches, which led to an increase of an additional 13 and 28 percent of the public who claimed Iraq was the most important problem facing the nation. The January speech is as expected.[34] The February speeches continued to sustain the public's attention to Iraq, providing some support for our reinforcement hypothesis. Indeed the coefficient for February 1991 is not the impact of any one speech but the cumulative impact of three speeches on public concern for Iraq. The president was much more successful affecting the media's attention to Iraq, with all but one intervention, the victory speech on March 6, 1991, generating significant increases in the number of stories devoted by the networks to Iraq. As we will discuss, it is impossible to distinguish between the effects of discrete presidential speeches and an ongoing military conflict, however.

TABLE 4.3.

Impact of nationally televised presidential speeches on public's and media's
Iraq policy agendas, January 1989–June 2008.

	Public agenda		Media agenda	
	Parameter estimates	Standard error	Parameter estimates	Standard error
G. H. W. Bush 8/90	−3.81	2.67	320.78*	21.28
G. H. W. Bush 9/90	−11.50*	3.27	102.87*	17.77
G. H. W. Bush 1/91	13.55*	2.65	79.87*	20.59
G. H. W. Bush 2/91	28.33*	2.46	54.99*	21.28
G. H. W. Bush 3/91	−1.54	2.22	12.86	25.40
Clinton 6/93	−0.34	1.95	4.16	16.07
Clinton 10/94	0.23	1.94	37.54*	15.97
Clinton 12/98	−3.25*	1.95	34.51*	16.16
G. W. Bush 10/02	−0.36	1.95	7.96	16.11
G. W. Bush 3/03	13.28*	2.49	65.71*	20.02
G. W. Bush 5/03	1.15	2.20	−22.47	18.09
G. W. Bush 12/03	2.33	2.06	14.01	17.00
G. W. Bush 1/05	0.85	2.12	26.32	16.99
G. W. Bush 6/05	−1.27	2.01	−1.03	16.31
G. W. Bush 12/05	−0.35	1.99	−0.77	16.09
G. W. Bush 01/07	2.04	1.95	28.27*	16.31
G. W. Bush 09/07	0.24	2.80	22.73	22.83
Media agenda$_{t-1}$	0.07*	0.01		
Public agenda$_{t-1}$			0.73	0.57
Approval	−0.10*	0.04	−0.08	0.32
First term	0.07	1.61	13.89	11.94
Reelection year	−0.55	1.14	−4.47	8.74
Events	0.67	1.20	−5.19	9.61
Misery index	0.37	0.41	−0.12	3.11
Constant	10.78	7.74	32.82	35.51
AR1	0.98*	0.02	0.95*	0.03
MA1	−0.27*	0.08	−0.36*	0.08
MA|5|	0.22*	0.07		
R-square	0.96		0.87	
Mean of dependent	7.04		41.33	
Box-Ljung Q	41.05		25.51	
N	234		234	

* $p < 0.05$, one-tailed test

Note: All speeches are pulse functions, indicating the short-term (same month) effect of the president's speech, with the parameter estimate reflecting the estimated number of stories increased in the month of the speech. There were no long-term effects.

Iraq was a clear foreign policy priority for the Clinton administration. The U.S. military patrolled the no-fly zones routinely, coming into conflict with Iraqi military. Additionally, Clinton backed U.N. requirements for inspections of Iraqi chemical and nuclear facilities, to which Iraq sometimes cooperated and other times balked. In response to a foiled assassination attempt on former President Bush, Clinton ordered missile strikes in June, 1993. In 1994, major deployments of Iraqi troops on the Kuwaiti border prompted the deployment of U.S. and allied ground troops to the region. These events led to a handful of national addresses: one that announced retaliation in 1993 for the attempted assassination of former President Bush, another that occurred in October 1994 during the midterm election campaign season, and the other two (coded in our study as one speech because they occurred within days of each other) announcing the beginning and end of air strikes in Iraq as retaliation for not cooperating with chemical weapons inspection teams in Iraq in December 1998 (Operational Desert Fox). The results in Table 4.3 reveal no positive impact of any of President Clinton's speeches on the public's agenda—these events and adjoining televised addresses had no measurable effect on public concern for Iraq (which remained near zero). Both the 1994 and 1998 speeches generated significant media attention, nevertheless, which is expected when presidents deploy troops or order the use of force abroad.

George W. Bush made Iraq a top policy priority, whether from the first day of his administration, as some contend (Suskind 2004), or soon after September 11, 2001 (Woodward 2002). The build-up to the war in Iraq, in which weapons inspectors were actively seeking information about weapons of mass destruction inside Iraq, included numerous attempts at presidential leadership in what we would characterize as a strategy of focused attention. This began with a national address to the American people on Iraq in October 2002, followed by numerous other speeches. These included an announcement of the beginning of the war in March 2003, the end of "major combat operations" in May 2003, reminders to the American people of the reason for being in Iraq in 2005, and the announcement of and updates on Bush's "surge" policy in 2007, which increased ground troops in and around Baghdad.

The conventional wisdom is that the Bush administration, especially early on in the Iraq War, drove news coverage (Bennet et al. 2007; Hayes and Guardino 2010; but see Baum and Groeling 2010). We find only limited support for this contention, at least in terms of setting and sustaining the media's agenda using a strategy of focused attention.[35] Mainly, the March 2003 speeches, reinforced and surrounded by an invasion, positively and significantly increased media attention to the war. Because two speeches were given during this month, this also supports our reinforcement hypothesis, that multiple addresses in a month should be most effective leading the agenda, at least in the short term. Additionally, the announcement of a new "surge" policy by Bush in January 2007 had a significant impact on media attention to Iraq.[36] We would have expected that if the conventional wisdom were correct that numerous addresses, and especially during the march to war, would have a similar impact. These results speak to the difficulties that presidents have leading the media's agenda even over foreign policy and war, at least during the George W. Bush administration.

We report similar results concerning President Bush's leadership of the public's agenda on Iraq. After controlling for media attention, which substantially increased public concern for the war in Iraq, President Bush had limited success using his national addresses to increase public concern for the war in Iraq. Only President Bush's dual addresses in March of 2003 had a significant and positive impact on public concern for Iraq, increasing about 13 percent of the public that cited Iraq as a most important problem. When presidents can announce the beginning of a policy action in a national address, as we saw in March 2003, then they are best situated to lead the public's agenda. This not only supports our salience hypothesis but also lends credence to the greater likelihood of presidential leadership on foreign than other policy areas.

As we have uncovered in other research (Peake and Eshbaugh-Soha 2008), however, it is virtually impossible to differentiate statistically between the announcement of military action and the military action itself (see Baum and Groeling 2010, 149). For our purposes, we recognize that we cannot discern whether the media response is specific to the president's speech (although it is undoubtedly referenced on the news) or whether the media focus their coverage on events on the ground after the announcement. Despite the difficulties this presents for the precision of our conclusions, we remind the reader that we are not interested in whether the media report on the president's speech but in whether they report on the president's policy priority, in this case Iraq. Moreover, we suggest that the president's speech, his agenda, and a media response are inseparable:

Military action is newsworthy because it is on the president's agenda, and it is on the president's agenda because it is important and relates to the president's constitutional authority as commander in chief.

Although a few individual addresses helped presidents lead the public and media agendas on Iraq, our findings also insinuate limits to a purely public relations strategy in setting the agenda on foreign policy (Peake 1999). As evidence for this, there exist coinciding new major policy events (that is, military action or troop deployments) in every case where we find a positive influence by speeches. In cases where the president delivers an address on Iraq without a corresponding dramatic event (such as George W. Bush's speech in October of 2002), we find no significant influence on the public or media agendas. It is likely that public concern for and media attention to Iraq would have increased at these times when major policy innovations occur regardless of whether or not the president went on national television.

To assess all addresses together and evaluate the presence of indirect presidential leadership of the public, we now evaluate whether a collapsed measure of all national addresses influences the public and media or vice versa. We present the results of reciprocal models in Table 4.4. Our findings show that, when coded as a single variable rather than as individual interventions, national addresses have no direct positive impact on the public's agenda (see model 1). Instead, presidential addresses tend to suppress public concern, perhaps given the significance of George H. W. Bush's myriad addresses toward the end of the Persian Gulf War. Rather than presidential speeches, it appears that media attention to Iraq drives public concern for the issue, given its significance in model 1 in Table 4.4. What is more telling is that the public's concern for Iraq increases the likelihood that a president will deliver a national address. This supports our expectation that prior public concern will diminish the likelihood of presidential leadership, as presidents seek to be responsive on issues of public concern. At the same time, it serves to undermine our expectation that presidents would have more capacity to lead the public on foreign than economic policy issues. Such differences may hold for the rare foreign policy event or use of force driven by the president of the United States; but a long-term conflict like the Iraq War serves to force

TABLE 4.4.
The interrelationships among national addresses, the public, and media on Iraq.

Model 1		Parameter estimates		Parameter estimates
Dependent variable	Public agenda		National address	
Independent variables	National address	−6.63 (4.924)	Public agenda	0.06* (0.018)
	Media agenda	0.12* (0.073)	Approval	0.05* (0.016)
	War deaths	0.27* (0.033)	First term	0.04 (0.435)
	Events	10.14 (8.193)	Events	0.68 (0.658)
	Misery index	−0.01 (0.672)	Misery index	0.03 (0.120)
	Constant	−15.42 (13.005)	Constant	−5.01* (1.235)
	R-squared 0.82	N = 234	Psuedo R-squared 0.23	N = 234
Model 2				
Dependent variable	Media agenda		National address	
Independent variables	National address	25.98* (9.931)	Media agenda	0.01* (0.004)
	Public agenda	0.98* (0.563)	Approval	0.03* (0.098)
	War deaths	0.44* (0.205)	First term	−0.27 (0.379)
	Events	40.96* (18.382)	Events	−0.05 (0.615)
	Misery index	3.92 (2.697)	Misery index	0.04 (0.098)
	Constant	37.86 (35.444)	Constant	−3.85* (0.979)
	R-squared 0.82	N = 234	Psuedo R-squared 0.19	N = 234

* $p < 0.05$, one-tailed test

Note: Models 1 and 2 are generalized probit models. Standard errors are in parentheses.

presidential responsiveness. For example, George W. Bush's addresses during the later years of the Iraq War are best conceived of as responses by the president to heightened public concern over the war's lack of progress.

Although national addresses do not directly affect the public's agenda, the generalized probit model in Table 4.4 (model 2) provides evidence of presidential leadership in two ways. First and foremost, nationally televised addresses have substantively positive effects on media attention to Iraq, even while controlling for the onset of major hostilities (the events measure) and war deaths, which are statistically significant. The effect is an estimated twenty-six additional stories. This relationship points to the possibility of an indirect impact because media coverage of Iraq also increases public concern for Iraq. After all, national addresses serve to affect media attention, and media attention increases the public's concern for Iraq. Thus, within the methodological limitations of our data, we conclude that presidents' national addresses on Iraq have influenced the public's agenda indirectly through the news media. Just as our results confirm that presidents are unlikely to directly lead the public's agenda when they respond to it, so too do our results provide evidence that a strategy of focused attention can be effective indirectly leading the public's agenda through the news media.

In sum, presidents tend to be slightly more successful using a focused strategy on Iraq than on economic policy issues given that a higher share of individual addresses on Iraq than the economy affect both the public's and media's agenda. This is unsurprising, given that presidential speeches on Iraq often corresponded with major developments in Iraq policy, including presidential decisions to use force. The differences end there, however. Like the economy, presidents are constrained by existing public concern for Iraq and tend to be responsive through their national addresses. Moreover, their speeches do not sustain the public's interest even with the handful of addresses that do induce public responsiveness. Like with the economy, we show fairly strong evidence that presidents influence the public indirectly by first increasing media attention to Iraq. Directly leading the public, however, is a highly unlikely outcome when using a strategy of focused attention regardless of policy area.

CONCLUSION

We set out in this chapter to explore the impact that a focused strategy of presidential agenda setting may have on the public and media. We present compelling evidence that this strategy does not guarantee influence, despite the many advantages the strategy affords the president; nor does it preclude leadership, in spite of its numerous disadvantages. Instead, presidents tend to respond to the public's agenda through their national addresses rather than lead the public directly. Our salience hypothesis is supported for both economic policy and Iraq. The analysis also supports our view that media are a central and intervening linkage between the president and public given that the president appears able to indirectly lead the public through the news media. The media, in this sense, is therefore not so noisy as to preclude focused presidential leadership of the public's agenda on the economy and Iraq. However, the tendency for presidents to respond to the public through nationally televised addresses speaks to the central role media play as gatekeepers, in that it is their decision—not the president's—that dictates whether or not the president has access to a national television audience in the first place.

Still, our results also reveal the limits of a strategy of focused attention. As we theorized, presidents are in their strongest position to lead the public in the absence of existing public concern. Presidents also have the discretion to use the national address as a tool of public leadership. Yet, in our examination of both the economy and Iraq, presidents directly respond to the public, which, according to our salience hypothesis, is a function of these issues' presence on the public's agenda prior to the national addresses. So even though presidents have discretion to strategically maximize their chances for leadership, we demonstrate that they do not typically lead through a strategy of focused attention. Rather, presidents respond strategically to existing public concern for issues in the highest-profile and most visible means possible. Because presidents are highly responsive through their national addresses, then, consistent with our salience hypothesis, it should be no surprise that presidents have much difficulty also leading public opinion through this strategy.

Our results speak clearly to the potential for effective leadership through a strategy of focused attention, nevertheless, especially on foreign affairs. At the beginning of an international event, presidents may be able to act in an entrepreneurial fashion to influence news coverage of their foreign policy agenda. Presidents are unlikely to be able to sustain public attention to the issue, however, unless they can buttress media attention through future national addresses. It complicates matters as well if an issue remains on the public and media agendas. Even if presidents have already led the public and media through an initial address, driving media attention and public concern further with another national address may prove futile, given the numerous limitations we have identified to such an approach. We see this clearly with the war in Iraq, when President George W. Bush led the agenda at the beginning of the conflict but could only respond to public concerns as the war dragged on. Indeed, if presidents choose to speak nationally with the intent of setting the media or public agendas, they should do so at the beginning of the policy cycle, not later in the process as media and public agendas become saturated with the issue and opinion may become less malleable. Although we can only make this conclusion in regards to the broad policy areas that we have examined in this chapter, there is no reason for us to believe that it will not extend to a larger examination of additional policy areas.

CHAPTER 5

A Sustained Strategy of Presidential Leadership

MODERN PRESIDENTS EXPEND substantial resources on public relations. This is most evident in recent presidents' frequent use of the bully pulpit. For example, President Clinton averaged 421 addresses and appearances per year during his two terms in office, and President George W. Bush averaged 360 (Ragsdale 2009). President Obama has continued the trend. During his first year in office, Obama made 333 addresses and appearances, which places him on par with President Bush's frequency of public activities.[1] These speeches come in a variety of forms, including weekly radio addresses, remarks to reporters, press conferences, nationally televised addresses, and public appearances in and out of Washington, D.C. They may be used to announce new policy initiatives, respond to public criticism, or claim credit for recent policy successes.

Presidents do not speak for the sake of speaking alone, of course. They engage in public speaking to achieve their goals, whether these include policy, reelection, or historical achievement. Although presidents may ultimately hope to affect the votes of legislators through speech making, one of their first concerns is reaching the public and news media. Given that national addresses are rare events, dwarfed by the several hundred speeches presidents give annually, the bulk of the president's efforts to lead the public and news media is through short remarks, minor speeches, or addresses aimed at specific constituencies. Presidents typically underscore a policy priority repeatedly in speech after speech, in what we call a strategy of sustained leadership.

A recent example of a sustained leadership strategy involves President Obama and the economy. Obama ended a very busy first week of February 2009 with a Saturday morning radio address focused on the economic stimulus bill. During the following week, he continued his attention to "economic stabilization" with speeches in Indiana, Florida, and Illinois. On February 9, the president devoted much of his first prime-time televised press conference to the economic crisis. In total, President Obama delivered twenty-one public remarks concerning the economy during the first two weeks in February.[2] Descriptive evidence suggests, as well, that the president's policy agenda for those weeks correlates highly with the media's and public's agendas. The media covered the economy throughout the month of February, as roughly 44, 47, and 40 percent of news coverage during the first, second, and third weeks in February, respectively, pertained to the economy.[3] Part of this coverage included five solo interviews with journalists from the major television networks, in which the president's economic agenda was prominent. Most importantly, the economy ranked highly on the public's policy agenda. By March, public concern for the economy—or those who viewed some aspect of the economy as the "most important problem"—reached 80 percent.[4] Just as the president spoke about the economy in a sustained fashion and the media gave it substantial coverage, so too was the economy high on the public's agenda.

One may look at these data and credit the president with successful leadership of the economy based on a typical scenario: The president speaks about an issue continuously, the news media cover it, and it reaches the public's agenda. But the causal ordering is likely to be more complicated. Was Obama leading the public's agenda, or was he responding to existing public concern about the economy? It is probable that the president was responding to the public's agenda given that public concern for the economy reached 77 percent right after the 2008 presidential election.[5] Concerning the media, did Obama's sustained public attention to economic issues encourage additional news coverage of it, or did Obama adjust his level of attention to economic issues based on media coverage of the economy? The economy's being a top issue on the network newscasts likely influenced the president's decision to address it during February and sustain his public attention to economic issues. Through this anecdotal evidence alone, however, we cannot be certain who led whom and what role the media played in the president's efforts at public leadership over the economy in 2009 or, more generally, in other instances.

The extent of the president's efforts to sustain public attention points to a straightforward empirical question: What are the effects of a sustained strategy of presidential speech making on the public and media agendas?

The frequency with which presidents deliver speeches suggests that presidents have the capacity and determination to lead both agendas. Yet, we know very little about the success of a sustained strategy because much of our understanding about the effectiveness of rhetorical leadership of the public centers on single-speech effects (see Canes-Wrone 2001; Cohen 1995; Rosenblatt 1998). Even scholars who question presidential leadership of the public rely predominantly on the single address strategy, as well, which focuses on a before and after research design to determine presidential effectiveness (for example, see Edwards 2003). Yet the many definitions and applications of public leadership, along with the implicit sentiment of the phrase "the permanent campaign," mean that the president's ability to lead the public through speech making is not a one-time, persuasive event. Successful leadership may require repeated and sustained presidential attention given that persistence is a central attribute of successful leadership (Rockman 1984). Effective leadership involves, to some extent, the president's ability to sustain attention—to engage in repeat and follow-up—even in the face of competing forces that may work to supplant their efforts. Because the literature is mostly silent on the question of presidential agenda-setting leadership of the public through a strategy of sustained attention, we not only examine the nature of the president's efforts to sustain the attention of the news media and public, we also ascertain whether the strategy is successful. As is also relevant, we explore whether presidents tend to respond rather than lead through this strategy and what impact existing public concern and media attention have on the effectiveness of a sustained leadership strategy.

SUSTAINED LEADERSHIP

A strategy of sustained presidential leadership of the media and public agendas entails repeated and continuous attention by presidents to a policy or topic in their public speeches. It does not mean that presidents will avoid other topics and engage only one at a time; clearly, presidents cannot meet public expectations by addressing exclusively one issue at a time, nor will they succeed on a multifaceted policy agenda by focusing on one issue at the exclusion of all others. Even so, the more presidents focus their own attention on one issue, the greater chance they have to influence and sustain the attention of the media and public. It is equally plausible that the expansion of media and public access to the presidency has served only to force greater responsiveness from presidents. Therefore, an analysis of the sustained leadership strategy must also account for the influence of the media and public on the president's emphasis on a particular issue.

Advantages to a Sustained Strategy

While it is clear that modern presidents speak frequently, why they do so is a question that has sparked considerable scholarly debate. We maintain that presidents speak frequently for a number of reasons (see Edwards 2003, 242–246). Primarily, public speaking is at the core of modern presidential governance and thus vital to presidential goal achievement. More precisely, speaking frequently in a sustained and continuous fashion may be an effective way to lead both the public and media agendas. Maintaining the attention of the public and media is especially important to presidential leadership given the tendency for the public and media to be distracted by other interests or stories. The president is newsworthy, but repeated presidential attention to a single policy area may be required to remind the public and media of the president's agenda. Although there are also limits, a sustained strategy of attention presents numerous advantages to presidents who seek to lead the media and public agendas.

Speaking frequently meets a principal condition of presidential agenda setting. By prioritizing an issue and feeding the news media and the public a consistent dose of attention to it, presidents increase their odds of penetrating a media business that may not always be responsive to presidential activities and a public that is usually out of touch with the presidency and public policy. Although the media do not always cover the president or report much of what is said by the president when they do (Barrett 2007), presidents regularly make the news, garnering as much as 80 percent of all government coverage on the network news (Farnsworth and Lichter 2006).[6] What is more, the public has a relatively high level of interest in presidential news, despite the public's tendency to disengage from political discourse.

All of this points to strong potential for a successful strategy of sustained presidential leadership. As we argued in Chapter 3, citizens rely on information short cuts to process vast amounts of information given their boundedly rational nature and limited interest in politics. The more a president speaks about an issue, the greater the public's accessibility is to the president's message and, therefore, the greater the likelihood is that the president will affect the public's policy agenda (see Wood et al. 2005). This accessibility—and the prospects for presidential leadership of the public—will be enhanced if speeches also increase news coverage of the president's agenda. Especially with a strategy of sustained attention, when presidents speak continuously and in a sustained fashion about a policy priority, they reduce the transaction costs associated with the public acquiring knowledge of the president's agenda (Baum 2003, 30). The more a president speaks, the less effort the public has to expend to be aware of—even if by accident—that president's agenda. Thus, presidents may have to repeat their message continuously to have an impact on the public. Some research shows that the frequency of presidential attention affects the public in the way we expect (Wood et al. 2005).

Accessibility is vital for presidential leadership of the public's agenda. But presidents rarely have the undivided attention of the public without news commentary. The most likely avenue for presidential leadership of the public's agenda may therefore be indirect and through the media's agenda. It is through the media, after all, that the public almost certainly learns what presidents are speaking about and what their top priorities are. It is rare for the public to be exposed directly to the president's entire message, essentially because media are likely to give the public direct access to the president's speeches only when they are delivered as part of a national address (see Chapter 4).[7] At best, the public will hear the president speak only briefly, as part of a short sound bite of not more than ten seconds on network news (Hallin 1992), limiting the direct impact that the president's own words may have on the public's agenda. Even if presidents are unable to maintain the public's attention directly and through multiple speeches, affecting media coverage may be sufficient for successful leadership given the strong link between the media and public agendas.

Indirect leadership of the public through news media requires presidents to first affect the media's agenda. Although there is evidence that presidents may have difficulty doing this (Edwards and Wood 1999; Wood and Peake 1998), others counter this claim (Bennett et al. 2007) and find substantial presidential influence over news coverage of a central foreign policy issue: the war in Iraq. The logic of presidential leadership of the news agenda is very similar to that of leadership of the public. Much as the public looks for information shortcuts, the news media look for low-cost ways to produce profitable news stories (Cohen 2010; Hamilton 2004). By sustaining attention to a policy priority, the president may remain accessible to the news media, making it easier (that is, reducing the associated transaction costs) for the media to tap the presidency for news. Given that the Washington press corps already devote substantial resources to covering the presidency wherever the president may be speaking, sustained attention means that when the media cover the president, the president increases the odds that they will also cover his agenda.

Another benefit of a sustained strategy of attention, unlike a focused strategy that suggests a short-term impact, is that it also provides presidents with the opportunity for long-term leadership. The goal of presidential leadership is not only to set the agenda but also to maintain a persistent impact over it for several months, perhaps also shaping the public's policy preferences or policy debates in Congress. By repeating and reinforcing his own message, the president increases the probability that the news media and public will continue to have access to his agenda. Think about it in this way: If, over the course of several months, the president speaks about the economy one week, health care the next, and energy security three weeks later, then the news media will cover a wide range of issues, any number of which could penetrate the public's agenda. Yet, if the president speaks about the economy one week, then continues to reinforce the economic message repeatedly and consistently over several months, then so long as the media cover the president's speeches they will cover the economy, increasing the likelihood that the public will also be thinking about the economy and not some other issue.

Even if presidents cannot direct the public's agenda through a strategy of sustained attention, a final benefit to this strategy is that it allows presidents to advertise their responsiveness to public concerns frequently. Just as accessibility is important to the president's efforts at leading the public's agenda, so too is it relevant to receiving credit for speaking about issues already on the public's agenda. That is, if the public are to know that the president cares about their economic concerns, then a primary means through which presidents can display this empathy is by speaking frequently and continuously about the economy. Lacking the national audiences that they once had, presidents may be better off speaking continuously about an issue so as to increase the likelihood that citizens notice that they are responsive to the public's agenda.

The success of a sustained leadership strategy requires presidents to be out in front of the public and news media on their policy priorities. Consistent with our theory, therefore, if presidents act as policy entrepreneurs and take it upon themselves to push an issue onto the national agenda, they are likely to drive coverage of this topic by the news media (see Edwards and Wood 1999; Peake 2001) and lead the public's agenda. Otherwise, presidential responsiveness is the most likely outcome. One way for presidents to lead on policy and attract initial media coverage is to tackle new issues or at least address old ones in inventive ways. Cohen (2008, 75) notes that an innovative policy agenda may stimulate news coverage, just as Edwards and Wood (1999) demonstrate this concerning health care reform in 1993–1994. Although the literature is clear that innovation may be an important first step for presidential leadership of the media and the public, being innovative is often at odds with maintaining and repeating one's policy preferences, as we will illustrate next.

Disadvantages to the Sustained Strategy

Although a potential boon to presidential leadership, given independent media and an uninterested public, the strategy of sustained attention suffers some basic limitations, which may undermine its potential effectiveness. The same conditions that help presidents penetrate media through a strategy of sustained attention may also render the strategy ineffective. To attract media coverage, for example, we have argued that it is important for presidents to tackle new issues or at least address old ones in inventive ways. Yet, the sustained strategy of leadership requires repeated follow-up and frequency. Something that is repeated continually by definition is likely to decrease in newsworthiness. As the novelty or timeliness of presidential speeches declines, their influence on the news and public opinion is likely to diminish (see Graber 2006, 99–101). The media and public simply do not always pay attention to presidents' myriad speeches and may be even less likely to pay attention when presidents offer little that is new. While President George W. Bush was able to generate significant national news coverage of Social Security reform early in his national tour in 2005, for example, the coverage declined as the novelty of the president's words and actions waned (Eshbaugh-Soha and Peake 2006).

There are other reasons that media hamper a strategy of sustained attention. Whether the president's policies are stale or new, the media are distracted easily by other stories and events. Kingdon (1995, 62) observes that media have limited "staying power" when it comes to issue coverage, which frustrates presidential efforts at leading the media's agenda (Edwards and Wood 1999). Moreover, when presidents make direct appeals to the public on legislation before Congress, news media often fail to cover them (Barrett 2007). The public's general inattention also matters. Just as sustained attention may pique the interest of the occasional viewer, viewers may need some enticement, such as a new and interesting policy proposal or related event, to engage them in presidential politics, which is something that repeated attention by the president may not provide over the long run.

Presidents may be beholden to events outside of their control to affect news coverage and the public's agenda. For example, even if the president talks repeatedly about the difficulties of fighting terrorism and argues that the U.S. military should engage this growing threat before it becomes too dangerous, he may be unable to convince the American people that terrorism should be important to them until something dramatic happens. Recall that Al Qaeda was deemed responsible for the U.S. embassy bombings in Africa and the attack on the USS *Cole* and that President Clinton targeted Osama Bin Laden with air strikes in August 1998. Clinton's rhetoric, even in the face of these events, was insufficient to engage the public in a conversation on international terrorism. Only when the issue hit home with the events of September 11, 2001, did the public prioritize terrorism.[8] In other words, even repeated and sustained efforts on the part of the president to set the public's agenda may fail without the appropriate conditions, especially a lack of public concern, for the president to lead it.

Even when the media cover the presidency, they may not cover what presidents want them to cover. For example, during late 1990 and early 1991, while the economy slumped, American forces built up in the

Persian Gulf region and eventually attacked Iraq. During this period of significant foreign policy events, news coverage focused on them—and President George Bush's speeches concerning Iraq—and not the slumping economy. The media focus on foreign policy clearly benefited Bush's approval ratings (see Edwards et al. 1995). As media shifted away from foreign policy to the economic recession following the war, the public's attention also shifted, to the detriment of the president. No matter how much President Bush might have liked to speak about his foreign policy successes, the economy dominated news coverage through the end of 1991 and into the 1992 presidential election campaign. He was expected to lead on the economy, even though the economic recession did not place him in a strong position to benefit from his speeches on it.

Related to this point are presidential responsibilities, which may limit presidents' ability to talk repeatedly about issues that they prefer. As we have discussed in Chapter 4, presidents have substantial discretion over which types of speeches to use and when. Yet, for a strategy of sustained attention to be effective, presidents may need to focus on one issue, repeatedly, and without much deviation. Presidents, however, are expected to address a number of issues. They have multiple policy proposals and priorities on their agendas and other goals that they hope to achieve. Moreover, the requirements of the office may cause presidents to address other priorities as they arise on the agenda, thus undermining their ability to engage in a sustained strategy on their top priorities. Along with general issues of newsworthiness and other distractions that drive media attention to other, nonpresidential stories, the president's own responsibilities, therefore, further compound the problems associated with this strategy's effectiveness.

In short, even though presidents are well positioned to affect agendas over the long term with a strategy of sustained attention, their own responsibilities, expectations, competing priorities, and events may limit the success of the strategy. Thus, if we find only short-term effects in the strategy of sustained attention, these competing responsibilities may be one reason for why the impact did not extend over the long term. However, it is these limitations that may require presidents to sustain attention to their policy priorities, and force them—even when innovation may be an important route to agenda leadership—to keep hammering the same message, day after day, and speech after speech. The president is rarely faced with a guarantee of influencing the public and media anyway, regardless of strategy, and sustained repetition may be his best option in a competitive political environment. It is our task, of course, to evaluate the effectiveness of this strategy in the remainder of this chapter, whether it is a successful one and whether it promotes leadership, responsiveness, both, or neither.

WILL A STRATEGY OF SUSTAINED ATTENTION BE SUCCESSFUL?

A strategy of sustained attention may be successful in part because the level of presidential commitment is a central feature of presidential leadership. Recall that most definitions of leadership, including those proffered by Rockman (1984) and Shull (1993), are centered on the notion of sustained commitment and assertiveness. That is, the more the president is committed to something, the more he is attempting to lead on it. This is important to those whom the president is trying to lead. Only if they notice signs of presidential commitment will others respond to the president's policy priorities (Kingdon 1995, 28). Thus sustained attention is essential for presidential agenda setting and for our definition of presidential leadership: affecting the policy priorities of others. Only if presidents maintain attention to an issue are they likely to sustain influence over the agendas of the media and public.

Our analysis accounts for several possibilities. First, presidents may lead the media by sustaining their public attention to issues important to them. If the news media report on presidential speeches or cover stories related to presidential policy priorities, then presidents are effectively leading the media's agenda. Second, such direct effects on media attention may carry over into indirect leadership of the public's agenda, one of the payoffs presidents are looking for when generating news coverage in the first place. Third, presidents may lead the public's agenda directly. Direct leadership of public attention through this strategy may be unlikely given that the public typically hears of presidential speeches only through news coverage. Indeed, only limited research holds that direct presidential leadership of the public is a distinct possibility (Wood 2007). Fourth, presidents may respond to public or media attention to issues. Such responsiveness would characterize a presidency focused on addressing those issues considered important to the public. As we have argued, presidents are responsive when they act on existing public concerns and issues that are already in the news.

Policy Variation

The policy context matters to presidential leadership. Because we do not expect the president's tendency to lead or respond to be uniform across policy areas, we examine two distinct policy priorities of recent presidents: the economy and Iraq. We have already outlined our general expectations in Chapters 3 and 4. These expectations do not vary according to a strategy of sustained attention. Nevertheless, we documented in Chapter 4 that presidents tend to give many more national addresses on foreign than on domestic policy. Therefore, there may be more opportunities for presidents to lead the public and media on foreign than on domestic policy using a strategy of focused attention. However, there is greater balance between presidential attention to foreign and domestic policy priorities when we examine all presidential speeches, which suggests that there is no inherent advantage to presidential leadership over foreign than domestic policy through a strategy of sustained attention.

That said, one of the primary motivations for selecting different policy areas is to ensure variation on the likely level of prior public and media interest in a policy area. The most important problem and media time series we introduced in Chapter 4 confirm substantial variation within and across both Iraq and economic policies. In addition, the nature of our economic data allows us to engage our central concern about prior salience more directly than we could in Chapter 4. Because we can disaggregate all presidential speeches into a variety of economic categories, we can also disaggregate economic policy into separate economic issues, which allows us additional variation on the level of prior public and media attention.

To do this, we need two subsets of economic issues, with at least one area that can be determined to be a priori salient to the public and another that can be determined to be a priori not salient to the public. Thus, we disaggregate our analysis of the economy to include two separate economic issues, unemployment and budget deficit and spending issues.[9] Public concern for economic issues most closely followed by the public, such as unemployment because it involves direct pocketbook issues, is most likely to affect presidential attention to the economy and encourage presidential respon-siveness. The public's agenda, alternatively, may be less likely to influence presidential attention to issues that involve esoteric economic attributes (submitting budgets and signing appropriations bills and related deficits) and therefore are not as closely followed by the public.[10] It is, perhaps, these less salient issues related to government spending and deficits that afford presidents the best opportunity to set the public's agenda because they are not usually salient or closely linked to personal economic conditions. During our time frame, presidents and Congress fought over the budget, perhaps creating opportunities for presidents to lead by heightening public concern for an issue of limited public interest at the outset of our analysis.

Conditional Leadership

The effectiveness of a sustained strategy of presidential attention should not only be affected by the news media and public, it should also be con-ditioned by the larger political environment. That is, the president's ap-proval ratings, reelection years, state of the economy, international events, and term in office may each affect his propensity to lead (or respond to) the public and media agendas. These variables should condition the ef-fectiveness of sustained leadership in ways similar to those we outlined in Chapters 3 and 4. We briefly restate these, here, but refer the reader to Chapter 4 for discussion of our measures. A higher presidential approval rating indicates a more favorable context for presidential leadership and may enhance presidential leadership on the economy or Iraq. Reelection years may condition whether presidents attend to the economy given its importance to presidential reelection chances. For similar reasons, presidents should behave differently during their first than during their second term in office over both issues. International events may serve to distract presidential attention from the economy but promote attention to foreign policy issues. The state of the economy, on the other hand, should increase the tendency for the president, media, and public to pay attention to economic issues but decrease their attention to Iraq. All in all, we treat these variables as exogenous controls that may influence the three-variable (president, media, and public) system. Although we include each control in the model, given the possibility that each could affect the interrelationships among the presidential, media, and public agendas, we report only those controls that are statistically significant.

Summary Expectations

A sustained strategy of presidential leadership provides presidents with a sound opportunity to lead the public and media agendas over the long term. This success should be conditioned not only by the policy area and political environment but also by existing public and media agendas. Consistent with our salience hypothesis, presidents are most likely to lead in the absence of existing public concern and media attention to policy issues. When presidents are forced to address an issue already on the public or media agendas, we are more likely to observe responsiveness. Even if presidents cannot sustain the public's agenda directly through their speeches, our indirect leadership hypothesis holds that increasing the public's exposure to the president's agenda through news coverage provides presidents with a potential opportunity to indirectly lead the public.

DATA

Our dataset is similar to what we analyzed in Chapter 4 to assess the dynamics of a focused strategy of presidential leadership. In addition, our rationale for choosing Iraq and the economy is the same for a sustained strategy of presidential leadership. Our analysis of Iraq covers the same time frame as in Chapter 4, from 1989 to June 2008, and includes three administrations (G. H. W. Bush, Clinton, and G. W. Bush). Our analysis of economic issues includes three presidential administrations as well (Reagan, G. H. W. Bush, and Clinton) over a slightly shorter, twenty-year period (1981–2000) than we used in Chapter 4. We chose this time period as a reasonable sample frame—240 monthly observations—given the labor-intensive nature of content coding the presidential papers. Identical to our measure in Chapter 4, we employ Gallup's most important problem (MIP) data to measure the public's concern for economic issues and Iraq. We measure media attention as the number of seconds per month that the television networks' (ABC, CBS, and NBC) nightly news programs devoted to economic policy and Iraq.[11]

There are two significant differences between the data we examine here and those we used in Chapter 4. First, we measure presidential attention to the economy and Iraq using a continuous measure of presidential attention through content analysis of *The Public Papers of the Presidents*. We count the number of paragraphs presidents devoted to economic issues (from January 1981 through December 2000) and Iraq (from January 1989 through June 2008) in their public statements by month, an approach employed by studies that use time series methods to examine the dynamics of presidential and media attention, yet do not model public opinion (Edwards and Wood 1999; Wood and Peake 1998).[12] Our measures account for presidents' efforts at public leadership, whereby presidents attempt to affect media attention and public priorities with regular speeches on economic issues and Iraq (see the Appendix for keywords used in the content analysis).

Second, our measures for economic policy are more refined than the measures we used in Chapter 4. While we examine the economic issues in the aggregate as we did in Chapter 4, here we also disaggregate our presidential, media, and MIP series into separate examination of budgetary and spending issues and unemployment. We examine the percentages of those Gallup respondents who find budgetary issues or unemployment separately as the most important problem. We also combine these categories with all other economic issues (including a general category and other economic issues, such as poverty or inflation) into a total MIP category. We have similar general and disaggregated time series for presidential and media attention to the economy, based on our content coding of the *Public Papers* and the Vanderbilt Television News Archive.[13] Here, we follow a similar process as outlined in Eshbaugh-Soha and Peake (2005).

Our controls for the objective economy are also more refined, as we are able to match each measure specifically to the area of the economy that we are assessing. Although we use a measure of economic growth for our general economic category, we employ more precise measures for each specific economic model: monthly unemployment rates for unemployment issues and the federal budget deficit (the monthly change in federal receipts minus outlays) for the deficits and spending model.[14] Finally, we combine inflation and unemployment rates into a monthly misery index to control for the state of the economy when evaluating the effectiveness of a strategy of sustained attention to Iraq.

METHODS

We use vector autoregression (VAR) analysis to examine the interrelationships among the president, media, and public. This method is particularly useful because it allows us to test for reciprocal causation, a central feature of our theoretical contribution. Recall that our conceptualization of leadership requires examination of both causal arrows, from the president to the media and public and from the media and public to the president. Thus, we treat continuous presidential attention as both a dependent and independent variable in our analyses, which is a primary benefit to using VAR. Moreover, we assume that presidents speak to influence both the public and the media and believe that part of explaining this puzzle requires consideration of the indirect linkages between the president and public. As we have argued, presidential leadership of the public could be conditioned by the president's ability to influence the media in the first place. Although this condition will not necessarily hold in our analysis, it is plausible that leadership effects could occur indirectly through news media, something that VAR allows us to examine quite parsimoniously.

VAR methodology helps us to evaluate the causal directions of the relationships among our measures of presidential statements, media attention, and public concern for the economy. VAR (Freeman, Williams, and Lin 1989; Simms 1980) is a multivariate extension of the Granger (1969) approach to causal inference. Each dependent variable is regressed on lagged values of itself and other dependent variables in the system, which provides an excellent control for history. We will conclude that one variable "Granger causes" another variable in the system when joint exogeneity tests indicate that changes in the first variable in one month independently affect the second variable. VAR is useful, therefore, because presidential leadership efforts may influence either public opinion or media attention to the economy, or it may be caused by public opinion or media attention.

We illustrate the direction and duration of the relationships using moving average response (MAR) graphs because the Granger tests we report only suggest causality. MAR graphs represent simulated responses in one variable to "shocks" in another variable of interest. MAR graphs account for feedback in the system, as well, an important attribute of agenda-setting theories and processes (Liu, Lindquist, and Vedliz in press). It is appropriate to inspect the MAR graphs whether or not causality is suggested by a statistically significant Granger F-test. According to Lutkepohl (1993) and reported by Wood (2007; 2009a), the Granger tests are not definitive evidence on the existence of a causal relationship. It is the MAR graphs that account for dynamic feedback that may suppress or accentuate relationships between the dependent variables. A simulated shock in our analysis represents increasing the independent variable by one-standard deviation.

In addition, we keep the variables measuring various conditional effects as a priori exogenous to the model, as theory suggests these conditions cause attention rather than respond to attention,[15] as illustrated by some of our findings in Chapter 4. The procedure is referred to as ARX modeling (Wood and Peake 1998, 177). We include the following exogenous variables in the models: reelection year, first term in office, events, presidential approval ratings, and the objective economy. One potential limitation to VAR modeling is that it can be overly parsimonious and, thus, unable to allow for interpretation of the exogenous variables through moving average response graphs. Nevertheless, we can assess the statistical significance and direction of the exogenous variables, providing us with some insight into the impact of these controls. At the very least, modeling the conditional influences as exogenous effects in the system is important to assuage any concerns that the results we do present are somehow spurious and are not driven by the variables endogenous to the system.[16] Nevertheless, any omitted variables are less of a concern in VAR than one might presuppose for other methods because the effects of all omitted variables are accounted for in the lagged dependent variables within the VAR system.

FINDINGS

The Economy

The economy is the most important policy area to a president's political success or failure. Just as the state of the economy is highly correlated with the president's likelihood of reelection and fluctuations in job approval ratings, the American public also expresses concern about the economy more than any other policy area. In turn, the news media have a strong incentive to cover not only the president's economic policies and rhetoric but also the broad contours of economic growth or decline. Without question, therefore, the economy is likely to be a top presidential priority, especially when it is in recession.

A general review of our data confirms these impressions. Presidents speak often on the economy, particularly when the media and public also express interest in economic issues. Take President Reagan's first term in office. As quarterly GDP growth hit its nadir of −6.4 percent during the first quarter of 1982, and 80 percent of the American people ranked the economy as the most important problem facing the nation, Reagan sustained a high level of attention to economic issues in his public speeches, devoting over 550 paragraphs to the economy in the first three months of 1982, his highest level of attention up to that point in his presidency. Not surprisingly, media coverage of increasing unemployment and the continuing recession reaches its zenith of 17,610 seconds during the same period. Under similar conditions, however, President George H. W. Bush took a different approach when the economy soured in 1991. Despite extensive media attention to the economy and high public concern for economic issues—the highest of each since the early 1980s—Bush spoke infrequently about the economy, as he prioritized foreign policy. Whether a strategy of sustained attention to economic issues, in order to appear responsive to public concerns, could have prevented Bush's reelection defeat in 1992 remains unknown. These two examples imply that presidents who face a poor economy on taking office may be better positioned to sustain their attention to public concerns and benefit from doing so, rather than if the economy sours toward the end of their term in office.

Concern about an economic recession is not the only motivation for presidents to prioritize the economy in their daily speeches. Presidents may speak about the economy, especially during reelection years and when the economy has improved, to claim credit for economic progress. Although Reagan did not speak as frequently as he had in 1982, he still devoted a fair amount, averaging seventy-three monthly paragraphs on the economy during 1984, to advertise an economy that was growing at over 7 percent per quarter in late 1983 and early 1984. Bill Clinton is the best example in our sample of a president who chose to speak primarily about an improving economy—and when media attention and public concern was relatively low. During his 1996 reelection campaign, Clinton devoted about 110 paragraphs per month on an economy that grew at 6.7 percent in the second quarter. This level of attention bested his previous high during the first half of 1993, a time when Clinton was responding to already heightened levels of public concern for the economy. Media attention on the economy increased in response to Clinton's efforts in 1996, to be sure, but it was much lower than the economic news coverage during the second quarter of 1993. Overall, this descriptive evidence reveals a strong relationship among the president, public, and media on economic issues, and not only when the economy is in recession.

To answer who led whom and who responded to whom on the economy, we systematically analyze our three indicators of the presidential, media, and public agendas across a broad economic category, unemployment issues, and deficit and spending issues in Table 5.1.[17] Model 1 displays the results of the Granger causality tests for the broadest category of economic policy. Primarily, we find that neither the president nor the media have direct influence over the public's concern for aggregated economic issues · evidenced by the statistically insignificant Granger tests. The second null

TABLE 5.1.

Granger tests for monthly presidential, media, and public economic agendas.

Independent variable	All economic issues (model 1)	Unemployment (model 2)	Deficits and spending (model 3)	Dependent variable
President	(0.005) →	(0.001) →	(0.026) →	
Media	(0.079) →	(0.002) →	(0.000) →	President
Public	(0.404)	(0.033) →	(0.130)	
State of economy				
President	(0.027) →	(0.201)	(0.000) →	
Media	(0.022) →	(0.005) →	(0.020) →	Media
Public	(0.032) →	(0.001) →	(0.031) →	
State of economy		+		
President	(0.685)	(0.554)	(0.088) →	
Media	(0.312)	(0.009) →	(0.134)	Public
Public	(0.000) →	(0.000) →	(0.000) →	
State of economy		+	−	

Note: Numbers in parentheses are p-values. The arrows indicate that the independent variable Granger causes the dependent variable at a significance level of 0.1. A plus or minus sign indicates direction of a statistically significant ($p < 0.1$, one-tailed) state of the economy coefficient, based on a t-test. Nearly all other exogenous variables are statistically insignificant and are not reported above. The N for each series is 240 (January 1981 to December 2000).

finding is interesting, especially because much research finds a causal link between what the media cover and the public's agenda. Our analysis holds that it is the media that respond to public concern for the economy, however. This responsiveness supports the general idea that news media are motivated by profit and want to address issues on the public's agenda to satisfy audience demand. We do find clear relationships between presidential and media attention to the economy. The president's economic agenda has a strong causal impact on the media's economic agenda. What is more, the relationship between the president and media is reciprocal, as each directly Granger causes the other's attention to economic issues.

The aggregate analysis shows that presidents do not respond directly to the public's economic agenda, either. This null finding suggests that a sustained strategy of presidential speech making may not be an effective leadership strategy when considering such a broad issue. However, because we find that media coverage of the economy increases as public concern grows, and because presidents are responsive to increased news coverage, they may at least use this strategy to respond to public concerns once the economy generates heightened news coverage.

To supply greater variation in the prior salience of economic issues, and to further test our salience hypothesis, we disaggregated the economy into the more specific subsets of unemployment and spending and deficit issues, both of which vary differently by public concern and media attention. We present the results for unemployment issues in model 2 of Table 5.1. Consistent with our expectations that high prior public salience will induce presidential responsiveness, the Granger causality tests reveal that presidents are highly responsive to the public on unemployment issues. The public's concern for unemployment Granger causes presidential attention to the issue. The converse, that presidents influence public concern for unemployment, is not supported. Thus, model 2 reveals strong support for the absence of presidential leadership when the president responds to an issue of generally high public concern. Support for our salience hypothesis also extends to the president's relationship with the news media, as presidents respond to but do not Granger cause the media's unemployment agenda. Further, the results show a strong reciprocal relationship between the media and public agendas on unemployment, as both Granger cause each other. Additionally, the objective unemployment rate increases both media attention and public concern for unemployment, as expected.

Deficits and spending issues also reveal a complex set of interrelationships that generally support our salience hypothesis. In model 3 (Table 5.1) we find that presidential attention to deficits and spending issues Granger causes both media attention to and public concern for deficits and spending. Moreover, the Granger F-tests suggest, although at a low p-value ($p = 0.134$), that increased media attention leads to greater public concern. This provides tentative evidence that presidents influence public concern for the deficit and spending issues both directly and indirectly through the news media and is the only set of Granger tests on economic issues that reveal both relationships. The media and president exhibit reciprocal causation, similar to the general economic model. Finally, the president does not respond to public concern for deficits and spending, according to the Granger tests, providing additional support for our theoretical argument that presidents will lead the public's agenda in the absence of presidential responsiveness to existing heightened public concerns.

We now turn to the moving average response graphs. Because the broad economic category provides overlapping support for our salience and indirect leadership hypotheses, we present the more specific models concerning unemployment and spending and deficit issues.[18] The MAR graphs present a more dynamic view of the Granger tests we presented in Table 5.1. Because they consider dynamic feedback, MARs may reveal additional evidence of presidential leadership or responsiveness missed by the Granger tests. Moreover, an insignificant Granger test does not alone reject the possibility for a significant causal relationship between two variables (Wood 2007).[19] Additional benefits to MARs are that they allow for a clearer examination of a variety of indirect relationships that may have been missed by the Granger tests and that they provide a clearer indication of the substantive impact of an increase in one variable on other variables in the system.

Figure 5.1 presents MAR graphs for unemployment issues. They confirm a primary set of findings revealed by the Granger tests. First, the president does not directly cause public concern for unemployment (column one, row three), as the confidence bands straddle zero. This is to be expected when presidents respond to the public's agenda, a second relationship revealed by

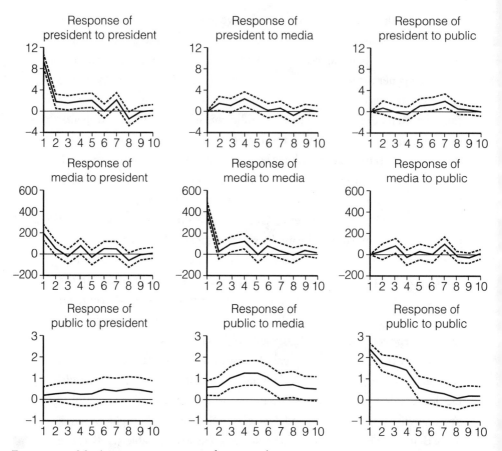

FIGURE 5.1. Moving average responses for unemployment.

Note: "president" is the total number of paragraphs per month that presidents devoted to unemployment; "media" is the number of seconds (per month) devoted to unemployment on the evening news; and "public" is the percentage of the public that considered unemployment to be the most important problem facing the nation. Dashed lines are 95 percent confidence intervals.

the Granger tests and confirmed in Figure 5.1 by the MARs. The box in the third column, first row, shows how this presidential response is typically delayed, rather than immediate. A delayed response suggests that presidents do not pander to public concerns about unemployment but instead respond to the public's agenda through a strategy of sustained attention only when unemployment becomes a chronic concern. Interestingly, our results reflect the deferred responsiveness of both Presidents George H. W. Bush and Barack Obama to unemployment. Each president delayed his response, contributing to the electoral defeat of Bush in 1992 and seriously undermining the public's confidence in Obama's handling of the economy in 2010.

In contrast to the Granger tests, the MARs present a more nuanced relationship between the president and public on unemployment issues, one that provides evidence in favor of our theory of indirect presidential leadership whereby the media play an important role. The graph in column one, row two, reveals that the media respond to the president on unemployment in the short term, with an immediate increase of 200 seconds per month in response to a one standard deviation increase in presidential attention and that this influence tapers off over two months. What is more, the public responds initially and in a sustained fashion to media attention (column two, row three). A one standard deviation increase in media attention leads to an estimated monthly increase of between 0.5 and 1 percent of the public that considers unemployment to be the most important problem.[20] This impact lasts about nine months and is cumulative such that a substantial percentage of the public is likely to consider unemployment a most important problem once it is covered heavily in the news.[21] Because we also find that presidents influence media attention to unemployment, the VAR results provide strong evidence that presidents indirectly lead the public's agenda on unemployment by affecting news coverage to unemployment given the sustained response by the public to the media. Therefore, even unemployment, which is a highly salient issue that precludes direct presidential leadership of the public, still provides for indirect leadership of the public's agenda through news coverage of unemployment issues. Taken together, Figure 5.1 supports both our salience and indirect leadership hypotheses.

The MAR graphs displayed in Figure 5.2 generally support our salience and indirect leadership hypotheses for spending and deficit issues as well. The direct public response to presidential attention to spending issues is positive, although not overwhelmingly so. The estimated increase in public concern in response to a shock in presidential attention is about 0.5 percent per month over a period of four months (column one, row three). The cumulative effects, therefore, are important given the relatively low percentage of the public that is concerned with spending issues on average. Because the president does not also respond to public concern for spending and

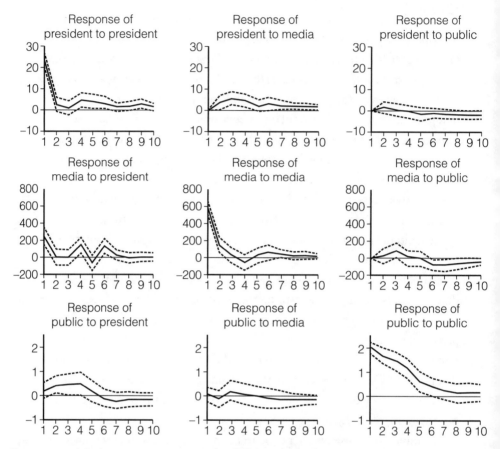

FIGURE 5.2. Moving average responses for deficit and spending issues.

Note: "president" is the total number of paragraphs per month that presidents devoted to deficit and spending issues; "media" is the number of seconds (per month) devoted to deficit and spending issues on the evening news; and "public" is the percentage of the public that considered deficit and spending issues to be the most important problem facing the nation. Dashed lines are 95 percent confidence intervals.

deficit issues (column three, row one), Figure 5.2 provides strong evidence of direct leadership of the public and support for our salience hypothesis.

Concerning the president's relationship with the media, the MAR graphs confirm a reciprocal relationship. On the one hand, a one standard deviation increase in presidential attention to spending issues leads to just over 200 seconds in news coverage about the issue during the first month (column two, row one). On the other hand, a one standard deviation increase in media coverage increases presidential attention by about two to five paragraphs per month over a period of four and a half months (column two, row one), and this effect is cumulative across time. This reciprocal relationship reveals that presidential leadership of media does not require a lack of prior media attention to these issues, unlike the relationships we have found between the president and public agendas. Moreover, that presidents influence news coverage on spending issues provides the possibility for indirect presidential leadership of the public's deficit and spending agenda, in addition to the direct relationship we have found. Although the public do not respond to increased media attention to deficits and spending as clearly as they do on unemployment, an increase in presidential attention still affects public concern indirectly through the president's leadership of news coverage revealed in the first column and second row box in Figure 5.2. Thus, on a low-salience issue, such as deficits and spending, presidents not only directly lead the public's agenda but also potentially lead indirectly through news coverage.

The public has never been highly concerned with deficit and spending issues throughout our time frame, which has provided presidents with substantial opportunity to lead the public's attention to these issues. Amid the government shutdown of late 1995 and early 1996, for example, President Clinton turned his attention to the budget, spending cuts, and the deficit. In January 1996 Clinton devoted 196 paragraphs, including a Saturday radio address, to spending issues. This level of attention did not affect media attention substantially, generating only 500 seconds of nightly news coverage that month and much less over the next several months. However, it led to a jump in public concern about spending issues from 7 to 20 percent in January 1996. Given the political benefit to President Clinton in winning reelection and policy success of budget surpluses at the end of the decade, Clinton not only directly led the public's agenda on the deficit and spending issues, he also translated that leadership into achieving two of his primary goals as president.

In sum, we present substantial evidence of both direct and indirect presidential leadership of the public's agenda, lending support for our primary expectations. Presidents are highly responsive to economic issues deemed most critical to voters (unemployment), and their attempts to increase attention to these issues have met with only limited success. On spending issues, however, presidents have greater opportunity to lead the public directly in part because the issue is rarely on the public's agenda. As expected, the president's agenda is not responsive to public concern for spending issues. Presidents indirectly lead the public agenda on both issues, not only providing support for our indirect leadership hypothesis but also adding a nuance to our salience hypothesis. In other words, presidents can indirectly lead the public through news coverage, even on issues of high public salience. This last contribution adds a significant wrinkle to our understanding of presidential leadership of and responsiveness to the public and news media and reinforces the importance of media to leading the public through a strategy of sustained attention.

Iraq

As we have already reviewed in Chapter 4, presidents have had several reasons to prioritize Iraq. Beginning with Saddam Hussein's invasion of Kuwait in August, 1990, George H. W. Bush addressed the invasion directly and frequently throughout the conflict, with a peak of 346 paragraphs in his public remarks related to Iraq delivered during the first month of the conflict. Although presidential attention predictably plummeted after the conclusion of the Persian Gulf War and the end of the first Bush administration, President Clinton, too, had several opportunities to speak about Iraq through his numerous monthly speeches, mainly as Iraq violated U.N. requirements for allowing international weapons inspections.

Post–September 11 foreign policy shifted hastily from terrorism, Osama Bin Laden, and Afghanistan to Iraq. According to various inside accounts of George W. Bush's foreign policy in general and Iraq and Afghanistan, in particular, he quickly made Iraq a top priority after the Taliban were overthrown in Afghanistan (Woodward 2002). The president took his case to the American people in August 2002 and continued to push for military intervention to topple the Saddam Hussein government. He made numerous speeches encouraging Congress to support a Use of Force resolution (which it eventually did), and then took his case to the United Nations. During his address to the U.N. General Assembly, Bush admonished the United Nations for failing to enforce previous resolutions restricting Iraq's acquisitions of weapons. Failure by the United Nations to act, Bush declared, will embolden Iraq to "bully and dominate and conquer its neighbors." Bush continued his efforts to maintain public and media attention to Iraq, even after the invasion in March 2003. During his 2004 reelection campaign, for example, he spoke frequently about Iraq, peaking at 730 paragraphs in October, the month prior to his reelection victory. During his second term, as he focused more on Social Security reform in early 2005 and news coverage of the war in Iraq grew increasingly negative, Bush never reached his first-term level of attention to Iraq. Even so, Bush continued to persist at public leadership on the issue, reaching 400 paragraphs on Iraq during the two months prior to the 2006 midterm elections. His focus was to keep attention on Iraq to build support for his intentions to increase the number of troops as part of his "surge" policy, which was officially announced during the 2007 State of the Union address.

The conventional wisdom is that presidents should affect the media and public agendas on Iraq. No better example comes from the assessment of the Bush administration's impact on the news media and its subsequent manipulation of public opinion (see Jacobson 2007, Chapter 5). Indeed, a virtual cottage industry of recent research has been built on the assumption that the Bush administration successfully swayed media coverage of the lead-up to the war in Iraq (Bennett et al. 2007; Howell and Pevehouse 2007). After all, practically no news outlet challenged Bush's contention that Iraq possessed weapons of mass destruction. As a result, much of the initial war coverage was decidedly positive (Farnsworth and Lichter 2006), with news organizations destined to promote the official line as embedded reporters flanked troops in the march on Baghdad. If we were to find, therefore, that presidents have led both the public and the media on Iraq policy since 1989, our findings would be unexceptional. Casual inferences drawn from case studies can be deceiving, however, and are not indicative of a causal relationship, especially because two of the three administrations we examine—the first Bush and Clinton administrations—were primarily reactive, in that they responded to events, whether the invasion of Kuwait, an assassination attempt, or Iraq's failure to comply with weapons inspections.

The VARs assess causal relationships more systematically and illustrate the more complex dynamics of the interrelationships among the president,

TABLE 5.2.
Granger tests for monthly presidential, media, and public Iraq agendas.

Independent variable	All presidents	George W. Bush administration	Dependent variable
President	(0.000) →	(0.000) →	
Media	(0.003) →	(0.103)	President
Public	(0.159)	(0.523)	
Reelection year	+	+	
Events	+		
Misery index	−		
President	(0.142)	(0.319)	
Media	(0.000) →	(0.000) →	Media
Public	(0.901)	(0.234)	
Events	+		
President	(0.001) →	(0.254)	
Media	(0.520)	(0.010) →	Public
Public	(0.000) →	(0.002) →	
Reelection year		+	
Events	+	+	
Misery index		−	
Approval	−	−	
First term		−	

Note: Numbers in parentheses are p-values. The arrows indicate that the independent variable Granger causes the dependent variable at a significance level of 0.1, two-tailed. A plus or minus sign indicates direction of a statistically significant ($p < 0.1$, one-tailed) effect for the conditional variables, based on a t-test. The N for the full model is 233 (January 1989 to June 2008) and 89 (February 2001 to June 2008) for the Bush Model.

media, and public on Iraq.[22] Beginning with the Granger F-tests reported in Table 5.2, we see that presidents have led the public's agenda on Iraq, with presidential attention increasing public concern for Iraq.[23] This relationship is not reciprocal, as we expected given our salience hypothesis. Although media also Granger cause presidential attention to Iraq, there is only a modest (albeit not statistically significant at $p < 0.1$) causal relationship in the other direction. In other words, the Granger tests support very limited presidential leadership of the news media on Iraq, even though the public responds directly to presidential attention. Media are particularly important in this depiction of agenda setting as their causal impact on the president's agenda supports the idea that presidents tend to respond to media coverage of international events across a wide range of foreign policy areas (Edwards and Wood 1999; Peake 2001). Attention to

Iraq is also affected somewhat by the exogenous environment and more so than we saw with the economy. Primarily, international events tend to buttress the presence of Iraq on all three agendas. Moreover, a worsening economy decreases presidential attention to Iraq, presumably because the president attends to that primary responsibility in response to problems in the economy. Finally, high approval ratings suppress public concern for Iraq.

Figure 5.3 presents the MAR graphs, which consider feedback and so allow for presentation of the direction and magnitude of the relationships.

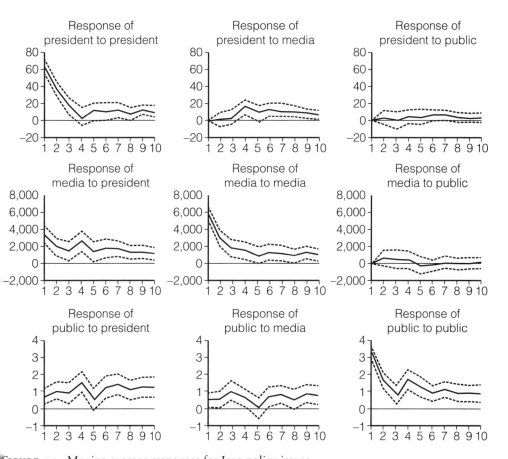

FIGURE 5.3. Moving average responses for Iraq policy issues.

Note: "president" is the total number of paragraphs per month that presidents devoted to Iraq; "media" is the number of seconds (per month) devoted to Iraq on the evening news; and "public" is the percentage of the public that considered Iraq to be the most important problem facing the nation. Dashed lines are 95 percent confidence intervals.

They corroborate most of the Granger findings. We see in the box in column one, row three, that a one standard deviation increase in presidential attention to Iraq leads to a sustained increase of about 1 percent of the public, per month, that considers Iraq a most important problem for at least ten months beyond the initial shock. This illustrates that presidents are successful maintaining public attention to Iraq, as the cumulative effects are impressive. This is consistent with what we expect from a successful strategy of sustained attention. Additionally, the public have no direct impact on the president's attention to Iraq. Both of these findings support our salience hypothesis and confirm our Granger tests.

The MARs differ from the Granger tests in one important respect. According to the box in column two, row three, media attention increases public concern for Iraq. This provides an opportunity for indirect presidential leadership of the public through the media, so long as the president also affects media attention through speeches. Indeed, the MARs reveal that presidential attention to Iraq substantially increases news coverage of Iraq to the tune of nearly 4,000 additional seconds (or over one hour) of Iraq news coverage in a month (column one, row two). This impact is not only immediate, it is also sustained over time, and therefore the cumulative effects are substantial. The reciprocal nature of this relationship is also revealing: The response of presidential attention to media attention is delayed and does not register until four months after a shock to media attention and then promptly declines. Finally, indirect presidential leadership of the public occurs through a second path, as a one standard deviation shock to presidential attention in column one traces through an increase in media attention (column one, row two) to a sustained increase in public concern (column one, row three), as the public responds to the media.

These findings comport nicely with what has occurred throughout our time series, particularly with developments toward the end of 1998. As we have already described in Chapter 4, President Clinton ordered missile strikes into Bagdad, as part of Operation Desert Fox, to punish Saddam Hussein for expelling U.N. weapons inspectors. Yet the news media began covering weapons inspections activity months before the president devoted much, if any public attention to it. During the several months before the operation, the news media reported frequently about the difficulties that U.N. inspectors faced in Iraq. In August, September, and October of 1998, for example, the networks devoted 2,680 seconds to coverage on Iraq. Over this same time frame, President Clinton discussed Iraq in only three paragraphs, with all of these coming during September. It was not until three months after the media turned their attention to weapons inspections in Iraq that the president devoted fifty-nine paragraphs to Iraq in November 1998, prior to ordering strikes against Iraq in December. Public concern for Iraq also increased immediately after the president's use of force, from 0 to 8 percent. Although the president was later able to drive news coverage with sustained attention to the missile strikes, the example shows how news media affected presidential attention to Iraq with a several month lag and how the president also drove the public's agenda on Iraq through both his rhetoric and actions.

Of course, much of the conventional wisdom about presidential leadership over Iraq policy concerns not the Clinton administration's brief emphasis on Iraq but the second Bush administration, given that the war in Iraq embroiled six of George W. Bush's eight years in office. For primarily this reason, we run a separate VAR for the George W. Bush administration (2001–2008). Our analysis suggests something other than clear evidence of sustained presidential leadership of the public and media for President Bush, however. The Granger tests reveal that Bush had no direct impact on either the public or the media. More striking, especially in comparison with the full Iraq model, is that the public appear to have been mostly impervious to the Bush administration's Iraq agenda, in that the public were neither affected by presidential speeches on Iraq, nor did the public's agenda influence the president's attention to Iraq. That said, the impact of the media on the level of public concern for Iraq is suggestive of the possibility for indirect presidential leadership of the public through the media. We find only modest evidence of such a relationship, however. Moreover, even if we infer that Bush led attention on Iraq early in the conflict given that he ordered the attack and placed it on the agenda, continued media attention to the war appears to have affected Bush's level of attention to Iraq later in the conflict, although this relationship barely misses statistical significance ($p = 0.103$).

Of course, much of the research that finds the media were compliant partners and rarely questioned administration policy (Bennett et al. 2007; Hayes and Guardino 2010) focuses on news coverage of the lead-up to the Iraq War. This research points to indexing as the theoretical reason, and the media had little to report that would counter the administration's policies given a relative lack of opposition in Congress. Given our data, we simply cannot address definitively whether the president was most successful leading the media's agenda during the build-up to and immediate aftermath of the Iraq invasion through a sustained strategy of attention. Even if we assume that the conventional wisdom is correct, that the media bought and sold the Bush administration's Iraq war policy, it did not occur over the length of his term in office, according to our results. At best, we can illustrate an indirect, short-term link, whereby presidential attention increased media attention in the short term, which translated into about a three-month increase in public concern for Iraq.[24]

Taking these findings together suggests several important conclusions. First, presidential leadership of the public is most likely when presidents do not also respond to the public's agenda. Yet a lack of responsiveness does not guarantee public leadership, as we see with the results for the George W. Bush administration. Second, and in addition to the direct effects we present, presidents have indirectly led the public's Iraq agenda by first increasing news coverage to Iraq. Both of these findings confirm our hypotheses and provide some evidence that presidents may more consistently affect the media and public agendas on foreign than other policy areas.

Our findings for the George W. Bush administration alone are not as strong as those for the entire time series and challenge the conventional wisdom that Bush directly led the public's agenda on Iraq. Indeed, painting a broad and systematic picture of presidential leadership reveals that even the Bush administration's war in Iraq did not entail one-sided news coverage as some suggest. As the war progressed and coverage soured (Aday 2010), the president could not dictate his agenda to the news media. Despite all of the resources that the contemporary White House may bring to lead the agendas of the media and public, it cannot compete with the stark reality of failure on the ground (Baum and Groeling 2010). Moreover, even the best communications operations may not help presidents overcome the difficulty they face sustaining agenda leadership over the extended long term and over the course of a protracted conflict. President Bush simply lost control of the Iraq War agenda as negative stories mounted; he tried to achieve other priorities, such as Social Security and immigration reform; and he had to respond to other major events, including Hurricane Katrina.

CONCLUSION

A strategy of sustained attention provides important opportunities for presidential agenda leadership. Concerning economic issues, recent presidents have had some success directly and indirectly leading the public's agenda. Direct leadership is most pronounced for the economic issues related to spending and deficits, an issue that is typically of low public salience. On this issue we do not find direct presidential responsiveness to the public, which supports our theoretical expectation that leadership is most likely when the president is unconstrained by existing public concern, which forces responsiveness. The president's best hope for leadership on issues that are typically much more salient is to lead the public's agenda indirectly through increased news coverage, as the media tend to respond to increased presidential attention to these issues and the public respond to the media's agenda. We see this on unemployment issues, where the president is also mostly responsive to the public's agenda. Except for the objective economy, political conditions matter little to agenda setting on the economy.

Our analysis of attention to Iraq produces similar, albeit clearer, evidence in favor of our general expectations. The president has led the public directly on Iraq policy in part because he was not also forced to respond to the public's agenda. Presidents have acted entrepreneurially through their public speeches, even though Presidents George H. W. Bush and Clinton reacted to real-world events, such as the Iraqi invasion of Kuwait and Iraqi resistance to U.N. weapons inspectors. We find evidence of indirect leadership of the public's agenda, as well, given the strong link between the president and media and the media and public on Iraq. Evidence of indirect leadership exists during the George W. Bush administration, as well, although only marginally. In contrast with economic issues, conditional variables matter more to the interrelationships among the president, media, and public agendas on Iraq. Moreover, a slumping economy decreases attention to this foreign policy issue, whereas international events, many of which related directly to Iraq, increase attention to Iraq.

The differences in our findings for all presidents and the Bush administration reveal a pattern of agenda-setting leadership and responsiveness that is consistent with the previous literature. Presidents are particularly well positioned to take advantage of the ebb and flow of short-term events in their efforts at agenda leadership. When external and significant events occur, like the Persian Gulf War, assassination attempts, or missile strikes on Baghdad, presidents have been able to lead the public's agenda on Iraq, even when they may respond initially to increased media coverage. However, when an issue is chronically on the media and public agenda, we see an absence of presidential leadership, similar to what Edwards and Wood (1999) report. Although George W. Bush took advantage of the initial invasion and influenced both the media and public agendas on Iraq through his national addresses, he lost control of the Iraq agenda over the long term, as the issue persisted even when the president had other priorities to address.

Just because we find only slight differences in leadership effectiveness by policy area, we do not conclude that policy differences are irrelevant to agenda leadership but rather infer that the gestation and duration of an issue helps explain the probability of presidential agenda leadership. Our examination of multiple policy areas—both in aggregated and disaggregated form—helps to improve the generalizability of our findings and should promote confidence in our results.

Although we find indirect leadership of the public, given that the public receive most of their information about the presidency through the news, it is still somewhat surprising that we find direct leadership of the public at all through a strategy of sustained attention. Other research reports similar direct presidential leadership of the public (Wood et al. 2005), suggesting that the public may increasingly gain access to the president's words from a variety of nonnetwork news sources. Such sources might include soft news television programs (Baum 2003), cable news, and the Internet—sources that we do not examine. Nevertheless, this possibility reinforces our contention that media play an intermediating role for presidents who wish to lead the public.

CHAPTER 6

Going Local as a Leadership Strategy

ON FEBRUARY 9, 2009, President Barack Obama traveled to Elkhart, Indiana, where he addressed a local audience at Concord Community High School to build support for the economic stimulus package moving through Congress. In the following two days he traveled to Fort Meyers, Florida, and Springfield, Virginia, delivering addresses on the economic stimulus plan to local audiences. The political battle over the $787 billion package was an early test for the new administration, a test the administration passed when Congress voted in favor of the legislation on February 11. The next day, Obama was on the road again trumpeting the passage of the stimulus package at the Caterpillar plant in East Peoria, Illinois. On February 17, the president signed the American Recovery and Reinvestment Act of 2009 before a local audience in Denver, Colorado. He followed that with a visit to Mesa, Arizona, where he announced a new mortgage initiative.[1] The economic recession dominated news coverage in late January and early February.[2] According to the Gallup Poll, 79 percent of the public cited some component of the economy as the most important problem in late January 2009 (Morales 2009). These realities suggest that Obama going local on the economy was in direct response to the public's and media's policy agendas.[3]

Even as the economy dominated the public's and media's agenda, President Obama turned next to his signature first-term domestic policy initiative: health care reform. As with the economic stimulus bill, Obama took his case to local communities throughout the nation. Starting with a town hall meeting in Green Bay, Wisconsin, on June 11, 2009, the president went local on health care reform, making thirteen stops outside of the Washington, D.C., area between June and September. Unlike the economy, which was already a public priority by the time Obama took the oath of office, the president prioritized health care reform absent previously high public concern and media attention. Whether Obama was successful in placing health care on the media and public agendas is a question we explore later in this chapter.

Obama's efforts on the economy and health care reform epitomize the going local strategy, whereby presidents use domestic travel to argue for their policy priorities. Going local is a relatively new strategy of presidential public leadership (Cohen 2010; Eshbaugh-Soha and Peake 2006). In this chapter we explore trends in going local on the part of recent presidents and discuss why presidents have opted to use the strategy. We compare going local by Presidents Bill Clinton and George W. Bush to demonstrate its wide-ranging recent use. Clearly, when presidents go local, they expect to influence the attention local media give to presidential policy priorities, hoping to also increase public attention. Presidents also use the strategy to respond to salient public concerns, as Obama did on the economy in early 2009. We end the chapter with an assessment of the effectiveness of going local as a strategy to influence the agendas of the media and public with three brief case studies: President George W. Bush on tax cuts in 2001 and Social Security reform in 2005 and President Barack Obama on health care reform in 2009. Our primary concern in this chapter is to determine whether presidents can break through the noise of news coverage and go local to affect the public's policy agenda.

THE GOING LOCAL STRATEGY

The modern White House devotes substantial time, energy, and other resources to cultivating a positive image with local news media. As evidenced by trends in targeted addresses and domestic travel, the attention presidents devote to managing local media has increased in recent years (Cohen 2010). Kumar (2007) illustrates how the Office of Media Affairs handles local media, in general, and she provides numerous anecdotes to support the importance of the local press to recent presidents' governing strategies. Among other examples, the Reagan White House used interviews with local media to buttress support for Robert Bork's nomination to the U.S. Supreme Court (Kumar 2007, 173). President George W. Bush, in particular, made targeting local news central to his media relations strategy throughout his tenure. Bush signaled his intentions to bypass what he called the filter of national news as early as March 27, 2001, during a speech at Western Michigan University, when he stated:

I find it's important to get out of town—at least out of the Nation's Capital—to take my message directly to the people who matter. You see, oftentimes, what I try to say in Washington gets filtered. Sometimes, my words in Washington don't exactly translate directly to the people, so I've found it's best to travel the country.[4]

To evade this "filter" of the national news media, recent presidents have taken their case directly to the American people by traveling outside Washington more frequently. The intent is not only to influence the public's priorities and opinions but also—and perhaps first—to affect news coverage of the president's priorities. Domestic travel has become fundamental to the permanent campaign (Cohen and Powell 2005; Cook 2002; Kernell 2007) and has risen dramatically over the past two decades. Figure 6.1 shows a clear increase in U.S. public appearances outside of Washington between 1949 and 2008 (Ragsdale 2009, 201–202).[5]

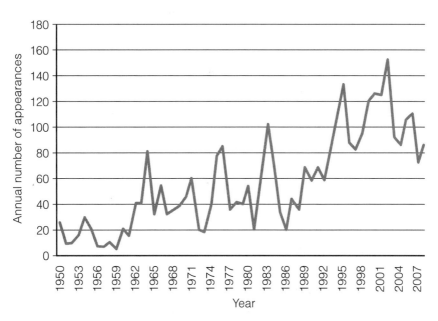

FIGURE 6.1. Domestic public appearances outside of Washington, DC, 1949–2008.

Source: Ragsdale (2009), updated by the authors.

The increase is especially apparent since 1992, with Presidents Clinton and George W. Bush averaging 102 yearly appearances in the states.[6] In comparison, their predecessors (1949–1992) averaged thirty-nine appearances per year outside Washington. Presidents Truman and Eisenhower averaged the fewest yearly appearances during the time frame, with only fifteen, and Presidents Johnson through George H. W. Bush averaged forty-eight yearly appearances. Clinton and George W. Bush travelled domestically twice as much as their more recent predecessors. President Barack Obama has continued the trend, traveling extensively across the United States during his first year in office (Doherty 2009).

Presidents Clinton and Bush Go Local

Going local has become a preferred leadership strategy of recent presidents (Cohen 2010). Because going local has been most prominent among the two more recent and completed presidencies, we examine more specifically the going local tendencies of Presidents Bill Clinton and George W. Bush. To do this, we counted the number of trips outside Washington, Maryland, and Virginia from 1993 through 2008.[7] We separated each of these trips based on the purpose of the president's visit and coded a visit as a policy trip when presidents made a policy-related speech. Policy-oriented travel typically involves the president appealing to a local audience or specialized constituency regarding specific policy proposals, the president's policy priorities, or recently enacted policies. It is these instances where presidents intend to affect local media and public opinion and, in particular, the agendas of the local media and public. We also counted trips taken for political or campaign purposes separately.[8] Although campaign travel often included policy-related remarks by the president, we categorize these events separately because of their obvious partisan nature. Finally, we counted trips related to the symbolic nature of the president's office in a third category.[9]

Domestic travel was central to each president's governing strategy. Clinton and Bush traveled extensively, averaging 8.4 monthly trips outside the Potomac region and their home states, with Bush averaging slightly more than Clinton, at 8.7 and 8.3 trips per month, respectively. A large percentage of the travel was policy related. Combined, the presidents made 1,622 trips outside of the D.C. area and their home states in sixteen years. Nearly half of the travel, 49.5 percent, involved the president making extensive policy-related remarks to local audiences or constituency groups. Much of the remaining travel related to campaigns, at 38.9 percent of the total number of trips, or was symbolic in nature. These trips accounted for 11.7 percent of the total.

Presidents Clinton and Bush differed in how they went local, with Bush speaking more frequently about policy. The majority of Bush's travel, at 52.4 percent, involved policy-related remarks or speeches, whereas President Clinton devoted 45.8 percent of his speeches to his policy priorities. In addition, Bush averaged 4.5 policy trips per month compared to Clinton's average of 3.9 policy trips. There is substantial variation around these means, nevertheless. President Clinton traveled most frequently to promote his policy initiatives during September 1995 and July 1999, with eleven and twelve trips respectively. During both of these months, Clinton discussed a broad range of policy priorities. President Bush was more focused in his efforts during his most-traveled months in office. In March 2001, most of Bush's thirteen local addresses dealt with his budget and tax cut proposals. Although Bush varied the topics of his fourteen local speeches delivered during January 2002, he focused once again on a specific policy priority, Social Security reform, in all but two of his fourteen trips in March 2005.

Both presidents traveled similarly according to the secular and electoral calendars. First, Presidents Clinton and Bush both reduced their policy-oriented travels at the end of each year because they typically spent the month of December with holiday travel. Indeed, Clinton took only nine total policy-related trips during the month of December over his eight years, whereas for Bush the total was eleven. Second, during the late months of even-numbered years both presidents were busy campaigning for either themselves or members of their political parties.

The president travels extensively during election years, especially as a part of their own reelection campaigns (Cohen 2010, 49; Doherty 2007). As Election Day nears, however, presidential travel takes on an entirely different character. Rather than delivering addresses that focus heavily on the president's policy priorities with the purpose of affecting the public's agenda, presidents address purely partisan audiences at campaign rallies and party fund-raisers. During the latter parts of the 1994, 1998, 2002, and 2006, both Presidents Clinton and Bush shifted their travel to emphasize helping their parties' congressional and gubernatorial candidates during the midterm elections. During their own reelection years (1996 and 2004), each president shifted his domestic travel away from policy to a campaign focus. Although campaign-oriented travel accounted for a substantial percentage of Clinton and Bush's domestic travel overall (39 percent), a hefty majority of travel focused on the president's campaign during each presidential reelection year (70.2 percent).

This descriptive presentation of the domestic travel of Presidents Clinton and Bush suggests that the amount of policy-oriented travel may be explained by two primary reasons. Mainly, a president might decide to travel more extensively across the nation when the public supports his job performance, hoping to translate higher approval ratings into more favorable news coverage (Cohen 2010, 165) or otherwise highlight his popularity to members of Congress on salient issues (Canes-Wrone and de Marchi 2002). President Bush, for example, traveled more often during early 2005 when his approval was at its second term peak, arguable for both of these purposes.

In addition, time may dictate the president's travel schedule in three ways. First, presidents are likely to travel more during both presidential and congressional election years. Second, however, presidents' policy-oriented travel is likely to diminish significantly as Election Day nears and throughout the remainder of the calendar year. Third, presidential term may matter. Absent the reelection incentive, second-term presidents may travel less frequently than they did during their first term in office. This appears to hold, at least for Bush. President Clinton continued to travel extensively during his last two years in office; however, Bush's travels declined significantly after the 2006 midterm elections.

REASONS FOR GOING LOCAL

Why has there been such a large increase in domestic travel by recent presidents? Perhaps the most widely accepted belief is that domestic travel generates extensive and positive news coverage in the local media. Positive local news coverage, presidents believe, will focus media and public attention on their policy priorities and generate public support for their policy agendas. Graber (2002, 332) asserts, for example, that national newsmakers, such as the president, "are eager to reach the hinterlands, where coverage tends to be gentler and more in tune with the newsmakers' agendas." Roberts and Eksterowicz (1996) write of "the widely held perception that local reporters will be kinder and gentler than national reporters." Similarly, Cohen and Powell (2005, 15) contend that local coverage of presidential trips "tends to be highly positive" and "highly visible." Moreover, domestic travel affords presidents opportunities to strategically target their speeches to specific "constituencies or to find locations suitable for sounding a particular theme" (Kernell 2007, 125). Ultimately, the White House communications team targets local media for two reasons. First, "the president generally receives positive coverage when he travels to localities around the country," and that coverage is typically comprehensive. Second, people generally trust their local media more than they trust national media outlets, which makes local media the primary source of news for most Americans (Kumar 2007, 97–99).

More domestic travel is the likely result of changes in national news coverage. As Cohen (2008) documents extensively, trends in national news coverage of the presidency do not favor the White House. Presidential news has grown more negative over time, and recent presidents have had greater difficulty than their predecessors in maintaining the attention of a more fragmented and national news media. To overcome these difficulties, Cohen (2010) contends that presidents go local regularly as part of their governing strategies and especially to target their party base, supportive interest groups, and supportive local constituencies. Going local offers presidents the opportunity to make a big splash in the local news given that local coverage of a local event will generally be much more favorable than coverage of the event by national news teams. In the words of Paul Begala, one of President Clinton's top political advisors, "What's not to like, if you're a politician, about cheering crowds and fawning press? It's like force-feeding sugar to an ant" (quoted in Bumiller 2002).

Working from these expectations, President George W. Bush visited more states during his first months in office than any of his predecessors. Although he received consistent coverage from local newspapers, national news coverage of his travels was limited (see Barrett and Peake

2007). One study that compared the first sixty days of Bush's coverage in the national press with that of President Clinton's, for example, showed much less coverage for Bush, despite his extensive domestic travel schedule (Edwards 2007, 80–89; Pew Research Center's Project for Excellence in Journalism 2001). The limited coverage in the national press was expected by the White House. After all, their target was the local press. In writing about President Bush's travels, White House press corps member Elisabeth Bumiller (2002, A24) of the *New York Times* writes:

A number of presidential trips got scant attention in the national news media . . . If the president travels and nobody notices, has he really taken a trip? The answer from the White House amounts to what, are you kidding? . . . The president, to use his favorite adjective, gets fabulous local news coverage, be it in Florida and Pennsylvania, states targeted for the 2004 election, or in Denver, where he spoke to cattle ranchers on Friday. Nicolle Devenish, the woman at the White House in charge of helping local reporters across the country, said that while Mr. Bush's remarks to the cattle ranchers had the impact of "throwing a pebble into a lake" for the national press, for the local news media it was "like rolling a boulder into a small pond" and made "a very big splash."

By going local, presidents hope to influence what the local and even perhaps the national media cover. In other words, presidents employ going local as a strategy to lead the agendas of local news media and affect the public's agenda and its support for the president's policy agenda. Analysis of local media coverage of domestic travel presents strong evidence that it leads to voluminous coverage in the local press. For example, a comparison of coverage in local newspapers to coverage in the *Washington Post* of local visits by President George W. Bush in 2001 indicates substantially more coverage in newspapers local to the president's events (Barrett and Peake 2007). Others show that presidential speeches significantly increase the amount of presidential news coverage, not only in local and regional newspapers but also in the *Washington Post* (Cohen 2010). Affecting local media, then, may prove to be an especially effective strategy for presidential agenda setting.

Recent research on newspaper coverage of President George W. Bush's domestic travel also provides support for positive local news coverage. In

2001, President Bush's domestic travel led to mostly positive local news coverage that was also more extensive than the coverage generated in national newspapers (Barrett and Peake 2007). Similarly, Bush's Social Security reform tour in 2005, a signature going local campaign, received ample and generally favorable coverage from newspapers local to the events in comparison with stories in the *Washington Post* (Eshbaugh-Soha and Peake 2006). A study of local newspaper coverage of President Bush in 2003 found that stories related to the president's visits were significantly more favorable than stories about Bush that were unrelated to the president's visits (Eshbaugh-Soha and Peake 2008). In fact, everyday coverage of President Bush unrelated to presidential visits in local media was largely negative, much as it is in the national media and prestige press (Eshbaugh-Soha 2010b; Peake 2007). Securing positive local press, then, requires presidents to travel frequently around the nation.

Going local generates extensive and positive local news coverage for several reasons. First, to a local community, a presidential visit is a unique event to local reporters and the newspaper's readers. This alone produces a newsworthy event that generates numerous local stories related to the president's visit. Second, local media's ability to cover the president differs from that of the national media. Local newspapers lack the resources that national newspapers have (Kaniss 1991). Because of this, they will rely more on what the White House provides them at staged media events, increasing the ease of coverage and the likelihood that it will reflect the president's perspective. Third, local events put on by the White House are almost entirely pseudoevents (Barrett and Peake 2007; Edwards 2007), fully controlled events designed to generate media attention (Boorstin 1961; Peake and Parks 2008). A pseudoevent staging allows the president to control the message and avoid uncomfortable questions from reporters and audience members, as evidenced by many successfully staged events by the George W. Bush White House (see Edwards 2007, 42–43). In addition, local reporters typically have less experience in public policy than national correspondents and therefore are less likely to write policy-oriented stories full of analysis. This, in turn, produces stories that are more descriptive and, thus, less negative than stories that analyze the pros and cons of a president's policy positions (Barrett and Peake 2007; Eshbaugh-Soha 2010b).

Local newspaper coverage of presidential travel is not uniformly positive, however. A consistent finding is that coverage varies depending on local political contexts, particularly local electoral support for the president. In supportive localities, press coverage tends to be significantly more favorable and extensive than press coverage in localities that did not vote for the president (Barrett and Peake 2007; Eshbaugh-Soha and Peake 2008). This relationship holds for everyday coverage of the president, irrespective of a presidential visit (Eshbaugh-Soha 2010b; but see Cohen 2010, 167). The relationship between support and news coverage results from the market forces that structure local news coverage of the president. To satisfy its readers' interests and maintain subscription numbers and profits, a newspaper serving a conservative audience is likely to cover a conservative president (such as, George W. Bush) more favorably than a newspaper serving a liberal audience (Eshbaugh-Soha 2010b; Gentzkow and Shapiro 2006; Peake 2007).[10] Local media also differ in terms of editorial board support for the president, ownership, and resources, which might influence the nature of local coverage. This variability in local media is central to understanding the overall success of a going local as a strategy of agenda leadership.[11]

STRATEGIC CONSIDERATIONS IN GOING LOCAL

Going local is an effective method for generating media coverage to promote the president's reelection and policy-making goals. In terms of reelection goals, presidents can focus their policy-oriented and symbolic domestic travel in states that are expected to be competitive in the next election. Much evidence supports this strategic behavior among recent presidents, a strategy commonly referred to as the permanent campaign (see Doherty 2007). President Bush targeted swing states early during his first term in office, visiting Ohio, Pennsylvania, and Florida more frequently than other states (Kornblut 2002).[12] During his first year in office, President Obama targeted his domestic travels in a similar fashion. For example, nine of the first sixteen states Obama visited had shifted from voting for Bush in 2004 to Obama in 2008 (Wilson 2009). Obama's press secretary, Robert Gibbs, remarked, "It's hard [to look] at a map and not see red, purple and blue states" (quoted in Wilson 2009, A1). Obama's first domestic trip to Elkhart, Indiana, was selected in part because it had the nation's worst unemployment rate. Indiana had also voted narrowly for Obama in 2008—the first time the state went Democratic in forty-four years (Wilson 2009).

While presidents use going local strategically to position themselves for reelection, they also travel for more short-term political benefits. Specifically, presidential travel increases the president's approval ratings. Cohen and Powell (2005, 23), in their study of state-level presidential approval ratings, report that presidents "can achieve a modest boost in state-level approval through strategically crafted public appearances." It remains unclear, nevertheless, whether these state-by-state increases in approval also translate into higher national approval ratings.

Presidents might also go local to influence opposition legislators who represent supportive local audiences. This logic stems from the expectation that positive and extensive local news coverage in areas that voted for the president may pressure opposition legislators to represent their constituents and support the president's policy proposals. Beckmann (2010, Chapter 3), for example, found that when President George W. Bush pushed his agenda on tax cuts in 2001, he focused his going local lobbying strategy on states represented by pivotal voters and leading Democrats in the Senate. In early 2001, Bush travelled to states that he won in the 2000 election but were also represented by key Democratic senators, in the hopes of pressuring those Democrats to support his tax cut proposals (Beckmann 2010; Edwards 2007; Kiefer 2001). Reviews on the success of Bush's strategy are mixed, however. Eleven of the twelve Democrats who voted in favor of the eventual tax cut passed in June were from states Bush visited (Hacker and Pierson 2005, 48). The strategy was trumpeted as a success by the administration, and passage of the tax cut was a major victory for the White House (Beckmann 2010, 103; Fortier and Ornstein 2003; Kiefer 2001). However, all but one of the Democratic senators who eventually voted for the compromise version of the bill voted against Bush's original version of the tax measure, the exception being Senator Zell Miller of Georgia, who had announced support for Bush's tax cut plan at the beginning of the year (Edwards 2007, 91).

Although presidents appear to consider their reelection and policy-making goals when deciding where to travel, these goals may be incompatible in guiding a going local strategy. Understanding that some local press is more fawning than others, presidents might choose to travel primarily to states where they have a high level of support with the expectation of positive press coverage. Doherty (2007) finds, indeed, that during their first three years in office presidents tend to visit states where they are popular. Even though this might help satisfy policy-making goals in the rare instance where presidents can parlay local support into a legislator's support, traveling to supportive locations would not help the president gain any additional electoral votes in his reelection campaign. Traveling to swing states for the potential benefit of additional electoral support may lead to more negative coverage, given the relationship between local opposition to the president and more critical coverage in the local press (Barrett and Peake 2007). Presidents are thus faced with a strategic decision: Target supportive locales to assist in short-term policy making through voluminous and positive news coverage, or target swing-states to enhance their reelection chances but receive more critical news coverage.

According to recent research, presidents target both goals and, in fact, travel broadly. For example, Barrett and Peake (2007, 8–9) show that President George W. Bush did not limit his first-year domestic travel to supportive communities. Out of a sample of sixty-one trips in 2001, Bush visited thirty-one communities where he received a lower percentage than the national average of the 2000 vote. The average vote for Bush in communities he visited during 2001 was 48.3 percent, barely higher than his national vote of 47.9 percent. Bush's travels in 2003 also targeted a broad range of communities and did not focus on competitive states or communities where his support was high (Eshbaugh-Soha and Peake 2008, 626n21). Once policy goals give way to the impending reelection campaign season, the nature of presidential travel changes starkly, as one might expect. Doherty (2007) shows, for example, that presidents eye electoral benefits during their reelection years and travel almost exclusively to competitive states. A second-term president, however, is free to emphasize his policy-making goals once again. For example, President Bush targeted primarily supportive states, those he won in the 2004 election, during his 2005 Social Security reform tour. Only six of President Bush's thirty visits were to states he lost in 2004, and only two were to states where he lost by more than five percentage points (Eshbaugh-Soha and Peake 2006, 699). Cohen (2010, 50–51) reports that Bush's reform tour targeted states that he won and that had Democratic representatives and senators in Congress.

Overall, presidents target their reelection and policy goals when they go local. They are likely to receive substantial benefits from this strategy given that they can count on voluminous local coverage. The strategy also tends to generate positive news coverage, which may help presidents achieve policy and reelection goals. We are curious as to whether going local is an effective way for presidents to lead the media's and potentially the public's policy agendas. The preceding discussion suggests that going local is likely to be an effective leadership strategy. Next, to test this expectation, we analyze the strategy's agenda-setting impact in three recent case studies.

THREE CASE STUDIES OF GOING LOCAL

Going local is an important agenda-setting strategy in which presidents highlight their policy priorities before local audiences. Although a growing body of research illustrates the effectiveness of these efforts on local and national news coverage, only one study examines systematically the effects of going local on public opinion (Cohen 2010, Chapter 8). No study of which we are aware tackles the questions of presidential agenda-setting leadership of the public, either directly through going local or indirectly through the news coverage that going local generates. Given a lack of local-oriented quantitative data on the public's agenda, we use three case studies to examine more carefully the going local efforts of Presidents George W. Bush and Barack Obama, their effectiveness in leading the media and public agendas, and what going locals means for successful passage of their policy priorities.

The three cases we examine are President Bush's efforts on behalf of tax cuts in 2001, Bush's Social Security reform tour in 2005, and President Obama's efforts to sell health care reform in 2009. We select these cases because they allow for a best test of presidential agenda leadership through a going local strategy. In each case, the president pushed a clear policy priority purposively through a significant going local effort. President Bush prioritized tax cuts and Social Security reform in the 2000 and

2004 presidential campaigns, respectively, and made these his signature issues at the beginning of each of his two terms in office. President Obama made health care reform a central part of the 2008 campaign, and it was a clear policy priority at the beginning of his presidency. Additionally, each going local campaign occurred during the first year of the president's term in office—a point where the president's political capital is highest and where we should see the greatest leadership success. In short, each case offers a best test for leadership effects because each president's political capital was relatively high at the beginning of each going local campaign, public and media salience of each issue was relatively low at the start of each presidential effort, and each represented a signature policy priority of the president.

As best test cases, these three going local campaigns help us to assess our two central hypotheses laid out in Chapter 3. First, the salience hypothesis holds that, if an issue is of low salience, presidents are most likely to lead the media and public agendas. Given that each effort was a top presidential priority, we expect presidents to lead both agendas. Any lack of agenda influence will illustrate the limits to going local as a leadership strategy.[13] Second, the indirect leadership hypothesis posits that presidents may influence the public's agenda indirectly if they can first turn the media's attention to their policy priorities. Given the substantial evidence in favor of presidential leadership of media through a strategy of going local, it is highly probable that going local will prove to be an effective strategy for indirect leadership, a claim to which we turn next.

President George W. Bush and Tax Cuts

President George W. Bush and his administration prioritized domestic travel as a strategy to influence the public and local media, especially on his signature proposals. Much as in later years when he campaigned extensively to reform Social Security, promote the war in Iraq, and push for additional tax cuts, Bush went local during his first year in office to sell tax cuts in the amount of $1.6 trillion and also to overhaul federal support for education. For the most part, Bush was successful on each proposal, even though he had to compromise by signing into law more modest tax cuts and more moderate education reforms than he had proposed.[14]

Bush's public relations campaign during 2001 was a quintessential going local effort, as evidenced by thirty-nine policy-oriented trips outside of Washington, D.C.; Maryland; Virginia; and Texas. Although a plurality of these trips focused on tax cuts (nineteen), Bush also used local trips to discuss education reform (with eight speeches), defense spending, health care, crime, the environment, energy, and his faith-based initiative. Overall, local newspaper coverage generated by President Bush's travel during his first six months was extensive and largely positive, especially when compared to coverage in the *Washington Post* (Barrett and Peake 2007).

Concerning his nineteen trips about tax cuts, Bush's travels generated 100 articles, including thirty-seven front-page articles, in the largest circulating newspapers local to the visit. Content coding of the front-page articles in local newspapers indicates that the coverage was primarily positive. On average, two-thirds of all statements that had a tonal element were coded positive.[15] In addition, an overwhelming 60.4 percent of the attributed statements in the local reporting reflected President's Bush's words or commentary by supportive Republicans. In comparison, only 18.5 percent of attributed statements were credited to Democratic politicians or other obvious opponents of the president.[16]

These statistics indicate that Bush was successful translating his policy message on tax cuts into local news coverage, his perspective dominated the coverage, and the coverage was largely positive.[17] A typical front-page article appeared in the *Pittsburgh Post-Gazette* the day after President Bush visited Beaver, Pennsylvania, on February 28 to push his tax cut proposal (O'Toole 2001). The headline reads, "Bush Easily Sells Budget on First Try in Vanport." The lead sentence quotes the president: "Part of my job as president—I might as well be very up front—is to travel the country ginning up support for this plan, and that's why I'm here." The article reports specifics regarding Bush's plan and quotes the president relating tax savings to voters in attendance. The event had all of the trappings of a staged pseudoevent, with a supportive audience and large banners stating "Tax Relief Now!" Following the president's visit to Portland, Maine, on March 23, the front-page of the *Portland Press Herald* led with a banner headline: "Bush Pitches Tax-Cut Plan in Portland." Below the headline, the article stated: "The president's ideas on the surplus and school spending are warmly received by his Chamber of Commerce audience." The article quotes extensively from Bush's remarks on his proposals to cut taxes and reform federal support for education (Bradbury 2001).

While it is clear that Bush's speeches generated numerous local news articles about his tax-cut proposal, what was the net effect of his strategy on the media and public agendas nationally? Bush's public relations efforts generated substantial media coverage of his tax cut proposals. Hundreds of newspaper articles on his tax cut proposal appeared in major newspapers across the country during each of the first six months of 2001.[18] The number of articles on tax cuts, where Bush appeared in the body of the article, was substantially higher during this period than at any other time during the Bush administration. According to our search on Lexis/ Nexis, the average number of articles mentioning tax cuts in the headline and Bush and tax cuts in the text averaged 228 for the first six months of 2001. The single highest month, with 359 articles, was March, which also coincided with the zenith of Bush's going local efforts on behalf of his tax cut proposals. This compares to an average of only thirty-nine articles per month for 2001 to 2008.[19]

The data suggest that the additional coverage is a result of Bush's going local efforts, the movement of his budget and tax proposals through the Congress, and a presidential address to a joint session of Congress in February in which Bush underscored his tax cut proposals. For 2001, the monthly number of public remarks in which Bush discussed tax cuts is highly correlated with the monthly number of newspaper articles (Pearson's $r = 0.84$).[20] While public statements by the president are correlated with media coverage, causation is unclear. To account for prior news coverage, we regressed the monthly number of news articles on monthly counts of Bush's remarks on tax cuts and the previous month's newspaper articles for 2001–2008. The R-squared is 0.60. The monthly count of Bush's remarks is statistically significant, with a coefficient estimate of 1.9, indicating that when the president mentioned tax cuts in his public remarks, newspapers published about two additional articles. This effect is much more significant in an analysis of 2001 alone where the significance of Bush's remarks increases considerably to an additional twelve newspaper articles. Furthermore, Bush's remarks on tax cuts have no significant impact on news coverage during the remainder of his administration, 2002–2008.[21] These results confirm that going local on tax cuts drove the media's agenda on tax cuts in 2001. In addition, they support our salience hypothesis: Tax cuts were relatively low on the media's agenda at the start of Bush's efforts, providing the president with ample opportunity to lead the media's agenda on the issue, which he did.

To address the public's agenda we examined aggregate responses to Gallup's most important problem (MIP) question. At the beginning of 2001, the economy was not a high priority, as net economic responses to the question hovered between 20 and 30 percent, relatively low percentages across the entire time series regarding concern for the economy. Among economic issues cited by respondents, taxes were not of much public concern, averaging only 5 percent during the first six months of 2001. A March poll, which happened to coincide with the president's tour to tout his tax cut plan, reveals that 7 percent of the public—the highest percentage during 2001—was concerned with taxes (Moore 2001). These data suggest, then, that Bush's efforts yielded a small impact on the public's agenda, likely a result of having influenced the media's agenda.[22] Nevertheless, his going local efforts failed to move public *support* for his policy, as only 56 percent of the public supported Bush's tax plan in April, the same level of support registered in February (Edwards 2007, 91).

Ultimately, President Bush was successful achieving tax cuts in 2001. Whether this is attributable to his going local strategy is a question left unresolved. Our results show mixed influence over the media and public, as going local increased media coverage on tax cuts in early 2001 but yielded less influence over the public. While our results lend support for our salience hypothesis, they offer only limited support for our indirect leadership hypothesis, as the resulting news coverage only marginally increased national public concern over taxes. The impact of going local on public support for tax cuts was also muted, perhaps because a majority already supported Bush's tax cut proposal prior to his going local efforts (see Kumar 2007, 284). This basic fact did not stop officials in the Bush administration from drawing the conclusion that their local strategy had worked in shifting public opinion and congressional support for tax cuts (Kiefer 2001). As such, they were just as eager to employ a going local strategy at the beginning of Bush's second term, with Social Security reform at the top of the president's agenda.

President George W. Bush's Social Security Reform Tour

Announced during his February 2, 2005, State of the Union address, the centerpiece of Bush's Social Security reform proposal would have allowed workers to divert portions of their Social Security taxes into personal retirement accounts, or investments in stocks or bonds. A major first step in his campaign to reform Social Security was to communicate to the public that the popular pension program was headed for fiscal crisis. Although the pending crisis was well supported by official reports, making the case for a major overhaul in Social Security was difficult. The impending bankruptcy of Social Security was decades off, after all, and so it was difficult for the president to increase immediate public concern, a potentially important variable in generating public support for his plan, or at least some version of Social Security reform. The difficulty in reaching the public persisted despite resounding success in setting the local and national news agenda on Social Security reform (Eshbaugh-Soha and Peake 2006).

Success on Social Security reform was even more daunting than Bush's case for tax cuts. Tax cuts were supported by Congress and the public independent of the president's leadership strategy. Clearly, the president's advisors' belief that going local helped secure success on tax cuts proved instrumental in their decision to go local on Social Security. When opinion polls indicated public support for reform of Social Security was lagging, the Treasury Department announced its widely publicized efforts to build support for reform, including administration visits to "sixty cities in sixty days" (Kumar 2007, 285). During the first six months of 2005, Bush made forty policy-oriented trips outside of the Potomac region, thirty of which focused on social security. Ultimately, Bush would hold campaign-style Social Security events in twenty-six states over the next several months following his State of the Union address, an effort that is "perhaps the most extensive public relations campaign in the history of the presidency" (Edwards 2007, 252).

Much like his previous attempt on tax cuts, his campaign-style speeches or "conversations" on Social Security reform typically involved a panel of hand-selected individuals predisposed to support the president's ideas and screened by White House staff to ensure that the president would receive mostly positive comments from those on stage. Local and national officials of both political parties also joined the president on center stage, with local media and, to a lesser extent, national media covering the president's visits. Presidential travel was only one component of a multifaceted effort to influence media coverage and public opinion on Social Security. The administration's efforts included outreach to conservative talk radio, extensive travel by other high-level administration officials, and coordination with supportive interest groups to build grassroots support. When the public relations efforts stalled as a result of other pressing events and issues, including increasing violence in Iraq and rising gas prices, President Bush held a prime-time press conference on April 28 at which Social Security was topic number one. It was his first prime-time press conference in over a year.[23]

Bush's efforts successfully increased news coverage of Social Security policy. Much like during his going local efforts on tax cuts in 2001, President Bush's Social Security reform tour generated extensive newspaper coverage in 2005, especially in newspapers local to the president's visits (Eshbaugh-Soha and Peake 2006). A broader sample of thirty major newspapers reveals an average of 175 articles per month on Social Security during the first six months of 2005.[24] The peak in coverage was in February, with 331 newspaper articles. In March, coverage remained substantial, with 246 articles. The coverage dropped in the months that followed, however, with 125 articles in April, ninety-two in May, and only fifty-eight in June. Once President Bush concluded his reform tour, Social Security no longer garnered substantial newspaper coverage, providing strong evidence that it was President Bush's speeches delivered to local audiences that generated substantial news coverage on Social Security. Going local effectively set the media's agenda, at least for a short period of time. Given that Social Security was not a salient issue prior to Bush beginning his public relations efforts, the success supports our salience hypothesis, which expects presidents to be better situated to lead on an issue that is not previously salient.

Much like tax cuts, our results disclose that leading the media's agenda was much easier than affecting the public's agenda. Examination

of Gallup's "most important problem" data shows that Bush's public relations efforts had some influence on public concern for Social Security,
nevertheless. In January 2005, prior to the reform tour, only 5 percent of
the public listed Social Security as a most important problem facing the
nation. In early February, after the president's State of the Union address
and a thirteen-day period where the president held Social Security reform
events in nine different states, the percentage citing Social Security as a
most important problem increased to 13 percent, a substantial increase.
The percentage remained steady at 12 through March, as the president
finished up another heavy period of travelling on the tour, holding twelve
Social Security events in eleven different states during the month. Bush
was unable to maintain this level of public concern for Social Security,
however, and by the time he finished his tour in June, the percentage citing Social Security had dipped back down to six, where it was prior to
the beginning of the tour.[25] Thus, the president had a difficult time maintaining public concern for Social Security.

A general examination of the interrelationships among the president,
media, and public confirms this modest leadership of public's Social
Security agenda.[26] Much as we conducted in Chapter 5, we use vector
autoregression (VAR) analysis to examine the interrelationships among
the president, media, and public regarding Social Security for the period
2001 through 2007. The VAR included the following three variables: the
monthly count of presidential remarks mentioning Social Security, the
monthly number of articles on Social Security in our Lexis/Nexis sample of major U.S. newspapers (see note 18), and the percentage of Gallup
Poll respondents citing Social Security as a most important problem. The
analysis indicates that President Bush was able to increase media attention to Social Security reform, but his public remarks had only a marginal
direct impact on the public's agenda.[27] Still, this supports our salience
hypothesis, especially in regards to media. Because the president affected
news coverage of Social Security reform and news coverage affected the
public's agenda, moreover, he indirectly led the public's Social Security
agenda through the news media, in support of our indirect leadership
hypothesis. These measurable effects were fleeting, however, as the issue
did not remain on the public's radar for very long.[28]

Given that Bush's arguments for reform hinged on the Social Security trust fund being in immediate peril, a better measure of the immediacy of the public's demand for Social Security reform may be the public's perception of whether the program faced a crisis. Polling from Gallup suggests that Bush performed worse on this measure (Newport and Saad 2005). Although 53 percent of the public believed that Social Security faced major problems, and 18 percent considered the Social Security system in crisis prior to the president's State of the Union address, these percentages remained virtually unchanged after the address. More directly for our purposes, a late February poll by Gallup revealed that only 38 percent of the public believed that the government should make changes in the Social Security system in the next year or two to ensure its long-term solvency. In an early January poll, taken prior to the president's reform tour, 49 percent of respondents cited the need to make changes within the next year or two. This number decreased by 11 percent *after* the tour began. Opinion was decidedly mixed on the question of the significance of Social Security as a problem. In early March, a Gallup poll asked respondents whether it is "necessary for the Congress and president to pass legislation this year to make changes to the Social Security system?" Only 51 percent of respondents claimed it was, while 46 percent claimed it was not necessary (Newport and Saad 2005). Thus, while President Bush's efforts appear to have modestly affected the public agenda according to our standard most important problem measure, these more nuanced opinion measures suggest a failure of framing the issue in a way attributable to the president's going local message.

Although we present some support for the effectiveness of going local as a strategy of presidential leadership of the media's and public's agendas on Social Security, we stop short of being able to explain why these successes did not translate into a signature policy victory. After all, President Bush clearly was unable to convince Congress, including members of his own political party, which had a majority in both chambers, to reform the "third rail" of American politics (Edwards 2007; Weiner 2007). Overhauling a popular policy with entrenched and powerful defenders is a monumental political undertaking, indeed (Ross 2007). Moreover, it appears that agenda leadership is less effective if presidents choose to go local on a policy that the public does not already support (see Canes-Wrone 2006). Absent other favorable conditions, therefore, going local provides no guarantee that presidents will achieve their policy goals, even if it tends to be an effective tool of agenda leadership.

President Barack Obama and Health Care Reform

Like his predecessors, President Barack Obama travelled domestically to build support for his key policy proposals early during his presidency. During his first year in the White House, Obama made forty-three policy-related trips outside of the Potomac region, including twenty-seven trips that were focused on his two key domestic policy priorities: economic stimulus and health care reform.[29] While his policy-oriented domestic travel is similar to Clinton's in scope, he did not travel domestically as often as George W. Bush, who made sixty-one trips in his first year in office. Obama, as is typical of modern presidents, also travelled for ceremonial and campaign purposes. He made seven fund-raising and campaign trips for Democratic candidates in 2009, delivered two commencement addresses, and spoke at two funerals. Overall, Obama's early travel is similar to his predecessors in the extent that it was focused on policy leadership.[30]

Although different from George W. Bush in terms of style, amount, and duration, Obama's effort on behalf of health care reform was a classic example of going local to increase public concern and build support for a top legislative priority. Obama clearly faced an uphill battle to reform health care, and his White House communications team pulled out all the stops to push health care reform onto the agendas of both the media and public. His efforts to place health care on the public agenda included numerous domestic trips where he held health care–related events. In addition to going local, Obama had an unprecedented nationally televised town hall meeting carried live on ABC News in June and delivered a nationally televised address before Congress in September on health care. Much like President Bush on tax cuts and Social Security reform, President Obama used all of the various public leadership tools available in his effort to lead on health care.

If Obama had an impact on the media, public, or both, then this would speak again to the benefits of a going local strategy.[31] As is typical for local media covering presidential visits, local newspaper coverage of President

Obama's twelve health care reform events outside of the Potomac region during 2009 was extensive. These twelve events led to sixty-four news articles in the largest circulating newspapers closest to the event and available on Lexis/Nexis, with twenty-four appearing on the front-page.[32] The coverage was similar in its makeup to the coverage received by President George W. Bush when he campaigned for tax cuts in 2001. President Obama's perspective dominated much of the policy-oriented coverage, and in each case at least one lengthy article detailed Obama's plan for health care reform. For example, the *Milwaukee Journal-Sentinel* led with the following headline the day after President Obama's visit to Green Bay on June 11: "Obama Puts Urgent Cast on Health Care Reform. In Visit to Green Bay, President Offers Few Specifics but Stresses Fast Timeline." President Obama is quoted at length, stressing the significance of the health care problem and the need to reform the system. " 'If we do nothing, within a decade we will be spending one out of every five dollars we earn on health care,' Obama said. 'In thirty years, it will be one out of every three. That is untenable, that is unacceptable, and I will not allow it as president of the United States' " (Borsuk and Boulton 2009). Three additional health care–related articles appeared in the Milwaukee paper on the day of and day after Obama's visit. President Obama's visit to the Cleveland area on July 23 led to eight articles related to his visit, three of which dealt specifically with health care reform, largely from the president's perspective, and two of these articles were on the front page of *The Plain Dealer*.[33]

President Obama led the media's health care policy agenda, as evidenced by substantial increases in the number of major U.S. newspaper articles discussing health care reform during his public relations campaign. Prior to going local, ninety-seven articles on health care reform appeared in major U.S. newspapers for the month of May.[34] The number of articles nearly doubled to 184 in June, the month Obama began going local on health care reform. As he continued to argue for reform, and as various reform bills moved through Congress, the coverage intensified. In July, the number of articles stood at 245 and increased to 485 in August. Part of the increase in coverage during August focused on several high-profile, raucous exchanges during congressional town hall meetings on health care reform (Pew Research Center's Project for Excellence in Journalism

2009a; 2009e). Thus, it would be inaccurate to say that all of the coverage either was favorable to the president or reflected his views fully. But the increases occur after the president began his public relations efforts and thus correlate highly with the president's policy agenda. September, the month in which Obama delivered his address before a joint session of Congress, generated 363 articles on health care reform, but by October, as the president shifted his focus to other issues, the number had fallen to 211 articles. Coverage remained high in October through December, even though Obama's local travels to tout health care reform effectively ended by October.

The Pew Research Center's Project for Excellence in Journalism's (2009c) News Coverage Index[35] provides an alternative measure of media coverage: the weekly percentage of the news hole devoted to a topic. Figure 6.2, which graphs the weekly percentage of the news hole devoted to health care from January through October 2009, corroborates our independent counts of newspaper articles. It indicates, too, that the news media turned their attention to health care reform as President Obama went local on health care reform. During August and again in September, health care stories accounted for fully one-third of the news hole, supporting our contention that Obama's public relations campaign on health care reform increased media attention to the issue. Regression analysis indicates that Obama's tour, along with his nationally televised speech, contributed significantly to increasing the amount of coverage devoted to health care. We regressed the weekly percentage of the news hole devoted to health care on the number of weekly health care reform trips (we included the Bristol, Virginia, trip in this analysis) and a dummy variable to account for his speech to Congress on September 9. The findings estimate that each trip increased the percentage of the news hole devoted to health care by four, a substantial impact. The speech to Congress is estimated to have increased the news hole focused on health care by 13 percent.[36]

Did Obama's influence over the media also affect the public's concern for health care? Obama's public campaign appears to have played a significant role in pushing health care reform onto the public agenda, according to the Gallup data. Between November 2008 and May 2009, an average of 8.3 percent of respondents cited health care as a most im-

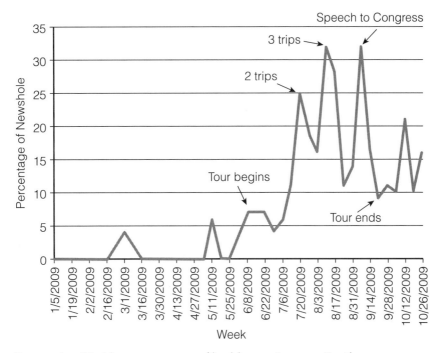

FIGURE 6.2. Weekly news coverage of health care, January–October 2009.

Source: Pew Research Center's Project for Excellence in Journalism, The News Coverage Index (establishment press); available at www.journalism.org/about_news_index/overview. The values include the percentage of the total newshole devoted to health care. The sources used by the index include network television, cable television, newspapers, websites and radio.

portant problem in the Gallup Poll. After the administration shifted its policy focus from the economy to health care reform, the percentage stood at 14 percent and 16 percent in June and July, respectively. Following additional speeches in August and September, the percentage increased to 25 percent and 26 percent, respectively, slipping to 22 percent in October and November. The public's concern for health care appears to have somewhat diminished public concern for the economy during this period. As health care reform increased in importance on the public's agenda, the percentage of the public citing some component of the economy as a most important problem went from 80 percent in March to just over 50 percent in September. Obama's efforts thus increased public concern for health care and, consistent with our salience hypothesis, led the public's agenda because it was not of prior public concern.

Although we cannot determine for certain whether Obama's public relations campaign directly increased public concern for health care reform, we can say that Obama appears to have at least indirectly influenced the public agenda on health care reform. Obama's speeches affected news coverage, as we have already described. Moreover, there is a high correlation between the number of major newspaper articles on health care reform and the percentage of respondents citing health care in response to Gallup's most important problem question (Pearson's $r = 0.92$), suggesting the increased media coverage contributed to increased public concern. These findings lend substantial support for our indirect leadership hypothesis. What is most striking about these results is that the president appears to have been successful in increasing public concern for health care, even though the economy still remained overwhelmingly important given the weight of the recession on the public's mind (Morales 2009; Saad 2009). We should note, however, that Obama failed to convince the public that immediate action was needed to reform health care. Fewer than half of respondents in a Gallup Poll indicated that Congress should pass a new health care reform law by the end of 2010 (Newport, Jones, and Saad 2009).[37]

Much as with President Bush's Social Security reform tour, President Obama was not able to generate a majority of public *support* for his health care policies by going local. This is important to the limits of a going local strategy to achieve policy goals, even though health care reform eventually passed Congress. For the best case going local scenarios, we return to President Bush's successful efforts to cut taxes in 2001 and President Obama's success on the economic stimulus during the first month of his presidency. In each case, the president had broad public support for his policy[38] and had healthy public approval ratings[39] early in his first term. These conditions appear to be equally as important to legislative success as using going local as a strategy to lead the agendas of the public and news media.

Even though we show agenda leadership on health care reform, the president's ultimate policy success may not have hinged on his having *led* the public's policy agenda. After all, it would be unreasonable to conclude that Obama's public relations efforts on behalf of the economic stimulus led public concern for the economy, as polls indicate it already dominated the public's agenda. As we discussed at the outset of this chapter,

Obama's economic priorities during 2009 were largely guided by existing public opinion, as over 80 percent of the public cited economic problems as most important at the start of his term. Thus, presidents can still achieve strategic victory by responding to issues of high public concern through a strategy of going local, even when they do not lead the agenda.

CONCLUSION

Given the necessity of news media to public leadership in the modern age and the tendencies for national news organizations to ignore or emphasize negative stories about the president, recent presidents have gone local to target local news media. They have done so extensively, as our data confirm, with the well-founded expectation that their efforts will generate extensive and positive local news coverage. In this chapter, we have examined going local as a leadership strategy for President Bush on tax cuts in 2001 and Social Security reform in 2005 and President Obama on health care reform in 2009. We explored not only whether going local is an effective strategy for generating news coverage but also whether going local is an effective strategy to reach the public.

We demonstrate that going local can be a useful strategy for presidential agenda leadership. In each of the three case studies, we show that going local is an effective tool for presidential leadership of the media's agenda. This includes affecting not only news coverage local to the president's visit but also exposure in newspapers throughout the nation. Going local still dictates local news coverage most consistently, as national news coverage is likely to decline rapidly after the beginning of a going local campaign (Eshbaugh-Soha and Peake 2006). Moreover, presidents have been modestly effective translating this news coverage into indirect leadership of the public's agenda, as we show for Social Security, health care reform, and, to a lesser extent, tax cuts. Presidents Bush and Obama also were more likely to have led, rather than to have responded to, the public's Social Security, tax cut, and health care reform agendas, given a lack of public concern for these issues prior to going local. We caution that these results require additional evidence and more rigorous analysis to confirm how increased media coverage through going local benefits the president's leadership of the public's agenda.

As with any presidential leadership strategy, translating agenda influence into legislative success by going local is another matter. As our case studies illustrate, political context matters greatly to the president's policy goal achievement. When it comes to Congress, the size of the president's majority is most important, regardless of whether he leads or responds to the public's agenda. Although President Obama influenced the public's concern for health care reform in 2009, health care reform would have undoubtedly failed without sizeable Democratic majorities in both houses of Congress. Moreover, President Bush succeeded on tax cuts in 2001 given a supportive legislature and even without substantially altering the public's policy agenda. Despite having Republican majorities in both houses of Congress, however, President Bush failed to reform Social Security in 2005. Determining exactly why Bush failed on Social Security reform is beyond the scope of this book, of course, but our analysis confirms that setting the public and media agendas on an issue is insufficient to position the president to succeed in Congress without clear public (Eshbaugh-Soha and Miles 2009) or congressional support. Bush's failure on Social Security reform reminds us, indeed, that influencing the agenda is only part of effective presidential leadership and is no guarantee for eventual policy success in Congress.

Certainly, even if presidents can increase the salience of issues to the public and news media by going local, they still face the predicament of being unable to move public support for these issues. Even if, as we have shown, presidents generate more positive local news coverage through their domestic travel, this may not necessarily affect the public's support or opposition to the president's priorities (but see Cohen 2010). As such, strategic presidents may be wise to prioritize those issues where the president's preferred policy is already popular with the public (Canes-Wrone 2006; Edwards 2009) and take advantage of existing support in Congress. A successful strategy of going local may therefore contain elements of both leadership and responsiveness. That is, presidents may be able to lead the public and media agendas by going local but are wise to go local on those policies with preexisting public support to translate agenda-setting leadership into increased legislative success. Furthermore, as we argue in our concluding chapter, going local may be most effective not as an exclusive strategy of agenda leadership but as one that is a blend of focused and sustained leadership efforts.

CHAPTER 7

Leadership and Responsiveness
in the Public Presidency

WE OPENED THIS BOOK with a claim from President Barack Obama that he "hasn't always been successful . . . breaking through the noise (of the media)" to reach the American people. President Obama's frustrations speak to the puzzle that has guided our exploration of presidential leadership of the public and news media. Modern presidents rely extensively on the bully pulpit, yet their efforts have yielded little in terms of moving public opinion. Why do presidents expend so much effort for such little payoff? Is President Obama correct that the media impede presidential leadership of the public? Are there any other benefits to presidential public relations absent clear evidence that the president has led either the public or news media?

Our examination reveals two potential payoffs for presidential public relations. First, we have argued that the news media provide opportunities for indirect presidential leadership of the public. Despite the difficulties presidents face leading the media and public, our theory and analyses show that the media are of central importance to presidential leadership of the public. Rather than providing a barrier to leadership, news media offer opportunities for presidential leadership of the public's agenda. By influencing what news media cover, presidents can affect the importance the public attributes to issues. Second, our theory and analyses make clear that responsiveness is a key component of the president's relationship with the public. Recent presidents respond to shifts in the public's agenda. Even when presidents are unable to lead the public's agenda, they still satisfy important conditions of democratic governance by responding to the policy concerns of the public. In short, although presidents may be unable to lead the public's policy preferences, we demonstrate the benefits of presidential speech making in setting the public's agenda indirectly through the news media. Additionally, we demonstrate the importance of the public's agenda in constraining leadership on the one hand while promoting responsiveness to the public's most pressing concerns on the other.

We conclude the book with a brief summary of our findings and what they mean more broadly for our understanding of the American presidency. We pay particular attention to the implications of our findings as they relate to the vast literature on going public, including what our findings suggest for presidential leadership of Congress and democratic responsiveness. In light of the many difficulties presidents face leading the public and news media, we suggest that future presidents would be well served to focus on agenda setting as a leadership strategy rather than on direct opinion leadership. We also underscore the limitations of the book, while offering suggestions for future research. Finally, we explore the normative implications of our work. Whether presidents lead the public's agenda may matter less to the president's goals than talking about policies that are important to the public. The bottom line is this: Policy salience is paramount to presidential leadership of the public and news media. It matters in that presidents are more likely to respond, rather than lead, through their public speeches when an issue is of high concern for the public. It also matters because a president who is able to increase the salience of an issue will have an opportunity to parlay public speech making into policy success for his priorities.

PRESIDENTIAL LEADERSHIP OF THE
PUBLIC AND NEWS MEDIA

Studies of presidential leadership of the public have produced mixed conclusions. For example, recent scholarship on public leadership indicates that presidents are effective leaders of the public (for example, Cohen 1997; Wood 2007). Other key works question the capacity of the presidency to lead the public, however (such as Edwards 2003; Wood 2009a; Young and Perkins 2005). To build on this literature, we set out to accomplish three tasks. First, we make prominent the role of the news media in our examination of presidential leadership of the public. Even if presidents cannot directly lead the public—as so much research has demonstrated—affecting news coverage provides presidents with an opportunity for indirect leadership of the public. Second, we have conceived of presidential leadership as a set of reciprocal relationships among the president, news media, and the public. Considering the impact that presidential speeches may have on the public and news media, while simultaneously accounting for the impact that the public and news media may have on presidential speeches, contributes to our understanding of these complex relationships. Third, to test the importance of media and these interrelationships systematically, we have examined leadership as agenda setting across three leadership strategies and several policy areas. This has allowed for a thorough test of the agenda-setting assumption put forth by proponents of the strategic presidency framework (Canes-Wrone 2006; Edwards 2009), for which we offer moderate but qualified support.

The Importance of News Media

We have argued throughout this book that media are an important, yet relatively unexplored, avenue for presidential leadership of the public. The media have important effects on public opinion, as so much research has demonstrated (for example, Iyengar 1991; McCombs 2004). The media clearly influence public opinion through their influence over the public's agenda. This truism of American politics suggests that, even in the absence of direct presidential leadership of the public, the news media may enhance public access to the president's agenda, thereby increasing the propensity for presidential leadership of the public's agenda. Out of this theoretical rationale, we derived an indirect leadership hypothesis. Presidents, even if they cannot directly lead the public's agenda through their public attention to policy issues, may do so indirectly so long as their speeches first influence what is on the nightly news.

Indeed, when we have found presidential leadership of the public, it tends to occur most frequently through the news media. Although relying on the news media presents its own complications and is no guarantee of presidential influence, our results indicate that presidents have substantial opportunity to affect the public's agenda for each of the public relations strategies we examined. In Chapter 4, we find little direct influence of presidential speeches on the public's concern for the economy. However, we find that nationally televised speeches on the economy had statistically significant effects on media coverage in about a third of our cases. When we examine the strategy in the aggregate, we find that national addresses tend to increase media coverage of the economy and that media coverage increases public concern for the economy. In each of our analyses, we find a clear relationship between media attention and public concern. Indirectly, therefore, national addresses affect the public's economic agenda. We report similar relationships for Iraq. Although direct, focused leadership of the public's agenda on Iraq has occurred rarely, typically coinciding with a major development in policy (such as a use of force), the analysis supports our argument that the media provide the president with an opportunity to indirectly influence the public's agenda on Iraq through media coverage of Iraq.

In Chapter 5, we examined a sustained strategy of attention. We assessed the relationships of all presidential remarks on the economy and Iraq to media attention and public concern for these issues. Our findings support our theoretical claims that the news media are critical to the president's leadership of the public. Concerning the economy, we find that, even in the absence of direct leadership of the public's agenda, presidential leadership of the news media's economic agenda affords presidents an indirect avenue to lead the public. Ignoring the news media's role in the presidential–public relationship would have understated the president's leadership influence. On Iraq, we find similar results. Presidential attention to Iraq increases media attention to it, which indirectly leads the public's agenda on Iraq over a period of several months.

A relatively new strategy of presidential leadership, termed going local, involves presidents using their domestic travel to influence both the media and public. In Chapter 6, we studied three recent cases of going local: George W. Bush on tax cuts in 2001 and Social Security reform in 2005 and Barack Obama on health care reform in 2009. We conclude that going local is an effective way for presidents to influence media coverage, consistent with previous research. However, increased media attention only slightly affected the public's agenda, as other key issues (especially in 2005 and 2009) focused public attention elsewhere. Thus, we conclude that, although going local provides a significant leadership opportunity over news coverage, the impact presidents had on the public's tax, Social Security, and health care reform agendas through increased news coverage is modest.

Our findings imply that failing to account for news coverage, which the White House devotes significant resources to influence, may understate the effectiveness of presidential public leadership. If presidents devote enough attention to a policy priority, offering an innovative and newsworthy policy agenda, then they have a good chance to lead the media. This affords presidents the opportunity to take advantage of the strong link between news coverage and public opinion in order to affect the public's agenda. These findings support the importance of news media to the presidency, offering a more nuanced view of the role that media play in presidential leadership of the public. After all, if we had not considered explicitly the news media in our analysis, we would have missed evidence of presidential leadership of the public's agenda.

The Importance of Reciprocal Causation

Our theory and analysis carefully consider the reciprocal nature of presidential leadership, which required us to account for presidential responsiveness. We simultaneously modeled the impact that presidents have on the public and news media *and* the impact the public and news media have on the president's own agenda. We argued that presidents are most likely to lead the media, public, or both when they can act entrepreneurially and target issues not currently of concern to either the news media or public. Raising awareness of new issues as part of an innovative policy agenda is especially likely to promote leadership rather than responsiveness. When the news is already saturated with coverage of an issue and public concern is sufficiently high, presidential agenda leadership is unlikely. This reasoning produced what we have called the salience hypothesis. Restated, presidential leadership is most likely in the absence of prior public concern or media attention to an issue, whereas presidential responsiveness is much more likely when an issue is high on the public and media agendas.

We find much support for our salience hypothesis throughout our three empirical chapters. The agenda-setting leadership capabilities of the presidency are partially a result of the public's existing agenda. Specifically, we report that presidential attention to the economy and Iraq is a function of the public's concern and that presidential agenda-setting leadership is not a likely expectation when these issues are already on the public's agenda. In Chapter 4, we find that nationally televised addresses do not directly influence public concern for the economy and that presidents are highly responsive to existing public concern in their decisions to deliver a nationally televised address. Put differently, when public concern for an issue is high, presidents are likely to respond to, rather than lead, the public through a strategy of focused attention.

In Chapter 5, we disaggregated our analysis of economic issues, providing a more thorough test of our salience hypothesis. We argued that unemployment is an economic issue to which citizens are highly attuned over time, and because of this high level of public salience presidents should be responsive to the public's concern for unemployment. We find that presidents increase their attention in response to the public's concerns for unemployment, and thus leadership is much less likely on highly salient issues. One recent example of this relationship is President Obama's efforts to address the economy. Even in early 2010, as Democrats in Congress were finalizing details on health care reform, a top Obama priority, steadily high unemployment numbers required a shift in the president's public remarks. He spoke heavily on jobs and what the administration intended to do to help create them. President Obama clearly responded to public concerns about unemployment by speaking more about job creation. To further assess the salience hypothesis, we separately examined federal spending issues, which are typically less salient to voters than unemployment. In that analysis, we find the clearest instance of presidential leadership on the economy, as both the public and media respond positively to presidential attention. Issues that typically lack salience afford presidents a strategic opportunity to lead the public and media.

We find the strongest evidence of presidential agenda leadership in the case of Iraq. Even though media covered events in Iraq independent of presidential action, presidents still affected media attention to Iraq when they chose to address Iraq in their public speeches. This leadership of the news also translated into indirect leadership over the public's agenda. It is in the case of Iraq that we find our strongest evidence of direct presidential leadership of the public's agenda through a strategy of sustained attention, and given a lack of prior public concern this is a finding strongly consistent with our salience hypothesis. Leadership effects waned during the George W. Bush administration, however, as the president found it difficult to maintain control over the agenda as the war in Iraq dragged on. In situations lacking either direct or indirect presidential leadership of the public's agenda, our tests demonstrate that the news media had the strongest and most direct impact on the public's concern for Iraq during the latter years of the Bush administration.

Our case studies of going local, presented in Chapter 6, also support the salience hypothesis, albeit not as clearly as our more sophisticated time series analyses. Social Security reform was not a public or media priority before President Bush pushed it onto the agenda in 2005. His reform tour clearly increased news coverage, but its influence over public concern, while noticeable, was short lived, as only a maximum of 14 percent of the public noted Social Security as the most important problem. He was unable to sustain attention to the issue, and his reforms died in Congress soon after. The public was clearly focused on other problems, most notably the Iraq War and the economy, and Bush's handling of Hurricane Katrina did little to maintain the public's focus on Social Security. President Obama, in taking on health care reform in 2009, successfully increased media attention to and public concern for health care. Health care was not on the public's agenda prior to the president's extended effort, but, as the tour ended, nearly a quarter of the public listed it as a most important problem. Even so, his success affecting public priorities was modest, given the public's overriding concern for the economy and the president's own incentives to show his responsiveness to public concern for the economy. We present the weakest evidence of going local leadership on tax cuts. Although taxes were not salient prior to President Bush's domestic travels, thus providing him with an opportunity to lead the public's agenda, public concern barely nudged upwards after a protracted effort by Bush, which included numerous local speeches.

Reciprocal causation in our models is important not only for fleshing out the precise relationships among the president, media, and public but also for larger concerns about the rationale for presidential responsiveness. Although we do not espouse that presidents are merely responding to public opinion and pandering to an unknowledgeable public, which may result in the formulation and adoption of bad policy (see Tulis 1987), we suggest that considering public concern about policies as presidents decide whether to prioritize them in their public speeches is in the rational self-interest of presidents who wish to further their political goals. Moreover, such responsiveness by modern presidents demonstrates the democratic nature of the office. Presidents may not change their policy preferences in response to public opinion (Jacobs and Shapiro 2000), but they set their policy priorities in response to public concerns. Such a pattern of responsiveness is consistent with important democratic ideals (Burns 1978; Dahl 1982, 6; Heith 2004) and is an important by-product of public speeches, even when presidential speeches do not lead the public.

Rather than pandering to public interests, our analysis suggests that presidents respond to critical issues facing the nation as democratic leaders are traditionally obligated to do (Burns 1978; Geer 1996; but see Wood 2009a). Presidents are concerned with meeting public expectations and responding to those issues the public finds important and in need of presidential attention. Because the public can drive presidential responsiveness on issues to which it is highly attuned, moreover, we contend that presidential speech making is limited as a strategic tool to secure policy goals. Presidents may not always have the luxury to lead on issues that are already popular with the public but may be forced by the public's agenda to focus on a policy regardless of the president's handling of the issue area. Obama's turn to unemployment and jobs in January and February 2010 reflects the necessity of presidential responsiveness in the face of high public concern.[1] Thus, our conclusion that presidents are responsive to public concerns adds an important component to the strategic presidency model: There are some instances when presidents cannot pick and choose on which issues to focus. Rather, presidents must respond when public concern is high, even if they are not thereby speaking about an issue where they have widespread public support. Presidents may want to emphasize issues where they are strong, but if public concern is high in an area where they are weak, they are still wise to respond.

The Importance of Different Strategies and Public Policy

The approach presidents take to lead the media or public matters, with substantial variation in leadership or responsiveness across the three strategies that we investigate. Our analysis in Chapter 5 shows, consistent with our expectations, that presidents are best able to sustain public and media attention to their policy priorities by speaking about issues frequently over several months. They tend to lead the public agenda through these efforts—directly and indirectly through the news media— most often when the policy lacks prior salience. Our analysis of national addresses in Chapter 4 indicates that a focused strategy produces mostly short-term effects. Moreover, presidents tend to use a focused strategy of attention to respond to rather than directly lead the public's agenda, especially on the economy, and to lesser extent on Iraq. This is another example of the dual expectations that presidents face. Just as presidents use their myriad speeches to lead, so too do they use the national stage to show the American people that they share the public's concerns for important national priorities.

In addition, going local, also a sustained effort at media and public relations, tends to affect both the media and public agendas. We show in Chapter 6 that presidents go local to focus the public and news media on the president's own priorities, which best fits traditional definitions of agenda leadership. In each of our cases, we find evidence of leadership, although the impact varies by effort, with President Obama having the clearest impact on health care reform. Given the limits of our case studies, we cannot determine precisely whether going local is an effective strategy of direct leadership of the public's agenda. Nevertheless, going local sustains media attention, which at least allows presidents to lead indirectly the public's agenda. Our results point clearly to going local as a strategy of presidential *leadership* rather than responsiveness, although there may be instances, such as Obama's travels on the economy in early 2009, which may produce clearer evidence of responsiveness for the reasons we have hypothesized.

Of course, presidents are not limited to a single strategy, and using all three strategies may be most helpful to the president's goal achievement. President Obama adopted a mixed strategy on both his economic stimulus and health care reform proposals in 2009. Although he went local often, he also delivered national addresses on both issues, gave lengthy television interviews to national media outlets to take advantage of his largely positive honeymoon with the media, and used a nationally televised town hall meeting on health care near the start of his public relations campaign. Obama's efforts on the economy were in direct response to the worst economic crisis since the Great Depression. Not only was the agenda set for him, but the public also largely supported his economic proposals at the outset. Circumstances were certainly propitious for Obama's early successes. Obama's initial experience supports the importance of presidential responsiveness to policy success and implies that presidents need not be the first to set the agenda to use the public's concern to their advantage in Congress. Indeed, being responsive to the public's agenda and speaking about it may present the president with an important opportunity to achieve policy goals.

What we do not find is significant variation in the relationships according to the two broad policy areas we examined. In other words, presidential agenda leadership and responsiveness on the economy and Iraq does not vary much according to the specific and substantive differences expected vis-à-vis the conventional two presidencies thesis. A lack of variation is especially pronounced in Chapter 4, even though recent presidents have been afforded more opportunities to speak on national television concerning Iraq than any other policy area. The primary reason that individual addresses on Iraq have been more influential over the public's agenda than have national addresses on the economy concerns the predominance of international events, which tend to force presidents to address a foreign policy issue (Wood and Peake 1998). Especially when presidents instigate force abroad, such as the U.S. invasion of Iraq, a national address is highly likely to lead the media and public agendas, at least in the short term. This is not to discount important differences suggested by the two presidencies framework but rather to illustrate that the expectations of the thesis are not as strong as we expected when it comes to leadership of the public agenda. We did find, nevertheless, that a strategy of sustained attention was effective in directly leading the public's Iraq agenda in the aggregate, something we did not find in our comparable analysis of the broad area of economic policy.

Policy differences are strongest in two other ways. First, policy matters as a function of prior public concern. It is the salience of the policy—the current importance of an issue to the public—that produces more variation than any differences in the substance of the policy itself. Nevertheless, we report that prior media attention does not preclude leadership, as the president–media relationship is often reciprocal. Second, policy variation is important in terms of the variety of political conditions that affect presidential leadership or responsiveness within a sustained strategy of attention. Whereas the interrelationships between sustained presidential attention, media, and public on the economy are unaffected by the political environment—with only the objective state of the economy driving media and public economic agendas—nearly all political conditions have some impact on attention to Iraq. Presidential decisions to prioritize Iraq through a strategy of sustained attention are much more variable than economic policy according to reelection years, international events, and the state of the economy. This is consistent with the general findings and expectations of previous research that holds that foreign policy agenda setting is driven heavily by external events and conditions (Wood and Peake 1998). In short, policy context is important to presidential agenda setting and influences the exogenous forces that condition the president's success as an agenda setter.

IMPLICATIONS

Our book has two important implications for the study of the public presidency beyond its immediate conclusions. First, our findings contribute to our understanding of going public as a strategy for presidential leadership and responsiveness. Second, our theory and analysis suggests that agenda setting may be the optimum public relations strategy for presidents in the face of the futility of direct public opinion leadership.

Presidential Leadership, Responsiveness, and Going Public

Going public is the central governing strategy of modern presidents (Canes-Wrone 2006; Cohen 2008, 2010; Edwards 2003; Kernell 1997). Although our study does not extend to presidential success in Congress, our findings speak to the prospects of going public as a successful governing approach in several respects. First, agenda setting is central to the effectiveness of going public. Recall that Canes-Wrone (2006) argues that if presidents can increase the public salience of or set the public's agenda on an issue where their position is already popular with the public, they should be able to parlay public speeches into increased legislative success. We present broad support for this agenda-setting assumption, depending on the president's choice of strategy and the issue's prior salience. If presidents have the flexibility to speak about issues that the public already supports and if they can affect the public's agenda, then they have an important source of power to affect not only the media and the public but also, potentially, Congress. Additionally, presidents need not influence the public's agenda directly but may succeed in "expanding the scope of conflict" through increased news coverage. We thus provide two distinct avenues for presidential leadership of the public's agenda, both of which speak to the effectiveness of going public as a leadership strategy.

Agenda leadership is central to presidential influence in the legislative arena. According to Neustadt (1990, 7), "Congressmen need an agenda from outside, something with high status to respond to or react against. What provides it better than the program of the president?" As Bond and Fleisher (1990) argued two decades ago, the key structural power presidents can use to affect legislation is by securing agenda space for their legislative proposals, something that they do quite well (Edwards and Barrett 2000). Presidential influence over the public agenda, therefore, should place presidents in an even stronger position to affect the legislative agenda, as they bring public concern to bear in their efforts to secure legislation. Even if presidents respond to existing public concern, as was clearly the case with President Obama and economic legislation signed in early 2009, they may still be able to use the public's agenda to set the legislative agenda and increase their policy success in Congress.

Second, our results imply that each of the public relations strategies we have studied should be used together for optimum impact over policy. To begin, national addresses are best situated to set the public agenda at the beginning of the policy process, that is, before the public and the news media become concerned with the president's priorities. We saw this at the start of the Iraq war in 2003, as Bush's national address (and associated invasion order) affected news coverage and public concern. It also appears to have benefited President Clinton's leadership of the news media in 1993 with health care reform (Edwards and Wood 1999). Given the relatively rare and short-term impact that national addresses have on the public's agenda and the tendency for presidents to use a national address to respond to the public's agenda, however, it makes sense for presidents to sustain their attention to their policy priorities subsequently through repeated efforts. Although not guaranteed to be effective, a sustained strategy can help presidents maintain an issue's salience, permeate news coverage regularly and, if need be, transfer existing public support into influence over what is often a long and arduous road to legislative victory. Whether presidents choose to give myriad speeches to specialized interest groups and their political party supporters, that is, going narrow (Cohen 2010), or to target locales throughout the nation, that is, going local, presidents are successful generating news coverage by sustaining attention to their policies. By affecting news coverage, moreover, we show that presidents should also be able to affect the public's agenda indirectly given the strong link between media and the public.

The difficulties of sustaining media attention abound, however, and should not be downplayed. From unexpected events to economic crises, other priorities may overshadow presidential leadership and force a presidential response. Issues other than presidential priorities have a way of forcing presidential attention or at least distracting media and public attention to the detriment of the president's agenda. As such, setting and sustaining the agenda in the way that we have described may be only a necessary but insufficient condition for effective legislative leadership. Because going public alone is an inadequate governing strategy—regardless of the many ways the president chooses to implement it—it may be wise, consequently, for presidents to use the national address to set the agenda early on, sustain the public's attention through a strategy of sustained attention or specifically by going local, and then use personal appeals and lobbying efforts on the eve of a congressional vote to optimize the president's legislative success (Beckmann 2010; Covington 1987). As Edwards has argued (2003, 2009), going public is no substitute for effective White House lobbying of legislators, even with the effective implementation of the three public leadership strategies we have identified and examined in this book.

Third, going public not only concerns presidential leadership of the public, news media, or Congress, it also concerns presidential responsiveness. Thus, even when presidential speeches fail to move the public's preferences or even set their agenda, going public may still prove to be a viable governing strategy in terms of satisfying public expectations. Our findings indicate that by responding to public concerns through speech making, presidents are able to meet the public's expectations for democratic leadership. The public expect presidents to be responsive. This is the case, even though presidents may be unable to move the public to support their policies or their presidency. For example, even if much of President Obama's going local efforts on the economy did not bolster public support or affect legislation before Congress, he was able to illustrate responsiveness to public concerns about the economy by claiming credit for past successes and offering assurances that he was working for the benefit of the American people. President Clinton may have benefited during the Kenneth Starr investigation during the Lewinski scandal by repeating publicly his claim that he was working on behalf of the American people—that he was being responsive to public concerns—even as voices called for his resignation or impeachment.

Although the strategic model of presidential leadership considers responsiveness, it seems to imply that presidents have the discretion to prioritize issues already popular with the public when they hope to translate speech making into increased legislative success. Yet we infer that presidents respond to public concern on issues, regardless of their popularity, due to their status as president and the public's expectations for presidents to address salient public policies. As elected leaders, presidents are not driven entirely toward affecting change on issues that they want to address. George H. W. Bush's response to the economic recession in 1992 is one example that comes to mind. He had to prioritize the economy, even though he may have preferred to revel in his Persian Gulf War victory and his strengths as a foreign-policy president. This is an important point. Although we find support for the agenda-setting assumption put forth by other scholars, we also confront basic notions of presidential leadership. There is more to leadership than attempting to prioritize those presidential policies that the public already supports. As democratic leaders, presidents are also elected to address the public's policy concerns. We conclude, therefore, that because the public expects presidents to be responsive on issues of high public concern presidents can go public to also meet this responsibility as democratic leaders. As such, going public concerns much more than leading the public; it is also geared toward democratic responsiveness.

Agenda Setting

Presidents are engaged in a permanent campaign, even as efforts by presidents and their massive communications operation to move public opinion have led to limited results (Edwards 2003). In light of our findings, and given the limited impact presidents have on the public's policy preferences according to other research, agenda setting may be the stage in the policy process that presidents should target with their speeches. Presidential success affecting the agenda is important to the goals of presidential leadership. We conclude, therefore, that a president's primary focus should be on influencing and responding to the public's agenda rather than their policy preferences. Targeting those issues that stand the best chance of becoming law given existing public and likely congressional support is an effective leadership strategy according to our formulation and that adopted by other scholars (Canes-Wrone 2006; Edwards 2009). Responding to public concerns to meet public expectations is also an important component of agenda setting, as we have argued, and can help presidents meet reelection goals and burnish their historical legacies.

Such a prescriptive claim is not something that is outside the bounds of what we understand about presidential leadership of the public. After all, we have long known of the complexities associated with elite leadership of the public's policy preferences, as this topic has been at the root of our understanding of public opinion (Achen 1975; Converse 1964; Zaller 1992). Presidents surely wish to convince the American people to support their policy preferences. But when they are unable to do so, presidents are compelled to lament their inability to communicate effectively, which they surmise is the reason for their failures (see Edwards 2003). Yet our reading of the literature suggests that changing public preferences should not be the first and primary goal of the modern White House communications operation. Instead, it should be to set the public agenda (Hult and Walcott 2004; Kumar 2007; Maltese 1994). Even Edwards's (2003, 6) characterization of President Reagan's communications difficulties speaks to policy priorities and the "seriousness" of key issues.[2] If President Reagan could have convinced the American people that Nicaragua was a serious issue, then maybe he could have framed the issue in such a way as to have generated enough support in Congress to fund the Contras. A stretch, perhaps, but the logic suggests that agenda setting is a first and most important step to tap public support as an end in itself or as a means to affect legislation. As we have argued, moreover, the president's most fruitful mission may not be reaching the public directly but influencing it through news coverage.

Setting the agenda through a strategy of public attention is no guarantee of successful leadership of the public, of course. George W. Bush's Social Security reform tour is a prime example. Having devoted considerable resources to an extensive public relations campaign, the president influenced media coverage of Social Security extensively; increased public concern about the issue, however slightly; and even mobilized interest groups to support and oppose his privatization initiative (Edwards 2007). Despite successfully affecting the agenda, Bush was unable to move the public to support his policy position. Instead, opinion moved away from the president, and the president lost control of the agenda as his tour continued. In the end, his efforts to reform Social Security stalled in the Republican-controlled Senate Finance Committee. Clearly, setting the agenda is only one step in the policy process, but on discretionary policies, especially, the failure of Social Security reform suggests that presidents are wise to target those issues that the public already supports to maximize their chances for policy success, acting strategically in the manner espoused by Edwards (2009) and Canes-Wrone (2006).

DIRECTIONS FOR FUTURE RESEARCH

Future research can build on our findings in several ways. First, future research should delve more deeply into potential variation by policy areas. Even though we find less than expected variation across the two broad policy areas we examine, our results reveal greater variation according to disaggregated economic issues and the specific going local cases we selected. Different characteristics of these policies, what we identify to be differences in a policy's initial salience, present different opportunities for presidential leadership or responsiveness. We think it is this variation on which future research should focus to further the generalizability of our findings.

Although we continue to maintain that studying variation by policy area is an important way to broaden our understanding of presidential leadership, we recognize that we do not offer a definitive examination of an exhaustive list of public policies. Indeed, our small subset of policies limits our ability to conclude authoritatively whether other policy attributes may produce divergent results, or, as we maintain, if the current placement of the policy on the public agenda drives presidential leadership or responsiveness. Some of our strongest evidence of leadership occurs through a going local strategy on very specific policy issues. That the administration actively selects the policies on which presidents will go local—devoting vast resources to their public relations efforts and strategically planning their potential effectiveness in White House meetings—limits variation in the types of policies that we can explore. Although our results generally show strong leadership over the media and, to a lesser extent, the public, the purposive nature of the going local strategy limits uncovering a policy area that may be more conducive to showing agenda responsiveness. If such a case exists, then future scholarship should explore it to further our understanding of how going local helps presidents achieve their goals through agenda leadership or responsiveness.

Given these limitations to our research design, we encourage future researchers to extend our analysis across a wider range of policies, with an eye toward additional variation in policy salience, much as Peake (2001) and Eshbaugh-Soha and Peake (2005) did to build on previous work on presidential agenda setting vis-à-vis the media and Congress (Edwards and Wood 1999). Doing so will help answer whether our results are specific to the policies we have selected or whether our expectations for prior salience and indirect leadership hold across other types of public policies. Expanding analysis to a broader range of—or at least different—policies can help underscore our results and enhance the generalizability of our contribution.

Second, scholars should look specifically at how the introduction of cable news and, more recently, the Internet affects presidential leadership. Our analysis does not account for either of these important latest developments, other than to suggest that presidential influence may be reduced as a result of smaller audiences in recent years. Part of the problem here is data availability. Even quality research on the twenty-four-hour news era (Cohen 2008) is limited in gauging systematically the effects that one of the major causes of this era—cable television news—has had on presidential leadership, given the dearth of available data. The typical measure, the percentage of households with cable television, is too broad a proxy to assess cable news effects, especially with the growing partisan and ideological divisions in viewers across cable news channels (Baum and Groeling 2010; Iyengar and Hahn 2009). Scholars must develop precise measures of cable news and new media effects to more clearly ascertain their impact on presidential politics. In short, our research illustrates what interrelationships among the president, the public, and traditional news media look like. Future research must now explore the differentiating impact that cable news and other new media may have on the relationship.[3]

Third, just as we show that presidential leadership of the public's agenda occurs primarily through the news media, we cannot speak to complexities that media add to presidential leadership of public *preferences* for policy solutions. Can presidents lead the public's policy preferences indirectly through the news media? Even though we show that presidents can indirectly set the public's agenda through news coverage, if the president cannot affect the direction of that news coverage, then the possibility of indirect leadership of public opinion seems remote. Baum and Groeling (2010) reveal the importance of news coverage to public support for foreign policy issues, but also limits to presidential influence over the tone of news. Cohen (2010) provides some initial evidence that presidents can affect news tone, which can affect public preferences. But these claims, too, require additional support.

Fourth, future research should add Congress explicitly to our equation given that a substantial portion of the political communications literature weighs Congress heavily in its consideration of political news coverage. The media tend to report the official line and, as such, are likely to reflect the government's position in much of their coverage, especially in foreign policy (Bennett 1990; Hallin 1984). When Congress disagrees with the president, however, this suggests an important impediment to presidential leadership of the news media (see Howell and Pevehouse 2007). Indeed, perhaps congressional opposition to Iraq or congressional Republicans' criticisms of President Obama's handling of unemployment drove the public's agenda related to these issues. Even though Congress may be unlikely to dictate agendas, as other research has found (Edwards and Wood 1999), it could at least limit presidential leadership given the media's appetite for conflict. What is more important is that when scholars extend their analysis of these complex interactions beyond the agenda-setting stage of the policy process to exploring public support or opposition to policies, they may be wise to include Congress in their analyses given the potential Congress has to counterbalance the president's views, perhaps undermining the president's ability to influence the public's agenda and their policy preferences. After all, as Edwards (2003) makes clear, the president is only one voice among many trying to break through the media to affect public opinion. Opposition voices often serve to counterbalance the president's argument and obfuscate the clarity of the president's message.

Our study also does not consider the role that interest groups play in affecting presidential leadership or responsiveness. This is a topic future research should consider. Cohen (2008) suggests that presidents are increasingly "going narrow," targeting specific interests in their numerous minor speeches (see Cohen 2010). To what extent do presidents attempt to influence the agendas of specific groups in their speeches? To what extent do presidents respond specifically to the policy priorities of interest groups in their speeches? Interest groups are clearly important to promulgating or undermining presidential messages (see Jacobs and Shapiro 2000), yet we do not account for them systematically. Interest groups may also be an important source of indirect presidential influence in Congress, especially because reaching the mass public is more difficult with increasingly fragmented news sources.

In all, there are important avenues for future research on the president's relationship with the media and public. The public presidency literature is advancing our knowledge of the topic at a considerable pace, yet much fertile ground remains to be tilled by future researchers.

THE PRESIDENCY AS A DEMOCRATIC INSTITUTION

The normative implications of the public presidency, including political pandering by presidents and, more importantly, demagoguery, have long been debated. When leading the public, should presidents be responsive to the policy concerns of the public? If presidents are responsive, is this pandering? If presidents lead the public's agenda, are they somehow manipulating public opinion? After all, presidents are charged with acting on behalf of the people as the steward of the public interest. In a democracy, the expectation is that leaders will respond to popular demands. How well have recent presidents managed these expectations, and what does our analysis say regarding the democratic nature of the office?

Concerns about demagoguery were clearly articulated by Hamilton and Madison in the Federalist Papers. A demagogue, by definition, gains power by arousing the emotions and passions of the people. The basic worry was that a demagogue would use divisive public appeals to promote tyranny. These early fears have diminished in the modern "rhetorical presidency," where public speech making has become a primary tool of presidential governance. That "a president ought to be a popular leader has become an unquestioned premise of our political culture" (Tulis 1987, 4). Given the modern evolution of polling, recent concerns have related more directly to pandering, where the president pursues a policy simply because it is popular, regardless of whether the policy is in the public interest (Canes-Wrone 2006; Jacobs and Shapiro 2000).

If presidents act as demagogues—if their appeals do indeed promote tyranny—then we would presumably see this play out in the latter stages of the policy process so that demagoguery would lead to policy that is not in the public's interest. We do not test, nor do we examine, whether Tulis (1987, 178; see Lowi 1985) is indeed correct that presidential public leadership has contributed to a "decay of public discourse." Nor do we examine leadership or responsiveness in regard to whether the public is informed about its interests (see Canes-Wrone 2006, 104). Instead, we have assumed—partially consistent with Canes-Wrone's definition of policy leadership—that presidents attempt to lead the national agenda because they believe it will help them achieve their goals, whether those be reelection or policy success. What is more, we have avoided the complication of defining what the public interest may or may not be but instead have assessed presidential leadership of the public *agenda* on a set of issues.

Even so, the broader considerations of this project speak to these larger, normative issues of democratic governance. Our results illustrate that presidents are responsive to public concerns. Our finding that presidents tend to emphasize in their public speeches those issues that are salient to the public and media should not be considered evidence in favor of demagoguery or pandering. After all, we limit our analysis to agenda setting. The nature of the president's policies—whether they promote the public or partisan interest (see Wood 2009a, 177) or neither—is beyond the scope of the book. Yet, the Constitution, as described by Hamilton in the Federalist Papers, numbers 71 and 72, incentivizes presidential behavior, targeting presidents' desire for power in such a way that they will act to benefit the public.

It is perhaps the presidents' broader goal for historical recognition that encourages them to remain responsive to public concerns even without a clear reelection incentive. Although it is commonplace to argue that presidents may be more likely to respond to public concerns when their reelection is at stake, that is, during their first term or in reelection years, we find little variation in the timing of presidential responsiveness. We contend that it is part of the fabric of the American presidency that presidents act in response to the concerns of public opinion, regardless of their immediate electoral concerns. When presidents do so, they may be remembered more favorably, as acting responsively may trump the many failures presidents experience throughout their tenure. It is, according to our results, the public and perhaps the media—but not consistently broader political conditions—that reliably predict whether the president will lead or respond. That presidents are no more or less likely to respond to the public's economic concerns through a national address during a reelection year supports the notion that presidents are not pandering.

We believe, as well, that media can help facilitate presidential responsiveness and democratic governance. Rarely do presidents have opportunities to address the nation on television. Although we have shown that presidents take advantage of this opportunity to respond to public concerns about the economy, the primary way by which presidents can demonstrate responsiveness to the public's agenda is through news coverage of their speeches. It is through the media that public accessibility to the president's policy agenda is greatest. Especially as new media become more fragmented, it is imperative that presidents consider creative and innovative ways to reach out and lead the American people. Just as media provide opportunity for indirect leadership of the public's agenda, so too they may help facilitate and promote a more democratic presidency.

Still, additional questions remain unanswered concerning the democratic nature of the presidency. For example, recent scholarship suggests that presidents respond primarily to their partisan supporters rather than to the general public and that presidential representation is based on "myth" (Wood 2009a). Our analysis of agenda setting is unable to tackle this important question directly. We do find evidence, however, that presidents respond to the policy agenda of the mass public in their going public efforts, which is indicative of presidential representation. While presidents may not always pursue policies favored by the general public, although quite a bit of evidence suggests that they do so regularly (Canes-Wrone 2006; Rottinghaus 2010), they do tend to address the broader public's policy agenda through their public rhetoric.

We conclude, therefore, that presidents act democratically using their primary tool of leadership in the modern age: their public speeches. Presidents also lead through their speeches, something that the public expect of them. The leadership we find, of course, is conditional and circumspect, but there are agenda leadership payoffs for the public presidency. The media, as the dominant linkage institution in American politics, also facilitate this relationship by linking the public with the president's agenda. Although the news media do not always provide presidents with an indirect road to public leadership, they are not so noisy as to preclude it, either. Indeed, a significant portion of the president's message rises above countervailing messages of the news media to provide the president an opportunity for leadership. Still, the nature of presidential leadership is premised on existing public opinion. When the public have well-developed concerns, we find that presidents respond. When public concern remains unfocused, however, presidents are in a much stronger position to lead the public's agenda and devise strategies to affect policy that they have decided are important to their presidencies, to be sure, but also the nation. Little more is needed to conclude that the presidency is a very public and very democratic political institution.

Appendix

Keywords Index

Public papers of the presidents	Most important problem	Vanderbilt TV News Archive
Economy		
Economy; Commerce; Deficit; Budget; Debt; Spending; Taxes; Unemployment; Employment; Inflation; Interest Rates; Monetary Policy; Business & Industry; Growth; Recession; Trade; Commerce-International; Economy-International; Country Name-US Trade	Economy (general); Deficit; Unemployment; Inflation; Spending; Trade relations; Trade; Recession; Interest rates; Other economic	Economy; Commerce; Deficit; Budget; Debt; Spending; Tax; Unemployment; Inflation; Interest Rates; Monetary; Fiscal Growth; Recession; International Commerce; Tariff; Trade
Iraq		
Iraq; Persian Gulf; Saddam Hussein; Kuwait	Kuwait; Iraq; Middle East crisis; Gulf crisis; Saddam Hussein; Persian Gulf; situation in Iraq; fear of war; feelings of fear in this country; War in Iraq	Iraq; Persian Gulf; Saddam Hussein

Note: The keyword list used for the public papers is developed from index headings and sub-headings provided by the hardbound copies. Index headings change from one administration to the next, so we included key words as the papers added them for subsequent presidencies. The Vanderbilt TV News Archive rely on electronic keyword searches. We read each keyword "hit" to determine its relevance to an economic topic and excluded any that were not germane to the economic issues addressed by the study. "Iraq" captured virtually all hits related to the topic. The keywords for the most important problem are those listed by the Gallup organization as responses to their questions.

Notes

1. See, for example, Blumenthal (1982) and Gergen (2000) on Reagan's public leadership abilities. Although a more tempered analysis, Greenstein (2000) indicates that Reagan's effective communication was a significant component to his success as president.

2. As Edwards (2003, 4) documents, President Clinton blamed ineffective public communication for the stunning defeat of Democrats in the 1994 midterm elections. Edwards, along with Jacobs and Shapiro (2000), suggests that the Clinton administration's belief in presidential leadership of public opinion on health care reform was a fundamental error that contributed to the president's failure.

3. Lest the reader believe we are cherry-picking our issue for Ronald Reagan, Edwards (2003, Chapter 3) extensively documents Reagan's inability to move public opinion on a range of priorities, including support for increased defense spending and tax cuts.

4. CBS News Poll (August 27–31, 2009, and September 19–23, 2009).

5. It actually declined to 39 percent (October 29–November 1, 2009) and then to 34 percent (November 19–22, 2009), rising again to 40 percent (January 28–31, 2010), according to the Ipsos/McClatchy Poll.

6. *Washington Post* Poll (February 4–8, 2010).

7. The Pew Research Center's Project for Excellence in Journalism (2009c) tracks the portion of the news hole devoted to top stories on a weekly basis. According to their weekly content analysis, health care reform was consistently a top story for the final six months of 2009 and into 2010.

8. A number of reasons for Obama's success on health care reform have been offered, including his personal lobbying of wavering Democratic legislators and final strategic decisions made by the president and Democratic leaders in Congress. Contemporary observers, including White House advisers, also point to Obama's public leadership. For example, David Axelrod, a senior Obama adviser, remarked in a televised meeting with Senate Democrats on February 3, 2010, that Obama has led on health care reform and that he had expended substantial political capital on health care reform: "Add up the number of trips, speeches, radio addresses . . . I spend a good part of every day with him, and I know he is still working hard on this issue" (Connelly 2010).

9. Our own research on the president and media suffers from similar shortcomings. For example, see Peake (2001), Eshbaugh-Soha and Peake (2005), and Peake and Eshbaugh-Soha (2008).

10. These numbers, provided by the Gallup Poll, are responses to the following question: "Do you approve or disapprove of the way President Bush is handling the situation in Iraq?"

11. Druckman (2006) makes the same observation in his book review of *Who Leads Whom?*

CHAPTER TWO

1. In our broad reading of the literature, we have found more instances where scholars fail to define leadership clearly as a concept. Kernell's (1997, 4–5) "going public" argument is about "strategies in leadership," and, although he writes about how going public affects a president's leadership style or what kind of leader he may be, there is no explicit definition of leadership, only an implication that presidential leadership exists when presidents act in a bargaining or going public fashion. Wood's (2007) book is about presidential leadership of the economy. But again, one can infer only that we know leadership when we see it: When presidential rhetoric affects the public evaluations of the economy or consumer and investor behavior, we find presidential economic leadership. This is not to undermine the value of these works but rather to illustrate how tackling this concept has not been easy by even the best studies of the public presidency and that our efforts to do so are important to the broader literature.

2. This can become diffuse quite quickly. For Andrew McFarland (1969), a leader who causes intended change is exercising power, whereas a leader who causes unintended change is exercising influence.

3. Edwards (2003, 85) notes one important exception. A study by Madsen and Snow (1991) shows limited evidence of charismatic leadership by Juan Peron, who was president of Argentina for two terms during the 1940s and 1950s.

4. Still others argue that presidential leadership is contingent more on a president's willingness to use the powers afforded him to act unilaterally more than on his ability to persuade. Clearly, presidents have "the ability to move first and act alone" on a range of policies (Howell 2003, 20–21) and can alter significant public policies with "the stroke of a pen" (Mayer 2001). According to this perspective, modern presidents have a number of unilateral powers, including issuing executive orders, proclamations, and national security directives and signing executive agreements, which by definition do not require persuasion to affect change. Careful analysis of presidential use of unilateral powers, however, indicates that presidents are still bound by their political context, especially the partisan makeup of Congress (see Howell 2003; Krutz and Peake 2009; Mayer 2001; Steele 2008; Warber 2006). Indeed, even when presidents are free to act alone (as they are with their use of unilateral action and rhetoric), their own behavior and successes are often structured by their political environment rather than by their own personal abilities.

5. This is not to say that personal attributes (such as charisma or rhetorical skill) of a president do not matter to public leadership. Our claim is that systematic analysis of these concepts, at least in a quantitative setting, is not very plausible. As Edwards (2009) has shown quite lucidly, even the most successful presidents did not rely on their personal attributes as leaders but instead exploited favorable conditions to lead.

6. Geer (1996, 24) does not, nor do we, tackle the more complicated question of politicians' intentions, including whether or not the president adjusts his position to reflect the public's or just happens to reflect the public's opinion.

7. One could argue that this was not always the case. Tulis (1987) and others suggest that premodern presidents were not responsive to public concerns in ways that modern presidents are. Simply put, the structure of presidencies in centuries past may not have been conducive to even the potential for a public display of responsiveness or representation. Thus, an examination of presidential responsiveness in the nineteenth century might render this assumption inappropriate.

8. This is by no means an exhaustive list of types of leadership, nor does it raise individual characteristics of what constitutes a leader (see Cronin 1984.) We do not, for example, employ Weber's leadership types (charismatic, bureaucratic, or legal-rationalistic). Even though we reference Burns (1978), we do not elaborate on his transformative or transactional forms of leadership in the context of our conceptual or operational definitions.

9. Even though they have offered an important study that considers the president, news media, and public opinion, Baum and Groeling's (2010) study serves as another example of the difficulties in exploring simultaneous and reciprocal relationships in examining opinion leadership.

CHAPTER THREE

1. Bush did not lose control of the agenda because he failed to prioritize the public's issue priorities. The end of the Persian Gulf War ended the immediate conflict and, more generally, public concern and interest in Iraq and foreign policy. Because a poor economy was lurking, the American people quickly focused on it before the president could adequately address it.

2. Although our focus is on public leadership, presidential agenda setting is far reaching within the institutional presidency. The institutional presidency provides presidents with myriad resources to promote their policies in Congress, whether through direct presidential lobbying (Edwards 1989), the Office of Legislative Liaison (Collier 1997), or coordinated legislative clearance through the Office of Management and Budget (Larocca 2006). Presidents also seek to influence the development of policy at the bureaucratic level through their political appointments, which can affect the priorities of various executive agencies (Wood and Waterman 1994).

3. Like Geer's (1996) understanding of Wilsonian leadership, Rottinghaus (2010) notes how higher salience constrains the president's ability to lead the public's policy preferences. We build on these observations in the sense that presidents are most likely to affect public concern for issues—or increase salience—when an issue is not initially important to the public.

4. This depends heavily on the subject, the level of public support for the president's position, and the availability of adversarial sources (see Hallin 1984).

5. For a similar conclusion regarding famine in Ethiopia, see Bosso (1989) and Rogers and Dearing (2000). Their arguments hinge on the media affecting opinion prior to provoking a government response. Livingston and Eachus (1995) challenge the veracity of the claim regarding Somalia in their study of the "CNN effect."

6. The 2008 Pew Biennial poll about news interest and knowledge shows that only 39 percent of the public follows international news "most of the time" (August 17, 2008), despite two ongoing wars. This varies, though, as 56 percent of respondents have an interest in international news "only when important." This suggests that media coverage of an international crisis or event should encourage public interest in international news.

7. According to Pew's (2009) News Interest Index, Jackson's death occupied 17 percent of the news hole for the week of July 15, whereas the economy, Obama's trip, and health care reform made up 11, 11, and 7 percent of the news hole, respectively. Differences in reported news interest were even greater, as 29 percent of the respondents named the Jackson story as one they were closely following, while 20 percent stated they were closely following the economy. Only 12 and 11 percent stated they were closely following stories on Obama's trip and health care reform.

8. Even though they account for the president, media, and public, in their ground-breaking study of the Iraq War, Baum and Groeling (2010) do not address the reciprocity that we identify.

9. Personal experience also matters to agenda setting (see Iyengar and Kinder 1987). Because we do not have individual-level data to assess personal experience, we cannot account for this effect directly. Nevertheless, objective conditions may serve as a proxy, in the aggregate, for this likelihood.

10. This changed briefly with the war in Iraq, as 52 percent said that they follow international news "most of the time" in April 2004. These data are from the Pew Research Center.

11. Although there are foreign policy elements to economic policy (such as trade with other nations), we view the economy primarily as a domestic policy issue and believe presidential leadership on the economy should differ from foreign and national security issues. Some scholars have referred to international economic issues as "intermestic," signifying their link to domestic politics and thus decreasing the probability of presidential leadership (Barilleaux 1985; Conley 1999; Steger 1997).

12. We could have examined other important foreign policy issues besides Iraq. Terrorism, although of great importance to presidents, was not of central importance until after the events of September 11, 2001, limiting the range of analysis. Presidential attention to the Arab–Israeli crisis and the U.S. relationship with Russia are also important. Yet presidents have devoted only sporadic attention to Arab–Israeli conflict, and U.S. relations with Russia have changed substantially after the Cold War. Furthermore, studies of foreign policy agenda setting have already addressed both the Arab–Israeli conflict and U.S.-Russian relations (Wood and Peake 1998) but not Iraq. Finally, we decided against examining a single, broad policy category of foreign policy, as some other research has done (for example, Cohen 1995) because foreign policy issues compete with one another for presidential and media attention (Wood and Peake 1998).

13. The yearly average percentage of the public stating some component of the macro-economy as the most important problem is 32 percent for the period of 1947–1999 (Policy Agendas Project 2010).

14. The yearly average percentage of the public stating some component of international affairs or defense categories as the most important problem is 25 percent for the period 1947–1999, according to the Policy Agendas Project. In the Policy Agendas Project coding scheme, wars and conflicts are listed under the defense category. Comparably, while salient at times, the monthly average percentage of the public stating Iraq as a most important problem between 1990 and 2008 was 7 percent, with a high of 38 percent in March 2007.

15. There is substantial variance for each issue. According to Gallup's most important problem data, an average of 11 percent of the public cites unemployment as a most important problem since 1950, whereas spending issues combine to reach an average of only 4 percent. Unemployment also ranges much higher (61 percent) than spending issues (20 percent), with substantial variance in both time series.

16. Each of these issues also varies in terms of issue salience. Taxes reached a high of 7 percent of the public citing it as a most important problem in 2001, while Social Security peaked at 12 percent in 2005. In late 2009, 26 percent of respondents indicated health care to be the most important problem facing the nation.

CHAPTER FOUR

1. We cannot tell from these data alone whether the media reinforced the impact of the president's speech. According to Edwards (2003, 198), only 38 percent of Americans watched the president's national address on illegal drugs, suggesting that media attention may have aided the president's leadership of the public's agenda.

2. President Kennedy, the first president to take advantage of television as a new technology, saw the potential of going directly to the public through televised addresses. He "exulted in the potential of television for going directly to the people when he told journalist Ben Bradlee that 'when we don't have to go through you bastards, we can really get our story to the American people'" (quoted in Edwards and Wayne 2010, 158).

3. Edwards (2003, 189) maintains that audience numbers indicate "that the president obtains the attention of a large percentage of the viewing public. Such a conclusion would be incomplete, however. The White House is interested in reaching the entire public, not just those who might be watching television." Such an expectation is unrealistic. The entire public does not vote, so presidents do not have to reach the entire public to benefit electorally from their national addresses. Moreover, Wood (2009a) argues that presidents do not represent even the median voter but rather their partisan supporters. Besides, if presidents hope to use a national address to move the public to influence legislation before Congress, they surely do not expect the entire nation to move to support them. Rather, if presidents can motivate a segment of society, this may help them achieve their policy goals through a strategy of focused attention (see West 1988).

4. See Pew Research Center's Project for Excellence in Journalism (2009d). Despite their decline in recent years, evening news network broadcasts still reach an average of 25 million viewers, considerably more than cable news (Bennett 2009, 229). Prime-time network audiences are substantially larger. We also do not directly assess the listening audience of National Public Radio, even though it is actually larger than cable news audiences. In fact, NPR's average national audience for "Morning Edition" is 7.6 million (Farhi 2009).

5. This includes *CSI* on CBS (ranked number one) and *Will and Grace* on NBC (a top-ten show).

6. Our list of national addresses on the economy and Iraq illustrate that presidents bifurcate their national addresses by policy areas in only a handful of instances. In 1975, President Ford delivered an address on the economy and energy; in 1990, President Bush delivered an address on the budget deficit (an economic issue) and Iraq.

7. The discretionary nature of national addresses is a function of presidential preferences and style, much as press conferences are an individual choice of presidents (Eshbaugh-Soha 2003; Kumar 2007). Despite the opportunity it affords presidents, a president may or may not choose to use it depending on his individual style and governing strategy.

8. This contrasts with Edwards (2003, 209), who argues that the more educated are better able to process complex information or translate the president's message into their increased support or opposition for it. We do not disagree with Edwards but note that he is examining opinion change, not agenda setting, which suggests the relationship we offer.

9. For example, for four of Reagan's first-term addresses, only an average of 69 percent of viewers could remember at least one point that the president made. However, only 60 percent of the public watched, heard, or read anything about the speeches, on average. That is, "31 percent of the 60 percent of the public who *were* exposed to an address could

not identify a single point the president had made. Thus, *a clear majority of the public could not remember anything The Great Communicator had to say, even in the immediate aftermath of the speech*" (Edwards 2003, 207–208, emphasis in original).

10. Local affiliates could carry the speech, as the CBS affiliate in College Station, TX, did.

11. See Edwards (2003, 212–214) for a brief history of presidential difficulties securing network airtime.

12. Some might argue that we should use economic approval ratings for our analysis of economic policy. We do not do so for two reasons. First, surveys that assess economic approval are sparse before 1980. We prefer to have a longer time series. Second, when approval ratings are likely to most influence economic addresses, they are likely to be highly correlated with economic approval, anyway (see Edwards et al. 1995). There appears to be little difference between the impact of speeches on economic and total presidential approval besides (Wood 2007, Chapter 5).

13. Edwards (2009, 81–82) finds another incentive for presidential speech making during reelection campaigns: Presidents who are successful raising public awareness of issues during a campaign may be more successful translating that awareness into policy victories once in office.

14. Network coverage of the economy and the unemployment rate correlate at $r = 0.45$.

15. There are numerous measures of events that could be used, including Brace and Hinckley (1992).

16. Wood (2007) uses public perception of the economy in his models. This makes sense given that he is looking at effects on the public's perception of the president's job performance. The objective economy is more relevant to agendas, nevertheless, which also has a much weaker correlation with presidential approval ratings ($r = < 0.32$) than with our agenda measures.

17. Using alternative specifications, such as changes in the gross domestic product (GDP), makes little difference to the results presented. The misery index is a better measure given our monthly unit of analysis.

18. Some might maintain that we should be examining cable television news instead of the networks. Although we admit that this is a hole in not only our research, but much of the literature, and encourage future research to explore this specific question, examining network news coverage is appropriate. Even though the audience for network television news has declined precipitously throughout the 1990s, it is still much higher at 25 million viewers than cable television news viewership (about 3 million in prime time). Network news averaged about 55 million viewers in 1990 and several million more in the 1980s (Bennett 2009, 229). See Baum and Groeling (2010, 174) for a similar justification. They also note that cable news, especially Fox, is more of a "niche news outlet."

19. We test each dependent variable in our time series analysis for stationarity. Augmented Dickey Fuller tests denote stationarity for the economy ($t = -1.09$; intercept and trend: $t = -2.61$; intercept only: $t = -2.66$, with the null of a unit root rejected at $p < .05$, Schwarz Information Criterion) and Iraq ($t = -1.60$; intercept and trend: $t = -3.50$; intercept only: $t = -3.26$, with the null of a unit root rejected at $p < .05$, Schwarz Information Criterion).

20. Intercoder reliability is quite high, both internally and externally. A comparison with our Iraq counts, for example, correlates at 0.997 with data reported by the Pew Research Center's Project for Excellence in Journalism.

21. As Woolley (2000) illustrates, media-related data should be used with care. Fortunately, many of the issues he raises, such as problems with indexes that may be biased by the increase in the number of pages in yearly volumes over time, are not problems with the Vanderbilt abstracts.

22. Ultimately, this matters very little as stories and seconds for Iraq correlate at $r = 0.94$.

23. Our measure thus contrasts with Wood's (2007) measure of the public's self-reported exposure to negative news stories but may be a viable alternative given Prior's (2009) argument.

24. We use Wood (2007, 47) as a guide for coding MIP data by the month. We found some discrepancies between his data set of economic responses and the data we pulled from Roper. We corrected these discrepancies, which amounted to a few divergent entries. Most of these discrepancies involved Wood's (2007) coding differently a handful of surveys (primarily in 1982) in which Gallup pressed respondents who mentioned the general economy among one of their initial choices to offer a more specific economic problem. Because Gallup does not do this in all surveys, counting these responses produces some inconsistent and inflated numbers. Using Wood's numbers instead of our corrected data produce negligibly different results, but we report results using the corrected data because they are based on more consistent coding across a lengthy time series.

25. Augmented Dickey Fuller tests denote stationarity for the economy ($t = -1.14$; intercept and trend: $t = -3.68$; intercept only: $t = -3.57$, with the null of a unit root rejected at $p < 0.05$, Schwarz Information Criterion) and Iraq ($t = -0.59$; intercept and trend: $t = -1.90$; intercept only: $t = -1.31$; fails to reject null of unit root). As the ADF also lacks statistical power, we reject the null of a unit root with a battery of other tests, including the Phillips-Perron test (intercept and trend: $t = -3.60$, with the null of a unit root rejected at $p < 0.05$).

26. Our treatment is broader because we examine three strategies of agenda leadership in the book, whereas prior research examines separately State of the Union addresses (for example, Cohen 1997) and nationally televised addresses (Peake and Eshbaugh-Soha 2008) or combines all public statements without differentiating by strategy (as in Edwards and Wood 1999).

27. To meet a basic condition of causality, we confirmed that each speech occurred before the subsequent Gallup Poll in that month. Thus, no speech in the model is lagged, but the time ordering is correct; that is, each speech occurs before the poll.

28. Battlefield deaths for the more recent Iraq war are taken from http://icasualties .org. For earlier periods of the time series, we rely on media reports and www.global security.org/military/ops/desert_storm-stats.htm.

29. Various alternative specifications, including those that rely on traditional Box-Jenkins time series methods and probit models, treated separately, produce nearly identical results. The findings that we present are actually more conservative given the restrictions on these methodological techniques, which account explicitly for simultaneity and thus do not result in biased or inconsistent estimates. See Amemiya (1978) and Keshk (2003) for more technical explanations of this technique. An additional three-stage least-squares regression that models the public's agenda and the media's agenda approximates the relationships we report.

30. We lag MIP in this model by one month to ensure the correct time ordering. Although it produces a statistically significant and positive result without changing the substantive meaning of the other coefficients, including a contemporaneous measure of

MIP would not definitively indicate that MIP affects media attention given that the survey questions for each respective month have occurred at various times and not necessarily before a speech in each month.

31. We find that Carter's 1978 national address on the economy significantly increased media coverage of economic issues, even though Gilberg and his coauthors (1978) find that Carter's State of the Union address of that year had no impact whatsoever on additional press coverage.

32. We also looked at changes in public concern that an especially large increase in a month may heighten the president's awareness of economic issues and affect a response. We do not find this.

33. To be sure, tempers flared in 1987 after the Iraqi Air Force attacked the USS *Stark*, an American Navy frigate, in which thirty-seven sailors were slain. The potential crisis was diffused by Iraq's speedy apology and agreement to pay reparations and the desire on the part of the Reagan administration to minimize the crisis as a "horrible error" (Lamar 1987).

34. Although we do not count it, the president's January 1991 State of the Union address clearly addressed Iraq, too. Moreover, we model all presidential attention devoted to Iraq in separate specifications. Whether lagged by one month (no impact on either media attention or public concern) or not (significant and positive impact on media attention only), the results presented in Table 4.3 hold.

35. We do not maintain that we have countered this perspective entirely. Much of the research is based on detailed qualitative assessments that show convincingly how the Bush administration was successful manipulating news coverage of the war in Iraq in the build-up to and immediate aftermath of the March 2003 invasion. Even so, our findings should be a call to future research to examine further the conventional wisdom.

36. Peake and Parks (2008, 98) analyzed the tone and frames of 136 front-page newspaper stories on the day after President Bush's "surge" speech. They report that, while extensive, coverage was primarily negative, with over half of the articles adopting the negative frame—that the president's policy had little support. It is important that readers keep in mind that the analysis presented here focuses on the president's ability to set the agenda, not frame coverage in a favorable fashion.

CHAPTER FIVE

1. We estimated Ragsdale's counts for Obama using the *Public Papers of the Presidents* available at The American Presidency Project. Kumar (2007, 10–11) shows similar patterns in public speechmaking for Clinton and Bush.

2. We derive these counts from *Public Papers of the Presidents* available at the American presidency Project.

3. Data are provided by the PEW Research Center's Project for Excellence in Journalism's (2009c) news index. Although we cannot determine how much of the news coverage was about Obama's speeches, he was the leading newsmaker for each of these weeks, at 16, 12, and 14 percent.

4. Data from March 5–8, 2009. Gallup did not ask an important problem question in February, closer to this week in the president's schedule.

5. The Gallup Poll, November 13–16, 2008.

6. Farnsworth and Lichter (2006) report only numbers from the first years of the Reagan, Clinton, and George W. Bush administrations. Presumably, this percentage would

be lower for all other years but still substantial, as a percentage of all government coverage on network news.

7. Cable news channels provide the public with more opportunity to view minor presidential speeches in part or full, regardless of news commentary and analysis. The audience for these speeches is still miniscule, however. The median daytime audience for Fox News Channel—the highest rated cable news network—averaged about 800,000 in 2007 (Pew Research Center's Project for Excellence in Journalism 2009d). This compares to a combined audience of 25 million for the nightly network newscasts (Bennett 2009, 229).

8. Terrorism did not register as a "most important problem," according to the Gallup Poll, at any time between 1998 and September 10, 2001. Unsurprisingly, 46 percent of Americans believed terrorism to be the nation's most important problem in an October 11–14, 2001, Gallup Poll.

9. We think of this conceptually in that some economic policy areas are more important than others. This is also verified by looking at Gallup's MIP data. In the MIP data, unemployment averages 11 percent since 1950, whereas spending issues combine at 4 percent.

10. Researchers, after all, typically use unemployment issues to tap economic voting behavior (Kiewiet 1981; Palmer and Whitten 1999).

11. Augmented Dickey Fuller tests denote stationarity for the economy ($t = -1.94$; intercept and trend: $t = -5.50$; intercept only: $t = -5.15$, with the null of a unit root rejected at $p < 0.05$, Schwarz Information Criterion) and Iraq ($t = -2.16$; intercept and trend: $t = -2.88$; intercept only: $t = -2.83$, with the null of a unit root rejected at $p < 0.05$, Schwarz Information Criterion).

12. Augmented Dickey Fuller tests denote stationarity for the economy ($t = -1.87$; intercept and trend: $t = -3.21$; intercept only: $t = -3.25$, with the null of a unit root rejected at $p < 0.05$, Schwarz Information Criterion) and Iraq (intercept and trend: $t = -2.62$; intercept only: $t = -2.54$; $t = -2.12$, with the null of a unit root rejected at $p < 0.05$, Schwarz Information Criterion).

13. We also examined inflation as a separate economic issue, which revealed relationships similar to unemployment. We have decided not to report these results, however, because autocorrelation plagues this particular model, remaining even after numerous attempts to purge it. This leaves us less confident in the results. These results are available from the authors.

14. Although we also have a theoretical reason for not including the objective economic indicators in our models, as others have done (Wood et al. 2005), we check and determined that the economic indicators are all exogenous to the system, given the impulse-response functions, which show statistically no impact on any of the other variables in the system, save itself. We also note that it made more sense for Wood to do this with consumer sentiment and approval ratings models (2007, Chapter 5) given that these are both measures of public perception.

15. Our measures of the state of the economy (the misery index, unemployment, GDP growth, and the budget) are broad, systemic measures of the economy's health and therefore are exogenous to public opinion, media, and presidential attention to the economy. Theory tells us that these conditions cause concern and attention, not vice versa.

16. We can also demonstrate statistically that the controls are not overwhelmingly influential such that they might nullify any of the relationships we report in the VARs. Simply applying unidirectional Box-Jenkins time series methods produces statistically insignificant results for many of the exogenous control variables.

17. We determine lag-lengths in each VAR using AIC and based on Simms (1980), estimating with a maximum lag-length of 16, which reveals lag lengths of five, seven, and five months for the total economy series, unemployment, and spending issues, respectively.

18. In brief, the MARs for the broad economic category effectively mirror the Granger tests and indicate that the relationships are positive. However, they provide more modest support for direct presidential leadership over the public's economic agenda given the absence of a corresponding response by the president to the public. Presidential attention also indirectly leads public concern about the broad economy through increased news coverage. The MAR graphs are available from the authors.

19. Interpretation of MARs is fairly straightforward. The reader should follow two rules of thumb. First, if the confidence bands (the dashed line in each graph) do not include zero, then there exists a relationship that is significantly different from zero. Second, if the statistically significant impact is greater than zero on the y-axis, then the effect is positive; if it is less than zero, the effect is negative.

20. The magnitude of the impact may not seem like much but is on par with the results other research produces concerning presidential leadership of public opinion (see Wood 2007).

21. While a 1 percent increase in the first month is rather small, the cumulative effects across time are substantial. Consider that the average share of the public specifically identifying unemployment as a most important problem is only 11 percent. The cumulative effects of a single shock are increased substantially if the media continue to heavily cover the issue, as this increased coverage continues to increase public concern for unemployment across time.

22. To supplement these findings, we also ran a basic regression of presidential attention and its separate impact on the public's concern for Iraq. This model shows that presidential attention to Iraq increases public concern for it but only without controlling for previous media attention to Iraq. Once we control for media attention, presidential leadership effects wash out, with only media affecting public concern. These supplemental results reinforce the importance of considering news media in models of presidential leadership of the public. They are available from the authors.

23. We determine lag lengths in each VAR using AIC and based on Simms (1980), estimating with a maximum lag-length of 16, which reveals lag lengths of five and three months for all presidents and the George W. Bush administration, respectively.

24. The MARs, which are available from the authors, reveal this evidence of indirect presidential leadership of the public's Iraq policy agenda through news coverage of Iraq, albeit at a marginal level of statistical significance.

CHAPTER SIX

1. Members of the president's administration went local on the economy, too. By October 2009, Vice President Biden had travelled to fourteen separate states to tout the economic stimulus (Elliot 2009).

2. According to Pew Research Center's Project for Excellence in Journalism (2009c), the economic crisis filled between 44 and 47 percent of the news hole during the last week of January and first two weeks of February.

3. Of course, going local was only part of a much larger sustained leadership strategy that we elucidate in Chapter 5.

4. President Bush made a similar claim one week later during a question-and-answer session with the American Society of Newspaper Editors (April 5, 2001): "Sometimes the Washington filter makes it hard for me to get my message directly to the people. And since I view you as people—[*laughter*]—I'd like to go directly to you." Bush continued to make this argument in 2003 during the early stages of the war in Iraq (see Eshbaugh-Soha and Peake 2008).

5. These data provide a broad representation of domestic speeches by presidents. Although this measure excludes more policy-driven, "minor" speeches also coded by Ragsdale (2009), this increase corresponds with other counts of domestic travel that do include more policy-specific appearances and days of domestic political travel (Kernell 2007, 122–129). The R^2 between year and yearly U.S. public appearances is 0.64.

6. Cohen (2010, 47–50) describes similar trends and identifies 1989 as the year in which presidents began to go local at a higher rate.

7. We also exclude Clinton's trips to his home state of Arkansas and Bush's visits to his home state of Texas as is typical of prior research (see Barrett and Peake 2007; Cohen and Powell 2005). A trip (or visit) is counted if the president delivered remarks that are listed in the *Public Papers of the Presidents*, available online at the American Presidency Project. Visits to a single state on the same day are counted as multiple trips if the president delivered remarks in separate cities at least fifty miles apart. When the president delivered separate remarks within the same city or in cities within fifty miles of one another, they were not counted as separate trips.

8. Campaign-related travel involved only the president speaking at a campaign rally or a party fund-raiser, whether for his own reelection or on behalf of his party's candidates. Many of Bush's (forty-one) and Clinton's trips (forty-one) included a campaign rally or fund-raising dinner in the same city as a policy-oriented address. We counted these trips as policy-related trips because a large reason for the trip fit the going local strategy. Each year, the president visits New York for two or more days to deliver an address at the United Nations. We count these as a single policy-related trip. While in New York, the president would often deliver remarks to local audiences, in addition to his address to the United Nations.

9. The symbolic trips included attendance at sporting events, holiday or memorial ceremonies, commencement addresses, troop rallies, and touring of natural disaster areas where the president made remarks. If a policy-oriented address was a major part of the president's remarks during the visit, it was coded as policy-related. Thus, several visits to troops are policy-related.

10. Local newspapers cover politicians differently in electoral settings, as well. Miller, Peake, and Boulton (2010) found a positive relationship between local support for Hillary Clinton and the tone of her local newspaper coverage during the 2008 Democratic presidential nomination race.

11. See Eshbaugh-Soha and Peake (2008, 612–614), Eshbaugh-Soha (2010b), and Cohen (2010, 78–80) for lengthier reviews of recent research on local media coverage of the presidency.

12. President Bush traveled to Florida, Pennsylvania, Ohio, Iowa, Missouri, and Wisconsin forty-six times, combined, during his first eighteen months in office (Kornblut 2002). In examining these trips, we find that only eight of Bush's public appearances during his first eighteen months in office were for electoral purposes. The campaign trips were on behalf of Republicans running for Congress in 2002, and only one of those occurred

in the swing states mentioned here (Florida). Therefore, his policy-oriented appearances early in his term were geared overwhelmingly to swing states.

13. A limitation to these cases is that they do not permit a true test of the responsiveness portion of our salience hypothesis. Although President Obama went local on the economy, arguably in a responsive fashion, this strategy was truncated at the beginning of his administration and included congressional pressures to act, which make this effort less comparable to our other cases. It may be difficult to find other responsive instances of going local because going local has been a purposive effort at leadership, used by recent presidents primarily to generate support for a policy priority of the president's choosing. President Clinton's health care reform tour in 1993–1994 is an early example.

14. Education reform, entitled No Child Left Behind, became law late in 2001. While clearly an important legislative success for Bush, the president did not get all of what he wanted in the legislation, having to compromise substantially on the bill (Rudalevige 2003).

15. The original data are from Barrett and Peake (2007). They counted all stories related to the trip appearing in the local newspaper on the day of and day after the president's visit. They content-coded all front-page articles in terms of relative tone, source attribution, and policy emphasis. See the article for a discussion of their newspaper selection and coding schemes. Barrett and Peake analyzed coverage of sixty-one trips by President Bush in 2001. Here, we discuss data only on the nineteen trips where Bush spoke primarily about his tax cut proposals during the first half of the year.

16. The remaining attributable statements were attributed to neutral sources (that is, policy experts) or local audience members and officials where a clear partisan allegiance could not be identified. Attributed statements included direct quotes and paraphrased sources.

17. Our analysis of the front-page articles used by Barrett and Peake (2007) indicates that the president's message on tax cuts framed much of the discussion.

18. We counted the number of newspaper articles using a key word search in Lexis/Nexis database, with Major U.S. Newspapers as our source. The keyword routine was: HEADLINE(tax* cut*) and BODY(tax* cut*) and BODY(Bush). We searched the following thirty newspapers: *Arkansas Democrat-Gazette, Chicago Sun-Times, Daily News* (New York), *Pittsburgh Post-Gazette, San Antonio Express-News, San Diego Union-Tribune, St. Louis Post-Dispatch, St. Petersburg Times, Star Tribune, The Atlanta Journal and Constitution, The Boston Globe, The Boston Herald, The Buffalo News, The Christian Science Monitor, The Columbus Dispatch, The Denver Post, The Houston Chronicle, The Milwaukee Journal Sentinel, The New York Post, The New York Times, The Oregonian, The Philadelphia Daily News, The Philadelphia Inquirer, The Plain Dealer, The San Francisco Chronicle, The Star-Ledger, The Tampa Tribune, The Times-Picayune, The Washington Post,* and *USA Today.*

19. In 2003, Bush proposed additional tax cuts in his budget. During the six-month period he was pushing his 2003 tax proposal our search routines on Lexis/Nexis found an average of 160 newspaper articles per month. His going local efforts on behalf of tax cuts in 2003 were not as extensive as they were in 2001. He made ten trips during the first six months of 2003 where he emphasized his tax cut proposals.

20. For 2002 through 2008, the correlation is statistically insignificant (Pearson's $r = 0.22$).

21. Of course, an N of twelve months is problematic. The full model (2001–2008) was reestimated with an indicator variable for 2001 and a variable interacting 2001 with the monthly number of presidential remarks on tax cuts. The results do not change, with

each public appearance by Bush where he remarked on tax cuts during 2001 yielding nine additional articles; whereas remarks during other years were statistically insignificant.

22. A 2 percent increase in national public concern could be considered an important impact, given that the measure is a national one and the president traveled only to select locations, targeting his efforts. Because we lack regional measures of public concern for issues, the targeted effects on public opinion of going local are difficult to measure.

23. See Edwards (2007, Chapter 6) for a lengthy description of the extent of the Bush White House public relations efforts on behalf of Social Security reform, including a detailed account of a typical Social Security town hall meeting. At the end of the public relations efforts, "the Treasury Department reported on its website that 31 administration officials had made 166 stops outside the beltway, visiting 40 states and 127 cities, and given more than 500 radio interviews in 50 states. Administration officials . . . participated in 61 town hall meetings" (Edwards 2007, 233).

24. See note 18 for specifics on the list of newspapers used in this search. For articles on Social Security, we used the following search routine on the Lexis/Nexis database: HEADLINE("Social Security") and BODY(reform OR private account* OR privatization).

25. See Eshbaugh-Soha and Peake (2006, 703–704) for a list of Social Security reform trips taken by President Bush.

26. We call this a general examination given the relatively small number of observations and absence of possible controls. Although these findings are thus suggestive, there is reason to expect that we'd find similar results with a longer time series.

27. We tested the impact of Bush's remarks in several ways. During the 2004 campaign, Bush cited Social Security reform as a major priority at just about every one of his campaign rallies. Thus, the series is inflated during August to November 2004, due to the campaign rhetoric. The campaign attention undoubtedly had an impact on media and public attention to the issue. The Granger causality test for presidential remarks (including campaign remarks) on media was statistically significant, whereas the president's impact on the public, while positive, was only significant at the $p < 0.1$ level. Media attention had a statistically significant impact on public concern for the issue. When campaign remarks are removed from the presidential remarks series, the direct impact of Bush's remarks diminishes, although they still affect media attention.

28. Moving average response graphs show that the all of the examined relationships are positive and disappear after two months. These graphs, as well as the Granger test tables, are available from the authors.

29. Through reading the president's remarks during each of the trips, we coded fifteen of the policy-related trips as focusing on the economy or economic stimulus and six as focusing on health care reform. Six trips included separate addresses on both topics or addresses where he discussed both priorities extensively. Obama's town hall in Bristol, Virginia, on July 29 was not included in this count because events held in D.C., Maryland, and Virginia are excluded in these analyses. Obama delivered five addresses before military audiences, extensively discussing administration policies on Iraq and Afghanistan. He also held five events on his renewable energy proposal, held three events on education, delivered an address at the United Nations in New York, addressed the nation on the Afghanistan war from West Point, and participated in the G-20 Summit in Pittsburgh.

30. Seventy-eight percent of Obama's domestic trips through October were coded as policy-related trips. This is a similar to Bush (81 percent) and Clinton (82 percent).

31. We examine only domestic trips on health care during 2009 because the agenda-setting stage of the process had clearly ended with passage of a health care bill by the Senate on Christmas Eve, 2009. Obama made six additional domestic trips where he made lengthy remarks on health care prior to its passage in March. We do not include these trips in our analysis.

32. The health care events and local newspapers examined include: Green Bay, WI (June 11, *Milwaukee Journal Sentinel*); Chicago, IL (June 15, *Chicago Sun-Times*); Shaker Heights, OH (July 23, *The Plain Dealer*); Raleigh, NC (July 29, *Raleigh News & Observer*); Portsmouth, NH (August 11, *The Union-Leader*); Belgrade, MT (August 14, *Billings Gazette*); Grand Junction, CO (August 15, *Denver Post*); Cincinnati, OH (September 7, *The Enquirer*); Minneapolis, MN (September 12, *The Star-Tribune*); Lordstown, OH (September 15, *The Plain Dealer*); Pittsburgh, PA (September 15, *Pittsburgh Post-Gazette*); and Troy, NY (September 21, *Albany Times Union*).

33. See, for example, Naymik and Tribble (2009).

34. We used the following search routine on Lexis/Nexis, with major U.S. newspapers as our source (see note 18): HEADLINE(health care) and BODY(reform).

35. Tracked since 2007, the Index includes coverage in newspapers and on broadcast television, cable television, the Internet, and radio.

36. Because the Durbin-Watson statistic indicated autocorrelation, we used the Prais-Winsten procedure. The adjusted R^2 for the model is 0.44, with an N of 42 and a model F-statistic of 17.2.

37. Moreover, the public's preferences on health care reform moved little during President Obama's public relations campaign. Numerous polls indicated that by October the president's efforts had failed to move the public to support his various health care reform proposals (Newport, Jones, and Saad 2009).

38. In February, 2001, the Gallup Poll indicates that 56 percent of the public supported Bush's tax cut and only 34 percent were opposed (Edwards 2007, 91). In February 2009 the Gallup Poll indicates that 59 percent of the public favored the economic stimulus package signed into law by Obama and 33 percent opposed it (Newport 2009).

39. In June 2001, Bush's approval ratings were 55 percent, but these had slipped from 62 percent in April. Obama, in the midst of his honeymoon, had an approval rating of 64 percent at the start of February 2009. Approval data are from Gallup's Presidential Job Approval Center; available at www.gallup.com/poll/124922/Presidential-Job-Approval-Center.aspx.

CHAPTER SEVEN

1. President Obama emphasized jobs during his State of the Union address on January 27, 2010, and devoted several speeches to unemployment, jobs, and the economy in February 2010. His focus on the economy came even as he had little public support for his handling of the economy. According to a February 5–10, 2010, *CBS News/New York Times* poll, only 42 percent of the public approved of the president's handling of the economy, just as 31 percent of the public believed that unemployment was the most important problem facing the nation (March 4–7, 2010, Gallup Poll). This was, again, even as health care reform was still under consideration in Congress.

2. The full quote reads as follows. "In his memoirs, Ronald Reagan—the 'Great Communicator'—reflected on his efforts to ignite concern among the American people regarding the threat of communism in Central America and mobilized them behind his

program of support for the Congress . . . 'Well, one of my greatest frustrations . . . was my inability to communicate to the American people and to Congress the seriousness of the threat we faced in Central America.'"

3. A fruitful avenue for analysis may include the web page of the White House, for example. Recent administrations have maintained extensive web pages, archiving presidential remarks on a range of presidential priorities, providing extensive video of administration officials, and publishing position papers and other information on the president's policy priorities that are useful for journalists and citizens alike, albeit subject to White House spin (Farnsworth 2009). President Obama's extensive e-mail list of supporters, Organizing for America, provides another important example of how the Internet provides additional opportunities for presidential communications (Lee 2009). The Internet, thus, may offer the president the opportunity to communicate with vast numbers of supporters or potential supporters without relying on the news media.

References

Achen, Christopher H. 1975. "Mass Political Attitudes and the Survey Response." *American Political Science Review* (December): 1218–1231.

Aday, Sean. 2010. "Chasing the Bad News: An Analysis of 2005 Iraq and Afghanistan War Coverage on NBC and Fox News Channel." *Journal of Communication* 60 (March): 144–164.

Alvarez, R. Michael, and Jonathan Nagler. 1998. "Economics, Entitlements, and Social Issues: Voter Choice in the 1996 Presidential Election." *American Journal of Political Science* 42 (October): 1349–1363.

Amemiya, Takeshi. 1978. "The Estimation of a Simultaneous Equation Generalized Probit Model." *Econometrica* 46 (September): 1193-1205.

Andrade, Lydia, and Garry Young. 1996. "Presidential Agenda Setting: Influences on the Emphasis of Foreign Policy." *Political Research Quarterly* 49 (September): 591–605.

Ansolabehere, Stephen, Roy Behr, and Shanto Iyengar. 1993. *The Media Game: American Politics in the Television Age.* New York: Macmillan Publishing.

Bailey, Michael, Lee Sigelman, and Clyde Wilcox. 2003. "Presidential Persuasion on Social Issues: A Two-Way Street?" *Political Research Quarterly* 56 (March): 49–58.

Barber, James David. 1972. *The Presidential Character: Predicting Performance in the White House.* New York: Prentice Hall.

Barilleaux, Ryan J. 1985. "The President, 'Intermestic' Issues, and the Risks of Policy Leadership." *Presidential Studies Quarterly* 15 (Fall): 754–767.

Barrett, Andrew W. 2004. "Gone Public: The Impact of Going Public on Presidential Legislative Success." *American Politics Research* 32 (May): 338–370.

Barrett, Andrew W. 2007. "Press Coverage of Legislative Appeals by the President." *Political Research Quarterly* 60 (December): 655–668.

Barrett, Andrew W., and Jeffrey S. Peake. 2007. "When the President Comes to Town: Examining Local Newspaper Coverage of Domestic Presidential Travel." *American Politics Research* 35 (January): 3–31.

Baum, Matthew A. 2003. *Soft News Goes to War: Public Opinion and American Foreign Policy in the New Media Age.* Princeton, NJ: Princeton University Press.

Baum, Matthew A., and Tim J. Groeling. 2010. *War Stories: The Causes and Consequences of Public Views of War.* Princeton, NJ: Princeton University Press.

Baum, Matthew A., and Samuel Kernell. 1999. "Has Cable Ended the Golden Age of Presidential Television?" *American Political Science Review,* 93 (March): 99–114.

Baumgartner, Frank, and Bryan D. Jones. 1993. *Agendas and Instability in American Politics.* Chicago: University of Chicago Press.

Beckmann, Matthew N. 2010. *Pushing the Agenda: Presidential Leadership in U.S. Lawmaking, 1953–2004.* Cambridge, UK: Cambridge University Press.

Behr, Roy L., and Shanto Iyengar. 1985. "Television News, Real World Cues, and Changes in the Public Agenda." *Public Opinion Quarterly* 49 (Spring): 38–57.

Bennett, W. Lance. 1990. "Toward a Theory of Press-State Relations in the U.S." *Journal of Communication* 40 (Spring): 103–125.

Bennett, W. Lance. 2003. *News: The Politics of Illusion*, 4th ed. New York: Pearson, Longman.

Bennett, W. Lance. 2009. *News: The Politics of Illusion*, 8th ed. New York: Pearson, Longman.

Bennett, W. Lance, Regina G. Lawrence, and Steven Livingston. 2007. *When the Press Fails: Political Power and the News Media from Iraq to Katrina.* Chicago: University of Chicago Press.

Blumenthal, Sidney. 1982. *The Permanent Campaign*, rev. ed. New York: Simon and Schuster.

Bogart, Leo. 1989. *Press and Public: Who Reads What, When, Where, and Why in American Newspapers*, 2nd ed. Hillsdale, NJ: Erlbaum.

Bond, Jon R., and Richard Fleisher. 1988. "Are There Two Presidencies? Yes, but Only for Republicans." *Journal of Politics* 50 (August): 747–767.

Bond, Jon R., and Richard Fleisher. 1990. *The President in the Legislative Arena.* Chicago: University of Chicago Press.

Bond, Jon R., Richard Fleisher, and B. Dan Wood. 2003. "The Marginal and Time-Varying Effect of Public Approval on Presidential Success in Congress." *Journal of Politics* 65 (February): 92–110.

Boorstin, Daniel. 1961. *The Image: A Guide to Pseudo-Events in America.* New York: Atheneum.

Borsuk, Alan J., and Guy Boulton. 2009. "Obama Puts Urgent Cast on Health Care Reform." *Milwaukee Journal Sentinel*, June 12: 1.

Bosso, Christopher J. 1989. "Setting the Agenda: Mass Media and the Discovery of Famine in Ethiopia." In *Manipulating Public Opinion*, ed. Michael Margoles and Gary A. Mauser. Pacific Grove, CA: Brooks-Cole, 153–174.

Box, George E. P., and George C. Tiao. 1975. "Intervention Analysis with Applications to Economic and Environmental Problems." *Journal of the American Statistical Association* 70 (March): 70–79.

Brace, Paul, and Barbara Hinckley. 1992. *Follow the Leader.* New York: Basic Books.

Brace, Paul, and Barbara Hinckley. 1993. "Presidential Activities from Truman through Reagan: Timing and Impact." *Journal of Politics* 55 (May): 382–398.

Bradbury, Dieter. 2001. "Bush Pitches Tax-Cut Plan in Portland." *Portland Press Herald*, March 24: 1A.

Brody, Richard. 1991. *Assessing the President: The Media, Elite Opinion, and Public Support.* Stanford, CA: Stanford University Press.

Bumiller, Elisabeth. 2002. "Presidential Travel: It's All about Local News." *The New York Times*, February 11: A24.

Burns, James MacGregor. 1973. *Presidential Government: The Crucible of Leadership.* New York: Houghton Mifflin Harcourt.

Burns, James MacGregor. 1978. *Leadership.* New York: Harper & Row.

Campbell, Angus, Philip E. Converse, Donald Stokes, and Warren Miller. 1960. *The American Voter.* New York: Wiley.

Campbell, Donald T., and Julian C. Stanley. 1963. *Experimental and Quasi-Experimental Designs for Research.* Boston: Houghton Mifflin.

Campbell, James E. 2000. *The American Campaign: U.S. Presidential Campaigns and the National Vote.* College Station: Texas A&M University Press.

Canes-Wrone, Brandice. 2001. "The President's Legislative Influence from Public Appeals." *American Journal of Political Science* 45 (April): 313–329.

Canes-Wrone, Brandice. 2006. *Who Leads Whom? Presidents, Policy, and the Public.* Chicago: University of Chicago Press.

Canes-Wrone, Brandice, William G. Howell, and David E. Lewis. 2007. "Toward a Broader Understanding of Presidential Power: A Reevaluation of the Two Presidencies Thesis." *Journal of Politics* 69 (January): 1–16.

Canes-Wrone, Brandice, and Scott de Marchi. 2002. "Presidential Approval and Legislative Success." *Journal of Politics* 64 (May): 491–509.

Canes-Wrone, Brandice, and Kenneth W. Shotts. 2004. "The Conditional Nature of Presidential Responsiveness to Public Opinion." *American Journal of Political Science* 48 (October): 690–706.

Cannon, Lou. 2004. "Why Reagan Was the 'Great Communicator.' " *USA Today*, June 6; www.usatoday.com/news/opinion/editorials/2004-06-06-cannon_x.htm.

Cater, Douglass. 1959. *The Fourth Branch of Government.* Boston: Houghton Mifflin.

Clines, Francis X. 1997. "On Split Screen Night, Clinton Gets Full Attention of Congress." *The New York Times*, February 4.

Cobb, Roger W., and Charles D. Elder. 1972. *Participation in American Politics: The Dynamics of Agenda-Building.* Baltimore: Johns Hopkins University Press.

Cohen, Bernard. 1963. *The Press and Foreign Policy.* Princeton, NJ: Princeton University Press.

Cohen, Jeffrey E. 1995. "Presidential Rhetoric and the Public Agenda." *American Journal of Political Science* 39 (February): 87–107.

Cohen, Jeffrey E. 1997. *Presidential Responsiveness and Public Policy-Making.* Ann Arbor: University of Michigan Press.

Cohen, Jeffrey E. 2008. *The Presidency in an Era of 24-Hour News.* Princeton, NJ: Princeton University Press.

Cohen, Jeffrey E. 2010. *Going Local: Presidential Leadership in the Post-Broadcast Age.* Cambridge, UK: Cambridge University Press.

Cohen, Jeffrey E., Michael A. Krassa, and John A. Hamman. 1991. "The Impact of Presidential Campaigning on Midterm US Senate Elections." *American Political Science Review* 85 (March): 165–178.

Cohen, Jeffrey E., and Richard J. Powell. 2005. "Building Public Support from the Grassroots Up: The Impact of Presidential Travel on State-Level Approval." *Presidential Studies Quarterly* 35 (March): 11–27.

Collier, Kenneth E. 1997. *Between the Branches: The White House Office of Legislative Affairs.* Pittsburgh, PA: University of Pittsburgh Press.

Conley, Richard S. 1999. "Derailing Presidential Fast-Track Authority: The Impact of Constituency Pressures and Political Ideology on Trade Policy in Congress." *Political Research Quarterly* 52 (December): 785–799.

Connelly, Cici. 2010. "61 Days from Near-Defeat to Victory; How Obama Revived His Health-Care Bill." *Washington Post*, March 23, A1.

Converse, Philip. 1964. "The Nature of Belief Systems in Mass Publics." In *Ideology and Discontent*, ed. David Apter. New York: Free Press, 206–261.

Cook, Corey. 2002. "The Permanence of the 'Permanent Campaign': George W. Bush's Public Presidency." *Presidential Studies Quarterly* 32 (December): 753–764.

Cook, Timothy E. 1998. *Governing with the News: The News Media as a Political Institution*. Chicago: University of Chicago Press.

Cooper, Phillip J. 2002. *By Order of the President: The Use and Abuse of Direct Executive Action*. Lawrence: University of Kansas Press.

Corwin, Edwards S. 1948. *The President, Office, and Powers, 1787–1948: History and Analysis of Practice and Opinion*. New York: New York University Press.

Covington, Cary. 1987. "Staying Private: Gaining Congressional Support for Unpublicized Presidential Preferences on Roll Call Votes." *Journal of Politics* 49: 737–755.

Crabb, Cecil V. Jr. 1982. *The Doctrines of American Foreign Policy*. Baton Rouge: Louisiana State University Press.

Crenson, Matthew, and Benjamin Ginsberg. 2007. *Presidential Power: Unchecked and Unbalanced*. New York: W. W. Norton.

Cronin, Thomas E. 1984. "Thinking and Learning about Leadership." *Presidential Studies Quarterly* 14 (Winter): 22–34.

Dahl, Robert A. 1982. *Dilemmas of Pluralist Democracy*. New Haven, CT: Yale University Press.

Davidson, Roger H. 1984. "The Presidency and Congress." In *The Presidency and the Political System*, ed. Michael Nelson. Washington, DC: CQ Press, 363–391.

DeRouen, Karl Jr., and Jeffrey S. Peake. 2002. "The Dynamics of Diversion: The Domestic Implications of Presidential Use of Force." *International Interactions* 28 (April–June): 191–211.

Doherty, Brendon J. 2007. "The Politics of Permanent Campaign: Presidential Travel and the Electoral College, 1977–2004." *Presidential Studies Quarterly* 37 (December): 749–773.

Doherty, Brendon J. 2009. "Barack Obama's First Six Months of International and Domestic Presidential Travel in Historical Context." Unpublished typescript available at http://whitehousetransitionproject.org/resources/briefing/SixMonth/Doherty-WHTP-Obama Six Month Travel-Revised 07-21-09.pdf

Dominguez, Casey B. K. 2005. "Is It a Honeymoon? An Empirical Investigation of the President's First Hundred Days." *Congress and the Presidency* 32 (Spring): 63–78.

Downs, Anthony. 1972. "Up and Down with Ecology: The Issue-Attention Cycle." *Public Interest* 28 (Summer): 38–50.

Druckman, James N. 2006. "Review: Who Leads Whom? Presidents, Policy, and the Public." *Public Opinion Quarterly* 70: 405–409.

Druckman, James N., and Justin W. Holmes. 2004. "Does Presidential Rhetoric Matter? Priming and Presidential Approval." *Presidential Studies Quarterly* 34 (December): 755–778.

Edwards, George C. III. 1989. *At the Margins*. New Haven, CT: Yale University Press.

Edwards, George C. III. 2003. *On Deaf Ears: The Limits of the Bully Pulpit*. New Haven, CT: Yale University Press.

Edwards, George C. III. 2007. *Governing by Campaigning: The Politics of the Bush Presidency*. New York: Longman.

Edwards, George C. III. 2009. *The Strategic President: Persuasion and Opportunity in Presidential Leadership*. Princeton, NJ: Princeton University Press.

Edwards, George C. III. 2010. "Barack Obama's Leadership of the Public." Presented at the Annual Meeting of the Midwest Political Science Association, Chicago, IL.

Edwards, George C. III, and Andrew Barrett. 2000. "Presidential Agenda Setting in Congress." In *Polarized Politics: Congress and the President in a Partisan Era*, ed. Jon R. Bond and Richard Fleisher. Washington, DC: CQ Press, 109–133.

Edwards, George C. III, William Mitchell, and Reed Welch. 1995. "Explaining Presidential Approval: The Importance of Issue Salience." *American Journal of Political Science* 39 (February): 108–134.

Edwards, George C. III, and Stephen J. Wayne. 2010. *Presidential Leadership: Politics and Policy Making*, 8th ed. Boston: Wadsworth.

Edwards, George C. III, and B. Dan Wood. 1999. "Who Influences Whom? The President, Congress, and the Media." *American Political Science Review* 93 (June): 327–344.

Elliot, Philip. 2009. "AP IMPACT: Obama's Travels Carry a Touch of Blue." October 13. Available at www.cbsnews.com/stories/2009/10/13/ap/politics/main5380874.shtml.

Erbring, Lutz, Edie N. Goldenberg, and Arthur H. Miller. 1980. "Front-Page News and Real-World Cues: A New Look at Agenda-Setting by the Media." *American Journal of Political Science* 24 (February): 16–49.

Erikson, Robert S. 1989. "Economic Conditions and the Presidential Vote." *American Political Science Review* 83 (June): 567–583.

Erikson, Robert S., Michael B. MacKuen, and James A. Stimson. 2002. *The Macro Polity*. Cambridge, UK: Cambridge University Press.

Eshbaugh-Soha, Matthew. 2003. "Presidential Press Conferences over Time." *American Journal of Political Science* 47 (April): 348–353.

Eshbaugh-Soha, Matthew. 2006a. "The Conditioning Effects of Policy Salience and Complexity on American Political Institutions." *Policy Studies Journal* 34 (May): 223–243.

Eshbaugh-Soha, Matthew. 2006b. *The President's Speeches: Beyond Going Public*. Boulder, CO: Lynne Rienner.

Eshbaugh-Soha, Matthew. 2010a. "The Politics of Presidential Speeches." *Congress and the Presidency* 37 (January): 1–21.

Eshbaugh-Soha, Matthew. 2010b. "The Tone of Local Presidential News Coverage." *Political Communication* 27 (April–June): 121–140.

Eshbaugh-Soha, Matthew, and Tom Miles. 2009. "George W. Bush's Domestic Policy Agenda." *American Review of Politics* 29 (Winter): 351–369.

Eshbaugh-Soha, Matthew, and Jeffrey S. Peake. 2004. "Presidential Influence over the Systemic Agenda." *Congress and the Presidency* 31 (Autumn): 161–181.

Eshbaugh-Soha, Matthew, and Jeffrey S. Peake. 2005. "Presidents and the Economic Agenda." *Political Research Quarterly* (March): 127–138.

Eshbaugh-Soha, Matthew, and Jeffrey S. Peake. 2006. "The Contemporary Presidency: 'Going Local' to Reform Social Security." *Presidential Studies Quarterly* 36 (December): 689–704.

Eshbaugh-Soha, Matthew, and Jeffrey S. Peake. 2008. "The Presidency and Local Media: Local Newspaper Coverage of President George W. Bush." *Presidential Studies Quarterly* 38 (December): 606–627.

Farhi, Paul. 2009. "Consider This: NPR Achieves Record Ratings." *The Washington Post* (March 24): C01.

Farnsworth, Stephen J. 2009. *Spinner in Chief: How Presidents Sell Their Policies and Themselves*. Boulder, CO: Paradigm.

Farnsworth, Stephen J., and S. Robert Lichter. 2006. *The Mediated Presidency: Television News and Presidential Governance*. New York: Rowman and Littlefield.

Fiorina, Morris, and Kenneth Shepsle. 1989. "Formal Theories of Leadership: Agents, Agenda-Setters, and Entrepreneurs." In *Leadership and Politics*, ed. Bryan D. Jones. Lawrence: University Press of Kansas, 17–40.

Fleisher, Richard, Jon R. Bond, Glen S. Krutz, and Stephen Hanna. 2000. "The Demise of the Two Presidencies." *American Politics Quarterly* 28 (January): 3-25.

Foote, Joe S. 1988. "Ratings Decline of Presidential Television." *Journal of Broadcasting & Electronic Media* 32 (Spring): 225-230.

Foote, Joe S. 1990. *Television Access and Presidential Power: The Networks, the Presidency, and the "Loyal Opposition."* New York: Praeger.

Fordham, Benjamin. 2005. "Strategic Conflict Avoidance and the Diversionary Use of Force." *Journal of Politics* 67 (February): 132–153.

Fortier, John C., and Norman J. Ornstein. 2003. "President Bush: Legislative Strategist." In *The George W. Bush Presidency: An Early Assessment*, ed. Fred I. Greenstein. Baltimore: Johns Hopkins University Press, 138–72.

Freeman, John R., John T. Williams, and Tse-min Lin. 1989. "Vector Autoregression and the Study of Politics." *American Journal of Political Science* 33 (November): 842–877.

Gans, Herbert. 1979. *Deciding What's News: A Study of CBS Evening News, NBC Nightly News, Newsweek, and Time.* New York: Vintage Books.

Geer, John G. 1996. *From Tea Leaves to Opinion Polls.* New York: Columbia University Press.

Gentzkow, Matthew, and Jesse M. Shapiro. 2006. "Media Bias and Reputation." *Journal of Political Economy* 114 (April): 280–316.

Gergen, David. 2000. *Eyewitness to Power: The Essence of Leadership.* Ithaca, NY: Cornell University Press.

Gilberg, Sheldon, Chaim Eyal, Maxwell McCombs, and David Nicholas. 1980. "The State of the Union Address and the Press Agenda." *Journalism Quarterly* 57 (Winter): 584–588.

Gormley, William T. 1986. "Regulatory Issue Networks in a Federal System." *Polity* 18 (Summer): 595–620.

Graber, Doris A. 2002. *Mass Media and American Politics*, 6th ed. Washington, DC: CQ Press.

Graber, Doris A. 2006. *Mass Media and American Politics*, 7th ed. Washington, DC: CQ Press.

Granger, Clive W. J. 1969. "Investigating Causal Relations by Econometric Models and Cross Spectral Models." *Econometrica* 37 (August): 424–438.

Greenstein, Fred I. 2000. *The Presidential Difference: Leadership style from FDR to Clinton.* New York: The Free Press.

Groeling, Tim. 2008. "Who's the Fairest of the Them All? An Empirical Test for the Partisan Bias on ABC, CBS, NBC, and Fox News." *Presidential Studies Quarterly* 38 (December): 631–657.

Groeling, Tim, and Samuel Kernell. 1998. "Is Network News Coverage of the President Biased?" *Journal of Politics* 60 (November): 1063–1087.

Grossman, Michael Baruch, and Martha Joynt Kumar. 1981. *Portraying the President: The White House and the News Media.* Baltimore: Johns Hopkins University Press.

Goldstein, Gordon M. 2009. "Five Questions for Obama on Afghan War." CNN, December 1; www.cnn.com/2009/OPINION/12/01/goldstein.five.questions.for.obama/index.html.

Hacker, Jacob S., and Paul Pierson. 2005. "Abandoning the Middle: The Bush Tax Cuts and the Limits of Democratic Control." *Perspectives on Politics* 3 (March): 33–53.

Hager, Gregory L., and Terry Sullivan. 1994. "President-Centered and Presidency-Centered Explanations of Presidential Public Activity." *American Journal of Political Science* 38 (November): 1079–1103.

Hallin, Daniel C. 1984. "The Media, the War in Vietnam, and Political Support: A Critique of the Thesis of an Oppositional Media." *Journal of Politics* 46 (February): 2–24.

Hallin, Daniel C. 1992. "Sound Bite News: Television Coverage of Elections." *Journal of Communication* 42: 5–24.

Hamilton, James. 2004. *All the News That's Fit to Sell: How the Market Transforms Information Into News*. Princeton, NJ: Princeton University Press.

Hansen, Liane. 2004. "Ronald Reagan: The Great Communicator." *National Public Radio*. June 6; www.npr.org/templates/story/story.php?storyId=1940534.

Hart, Roderick. 1987. *The Sound of Leadership: Political Communication in the Modern Age*. Chicago: University of Chicago Press.

Hayes, Danny. 2008. "Does the Messenger Matter? Candidate-Media Agenda Convergence and Its Effects on Voter Issue Salience." *Political Research Quarterly* 61 (March): 134–146.

Hayes, Danny, and Matt Guardino. 2010. "Whose Views Made the News? Media Coverage and the March to War in Iraq." *Political Communication* 27 (January–March): 59–87.

Heith, Diane J. 2004. *Polling to Govern: Public Opinion and Presidential Leadership*. Stanford, CA: Stanford University Press.

Hess, Stephen, and Marvin L. Kalb, eds. 2003. *The Media and the War on Terrorism*. Washington, DC: Brookings.

Hill, Kim Quaile. 1998. "The Policy Agendas of the President and the Mass Public: A Research Validation and Extension." *American Journal of Political Science* 42 (November): 1328–1334.

Hill, Kim Quaile, and Patricia A. Hurley. 1999. "Dyadic Representation Reappraised." *American Journal of Political Science* 45 (February): 109–137.

Hoge, James F. Jr. 1997. "Foreign News: Who Gives a Damn?" *Columbia Journalism Review* 36 (November–December): 48–52.

Holbrook, Thomas M. 1994. "Campaigns, National Conditions, and U.S. Presidential Elections." *American Journal of Political* 38 (November): 973–998.

Holian, David B. 2006. "Trust the Party Line: Issue Ownership and Presidential Approval from Reagan to Clinton." *American Politics Research* 34 (November): 777–802.

Holsti, Ole R. 2004. *Public Opinion and American Foreign Policy*. Ann Arbor: University of Michigan Press.

Hornick, Ed. 2008. "Can Lincoln's Playbook Help Obama in the Years Ahead?" CNN, November 19; www.cnn.com/2008/POLITICS/11/18/obama.lincoln/index.html.

Howell, William G. 2003. *Power without Persuasion: The Politics of Direct Presidential Action*. Princeton, NJ: Princeton University Press.

Howell, William G., and Jon C. Pevehouse. 2007. *When Dangers Gather: Congressional Checks on Presidential War Powers*. Princeton, NJ: Princeton University Press.

Hult, Karen M., and Walcott, Charles E. 2004. *Empowering the White House: Governance under Nixon, Ford, and Carter*. Lawrence: University Press of Kansas.

Hurwitz, Jon, and Mark Peffley. 1987. "The Means and Ends of Foreign Policy as Determinants of Presidential Support." *American Journal of Political Science* 31 (May): 236–258.

Iyengar, Shanto. 1991. *Is Anyone Responsible?* Chicago: University of Chicago Press.

Iyengar, Shanto, and Kyu S. Hahn. 2009. "Red Media, Blue Media: Evidence of Ideological Selectivity in Media Use." *Journal of Communication* 59 (March): 19–39.

Iyengar, Shanto, and Donald R. Kinder. 1987. *News That Matters: Television and American Opinion*. Chicago: University of Chicago Press.

Iyengar, Shanto, and Jennifer A. McGrady. 2007. *Media Politics: A Citizen's Guide*: New York: W. W. Norton.

Iyengar, Shanto, Mark D. Peters, and Donald R. Kinder. 1982. "Experimental Demonstrations of the 'Not-So-Minimal' Consequences of Television News Programs." *American Political Science Review* 76 (December): 848–858.

Jacobs, Lawrence R., and Robert Y. Shapiro. 1994. "Issues, Candidate Image, and Priming: The Use of Private Polls in Kennedy's 1960 Presidential Campaign." *American Political Science Review* 88 (September): 527–540.

Jacobs, Lawrence R., and Robert Y. Shapiro. 2000. *Politicians Don't Pander*. Chicago: University of Chicago Press.

Jacobson, Gary C. 2007. *A Divider, Not a Uniter: George W. Bush and the American People*. New York: Pearson Longman.

Jones, Bryan D. 1989. "Causation, Constraint and Political Leadership." In *Leadership and Politics*, ed. Bryan D. Jones. Lawrence: University of Kansas, 3–14.

Jones, Bryan D. 1994. *Reconceiving Decision-Making in Democratic Politics: Attention, Choice, and Public Policy*. Chicago: University of Chicago Press.

Jones, Bryan D., and Frank Baumgartner. 2005. *The Politics of Attention: How Government Prioritizes Problems*. Chicago: University of Chicago Press.

Jones, Jeffrey M. 2009. "Economy, Health Care Top 'Most Important Problem' List." *Gallup*, September 9; www.gallup.com/poll/122885/Economy-Healthcare-Top-Important-Problem-List.aspx.

Kaniss, Phyllis. 1991. *Making Local News*. Chicago: University of Chicago Press.

Kennon, George F. 1993. "Somalia through the Glass Darkly." *New York Times*, September 30, A25.

Kernell, Samuel. 1978. "Explaining Presidential Popularity: How Ad Hoc Theorizing, Misplaced Emphasis, and Insufficient Care in Measuring One's Variables Refuted Common Sense and Led Conventional Wisdom Down the Path of Anomalies." *American Political Science Review* 72 (June): 502–522.

Kernell, Samuel. 1997. *Going Public: New Strategies of Presidential Leadership*, 3rd ed. Washington, DC: CQ Press.

Kernell, Samuel. 2007. *Going Public: New Strategies of Presidential Leadership*, 4th ed. Washington, DC: CQ Press.

Keshk, Omar M. G. 2003. "CDSIMEQ: A Program to Implement Two-stage Probit Least Squares." *The Stata Journal* 3 (2): 1–11.

Key, V. O. 1961. *Public Opinion and American Democracy*. New York: John Wiley.

Kiefer, Francine. 2001. "Bush's Travel Itinerary—Surprise!—Is to Swing States." *Christian Science Monitor*, June 6, 2.

Kiewiet, D. Roderick. 1981. "Policy-Oriented Voting in Response to Economic Issues." *American Political Science Review* 72 (June): 448–459.

Kingdon, John W. 1995. *Agendas, Alternatives, and Public Policies*, 2nd ed. Boston: Little, Brown.

Kornblut, Anne E. 2002. "Bush Following a Map to '04: Presidential Travels Trace a Route Critical to Victory." *The Boston Globe*, July 5, A1.

Krosnick, Jon A., and Donald R. Kinder. 1990. "Altering the Foundations of Support for the President through Priming." *American Political Science Review* 84 (June): 497–512.

Krutz, Glen S., and Jeffrey S. Peake. 2009. *Treaty Politics and the Rise of Executive Agreements: International Commitments in a System of Shared Powers.* Ann Arbor: University of Michigan Press.

Kumar, Martha Joynt. 2003. "Communications Operations in the White House of President George W. Bush: Making News on His Terms." *Presidential Studies Quarterly* 33 (June): 366–380.

Kumar, Martha Joynt. 2007. *Managing the President's Message: The White House Communications Operation.* Baltimore: Johns Hopkins University Press.

Lamar, Jacob V. Jr. 1987. "Why Did This Happen?" *Time* 129 (June 1): 16–19.

Lammers, William. 1982. "Presidential Attention-Focusing Activities." In *The President and the Public,* ed. Doris Graber. Philadelphia: Institute for the Study of Human Issues, 145–171.

Laracey, Mel. 2002. *Presidents and the People: The Partisan Story of Going Public.* College Station: Texas A&M University Press.

Larocca, Roger T. 2006. *The President's Agenda: Sources of Executive Influence in Congress.* Columbus: Ohio State University Press.

Lawrence, Adam B. 2004. "Does It Matter What Presidents Say? The Influence of Presidential Rhetoric on the Public Agenda, 1946–2003." PhD dissertation, University of Pittsburgh.

Lee, Carol E. 2009. "Team Obama Mobilizing E-Mail List." *Politico.* January 30; available at www.politico.com/news/stories/0109/18208.html.

Leighley, Jan E. 2004. *Mass Media and Politics: A Social Science Perspective.* Boston: Houghton Mifflin.

Light, Paul. 1999. *The President's Agenda,* 3rd ed. Baltimore: Johns Hopkins University Press.

Lindsay, James M. 1994. *Congress and the Politics of U.S. Foreign Policy.* Baltimore: Johns Hopkins University Press.

Linsky, Marin. 1986. *Impact: How the Press Affects Federal Policymaking.* New York: W. W. Norton.

Liu, Xinsheng, Eric Lindquist, and Arnold Vedlitz. In press. "Explaining Media and Congressional Attention to Global Climate Change, 1969–2005: An Empirical Test of Agenda-Setting Theory." *Political Research Quarterly.*

Livingston, Steven, and Todd Eachus. 1995. "Humanitarian Crises and U.S. Foreign Policy: Somalia and the CNN Effect Reconsidered." *Political Communication* 12 (October–December): 413–429.

Lowi, Theodore J. 1972. "Four Systems of Policy, Politics, and Choice." *Public Administration Review* 32 (July–August): 298–310.

Lowi, Theodore J. 1985. *The Personal President.* Ithaca, NY: Cornell University Press.

Lutkepohl, Helmut. 1993. *Introduction to Multiple Time Series Analysis.* Berlin, Germany: Springer Verlag.

Madsen, Douglas, and Peter G. Snow. 1991. *The Charismatic Bond: Political Behavior in Time of Crisis.* Cambridge, MA: Harvard University Press.

Maltese, John Anthony. 1994. *Spin Control: The White House Office of Communications and Management of Presidential News.* Chapel Hill: University of North Carolina Press.

Marshall, Bryan W., and Richard L. Pacelle, Jr. 2005. "Revisiting the Two Presidencies: The Strategic Use of Executive Orders." *American Politics Research* 33 (January): 81–105.

Matthews, Donald R., and James A. Stimson. 1975. *Yeas and Nays: Normal Decision-Making in the US House of Representatives.* New York: John Wiley & Sons.

Mayer, Kenneth R. 2001. *With the Stroke of a Pen: Executive Orders and Presidential Power*. Princeton, NJ: Princeton University Press.

McCombs, Maxwell E. 1976. "Agenda-Setting Research: A Bibliographic Essay." *Political Communication Review* 1(1): 1–7.

McCombs, Maxwell E. 2004. *Setting the Agenda: Mass Media and Public Opinion*. Cambridge, UK: Polity Press.

McCormick, James M., and Eugene R. Wittkopf. 1990. "Bipartisanship, Partisanship, and Ideology in Congressional-Executive Foreign Policy Relations, 1947–1988." *Journal of Politics* 52 (November): 1077–1100.

McCormick, James M., and Eugene R. Wittkopf. 1992. "At the Water's Edge: The Effects of Party, Ideology, and Issues on Congressional Foreign Policy Voting, 1947–1988." *American Politics Quarterly* 20 (January): 26–53.

McFarland, Andrew S. 1969. *Power and Leadership in Pluralist Systems*. Stanford, CA: Stanford University Press.

McLeary, Richard, and Richard Hay. 1980. *Applied Time Series Analysis*. Beverly Hills, CA: Sage.

Meernik, James. 1993. "Presidential Support in Congress: Conflict and Consensus on Foreign and Defense Policy. *Journal of Politics* 55 (August): 569–587.

Miller, Joanne, and Jon Krosnick. 2000. "News Media Impact on the Ingredients of Presidential Evaluations: Politically Knowledgeable Citizens are Guided by a Trusted Source." *American Journal of Political Science* 44 (April): 301–315.

Miller, Melissa K., Jeffrey S. Peake, and Brittany Ann Boulton. 2010. "Testing the Saturday Night Live Hypothesis: Fairness and Bias in Newspaper Coverage of Hillary Clinton's Presidential Campaign." *Politics and Gender* 6 (June): 169–198.

Miller, Warren E., and Donald E. Stokes. 1963. "Constituency Influence in Congress." *American Political Science Review* 57 (March): 45–56.

Miroff, Bruce. 1990. "The Presidency and the Public: Leadership as Spectacle." In *The Presidency and the Political System*, 3rd ed., ed. Michael Nelson. Washington: CQ Press, 255–280.

Mondak, Jeffrey J. 1993. "Source Cues and Policy Approval: The Cognitive Dynamics of Public Support for the Reagan Agenda." *American Journal of Political Science* 37 (February): 186–212.

Monroe, Alan D. 1998. "Public Opinion and Public Policy, 1980-1993." *Public Opinion Quarterly* 62 (Spring): 6–28.

Moore, David W. 2001. "Lower ratings of the Economy Continue, Little Changed from Last Month." *Gallup News Service*. June 19; available at www.gallup.com/poll/4522/Lower-Ratings-Economy-Continue-Little-Changed-from-Last-Month.aspx.

Morales, Lymari. 2009. "Economy Declines Further as Top Problem; Health Care Rises." Gallup.com. August 14. Available at www.gallup.com/poll/122339/Economy-Declines-Further-Top-Problem-Healthcare-Rises.aspx.

Mueller, John. 1973. *War, Presidents, and Public Opinion*. New York: Wiley.

Nadeau, Richard, and Michael S. Lewis-Beck. 2001. "National Economic Voting in US Presidential Elections." *Journal of Politics* 63 (February): 159–181.

Naymik, Mark, and Sarah Jane Tribble. 2009. "Obama Uses Shaker Rally to Push Health Reforms." *The Plain Dealer*, July 24: A1.

Neuman, W. Russell. 1986. *The Paradox of Mass Politics: Knowledge and Opinion in the American Electorate*. Cambridge, MA: Harvard University Press.

Neustadt, Richard E. 1990. *Presidential Power and the Modern Presidents: The Politics of Leadership from Roosevelt to Reagan.* New York: The Free Press.

Newport, Frank. 2009. "Obama Signs Stimulus into Law with Majority Support." Gallup. com, February 17; available at www.gallup.com/poll/114691/obama-signs-stimulus-law-majority-support.aspx.

Newport, Frank, Jeffrey M. Jones, and Lydia Saad. 2009. "Americans on Healthcare Reform: Five Key Realities." Gallup.com, October 30; available at www.gallup.com/poll/123989/Americans-Healthcare-Reform-Five-Key-Realities.aspx.

Newport, Frank, and Lydia Saad. 2005. "What Does the Public Really Think about Social Security Reform?" *Gallup News Service.* March 17; available at www.gallup.com/poll/15283/What-Does-Public-Really-Think-About-Social-Security-Reform.aspx.

Nicholson-Crotty, Sean. 2009. "The Politics of Diffusion: Public Policy in the American States." *Journal of Politics* 71 (January): 192–205.

NielsenWire. 2009a. "40.8 Million Watch President Obama's Speech on Afghanistan." December 2; available at http://blog.nielsen.com/nielsenwire/media_entertainment/40-8-million-watch-president-obama's-speech-on-afghanistan/.

NielsenWire. 2009b. "32.1 Million Watch President Obama's Health Care Address to Congress on TV." September 10; available at http://blog.nielsen.com/nielsenwire/media_entertainment/31-8-million-watch-president-obamas-health-care-address-to-congress-on-tv/.

O'Toole, James. 2001. "Bush Easily Sells Budget on First Try in Vanport." *Pittsburgh Post-Gazette,* March 1: A1.

Packer, George. 2010. "One Year: Obama Pays the Price." *The New Yorker,* January 20; www .newyorker.com/online/blogs/georgepacker/2010/01/one-year-obama-pays-the-price.html.

Page, Benjamin, and Robert Shapiro. 1983. "Effect of Public Opinion on Policy." *American Political Science Review* 77 (March): 175–190.

Page, Benjamin, and Robert Shapiro. 1985. "Presidential Leadership through Public Opinion." In *The Presidency and Public Policy Making,* ed. George C. Edwards III, Steven Shull, and Norman Thomas. Pittsburgh: University of Pittsburgh Press, 22–36.

Page, Benjamin, and Robert Shapiro. 1992. *The Rational Public: Fifty Years of Trends in Americans' Policy Preferences.* Chicago: University of Chicago Press.

Palmer, Harvey D., and Guy D. Whitten. 1999. "The Electoral Impact of Unexpected Inflation and Economic Growth." *British Journal of Political Science* 29 (October): 623–639.

Patterson, Thomas E. 2000. "Doing Well and Doing Good: How Soft News and Critical Journalism Are Shrinking the News Audience and Weakening Democracy—And What News Outlets Can Do about It." The Joan Shorenstein Center for Press, Politics, and Public Policy, John F. Kennedy School of Government, Harvard University.

Peake, Jeffrey S. 1999. "Presidential Agenda Setting in Foreign Policy." PhD dissertation, Texas A&M University.

Peake, Jeffrey S. 2001. "Presidential Agenda Setting in Foreign Policy." *Political Research Quarterly* 4 (March): 69–86.

Peake, Jeffrey S. 2007. "Presidents and Front-Page News: How America's Newspapers Cover the Bush Administration." *Harvard International Journal of Press/Politics* 12 (October): 52–70.

Peake, Jeffrey S., and Matthew Eshbaugh-Soha. 2008. "The Agenda-Setting Impact of Major Presidential TV Addresses." *Political Communication* 25 (April–June): 113–137.

Peake, Jeffrey S., and Amanda Jo Parks. 2008. "Presidential Pseudo-Events and the Media Coverage They Receive." *American Review of Politics* 29 (Summer): 85–108.

Pew Research Center. 2008. *Pew Research Center Biennial News Consumption Survey.* Available at www.people-press.org/reports/pdf/444.pdf

Pew Research Center. 2009. "Americans Remain Focused on Michael Jackson." *News Interest Index.* July 15: http://people-press.org/report/529/americans-remained-focused-on-michael-jackson.

Pew Research Center's Project for Excellence in Journalism. 2001. "The First 100 Days: How Bush and Clinton Fared in the Press." April 30; available at www.journalism .org/node/312.

Pew Research Center's Project for Excellence in Journalism. 2009a. "Anger and Rancor Fuel Cable's Health Care Coverage." *PEJ News Coverage Index:* August 10–16, 2009; available at www.journalism.org/index_report/pej_news_coverage_index_august _1016_2009.

Pew Research Center's Project for Excellence in Journalism. 2009b. "Obama's First 100 Days." April 28; www.journalism.org/analysis_report/obamas_first_100_days.

Pew Research Center's Project for Excellence in Journalism. 2009c. "PEJ News Coverage Index"; www.journalism.org/news_index.

Pew Research Center's Project for Excellence in Journalism. 2009d. "The State of the News Media: An Annual Report on American Journalism"; available at www.stateofthemedia.org/2009/narrative_cabletv_audience.php.

Pew Research Center's Project for Excellence in Journalism. 2009e. "Town Hall Showdowns Fuel Health Care Coverage." *PEJ News Coverage Index:* August 3-9, 2009; available at www.journalism.org/index_report/pej_news_coverage_index_august_39_2009.

Pfiffner, James A. 1988. *The Strategic Presidency: Hitting the Ground Running.* Chicago: Dorsey Press.

Pitkin, Hannah F. 1967. *The Concept of Representation.* Berkeley: University of California Press.

Policy Agendas Project. 2010. "Gallup's Most important Problem." Available at www .policyagendas.org/page/datasets-codebooks.

Powell, Richard J. 1999. " 'Going Public' Revisited: Presidential Speechmaking and the Bargaining Setting in Congress." *Congress and the Presidency* 26: 153–170.

Prins, Brandon C., and Bryan W. Marshall. 2001. "Congressional Support of the President: A Comparison of Foreign, Defense, and Domestic Policy Decision Making during and after the Cold War." *Presidential Studies Quarterly* 31 (December): 660–678.

Prior, Markus. 2007. *Post-Broadcast Democracy.* Cambridge, UK: Cambridge University Press.

Prior, Markus. 2009. "Improving Media Effects Research through Better Measurement of News Exposure." *Journal of Politics* 71: 893–908.

Ragsdale, Lyn. 1984. "The Politics of Presidential Speechmaking, 1949–1980." *American Political Science Review* 78 (December): 971-84.

Ragsdale, Lyn. 1997. "Disconnected Politics: Public Opinion and Presidents." In *Understanding Public Opinion*, eds. Barbara Norrander and Clyde Wilcox. Washington, DC: CQ Press, 229–251.

Ragsdale, Lyn. 2009. *Vital Statistics on the Presidency: George Washington to George W. Bush*, 3rd ed. Washington: CQ Press.

Rieck, Donald. 2009a. "Media Boost Obama, Bash His Policies." *Center for Media and Public Affairs*, April 27; www.cmpa.com/media_room_4_27_09.htm.

Rieck, Donald. 2009b. "Study: Obama's Media Coverage Sours." *Center for Media and Public Affairs,* September 27; www.cmpa.com/media_room_9_14_09.html.

Rivers, Douglas, and Nancy L. Rose. 1985. "Passing the President's Program: Public Opinion and Presidential Influence in Congress." *American Journal of Political Science* 29 (May): 183–196.

Roberts, Robert N., and Anthony J. Eksterowicz. 1996. "Local News, Presidential Campaigns, and Citizenship Education: A Reform Proposal." *PS: Political Science and Politics* 29 (March): 66–72.

Rockman, Bert A. 1984. *The Leadership Question: The Presidency and the American System.* New York: Praeger.

Rogers, Everett M., and James W. Dearing. 2000. "Agenda-Setting Research: Where Has It Been, Where Is It Going?" In *Media Power in Politics,* 4th ed., ed. Doris A. Graber. Washington, DC: CQ Press, 68–85.

Rosenblatt, Alan J. 1998. "Aggressive Foreign Policy Marketing: Public Response to Reagan's 1983 Address on Lebanon and Grenada." *Political Behavior* 20 (September): 225–240.

Ross, Fiona. 2007. "Policy Histories and Partisan Leadership in Presidential Studies: The Case of Social Security." In *The Polarized Presidency of George W. Bush,* ed. George C. Edwards III and Desmond S. King. New York: Oxford University Press, 419–464.

Rottinghaus, Brandon. 2006. "Rethinking Presidential Responsiveness: The Public Presidency and Rhetorical Congruency, 1953–2001." *Journal of Politics,* 68 (August): 720–732.

Rottinghaus, Brandon. 2009. "Strategic Leaders: Determining Successful Presidential Opinion Leadership Tactics through Public Appeals." *Political Communication* 26 (July–September): 296–316.

Rottinghaus, Brandon. 2010. *The Provisional Pulpit: Modern Presidential Leadership of Public Opinion.* College Station: Texas A&M University Press.

Rozell, Mark J. 1996. *The Press and the Bush Presidency.* Westport, CT: Praeger.

Rudalevige, Andrew. 2003. "The Politics of 'No Child Left Behind.'" *Education Next* 3 (Fall): 63–70.

Rudalevige, Andrew. 2005. *The New Imperial Presidency: Renewing Presidential Power after Watergate.* Ann Arbor: University of Michigan Press.

Rudolph, Thomas J. 2003. "Who is Responsible for the Economy? The Formation and Consequences of Responsibility Attributions." *American Journal of Political Science* 47 (October): 698–713.

Saad, Lydia. 2009. "U.S. Satisfaction Sinks to Six-Month Low." Gallup.Com, October 14; available at www.gallup.com/poll/123662/U.S.-Satisfaction-Sinks-Six-Month-Low.aspx.

Schattschneider, E. E. 1960. *The Semi-Sovereign People.* New York: Holt, Rinehart, and Winston.

Schlesinger, Arthur M. Jr. 1973. *The Imperial Presidency.* Boston: Houghton Mifflin.

Scheufele, Dietram A. 2000. "Agenda-Setting, Priming, and Framing Revisited: Another Look at Cognitive Effects of Political Communication." *Mass Communication and Society* 3 (August): 297–316.

Shull, Steven A. 1993. *A Kinder, Gentler Racism? The Reagan-Bush Civil Rights Legacy.* Armonk, NY: M. E. Sharpe.

Sigelman, Lee. 1980. "Gauging the Public Response to Presidential Leadership." *Presidential Studies Quarterly* 10 (Summer): 427–433.

Simon, Dennis M., and Charles W. Ostrom Jr. 1989. "The Impact of Televised Speeches and Foreign Travel on Presidential Approval." *Public Opinion Quarterly* 53 (Spring): 58–82.

Simms, Christopher A. 1980. "Macroeconomics and Reality." *Econometrica* 48 (January): 1–48.

Skowronek, Stephen. 1993. *The Politics Presidents Make: Leadership from John Adams to George Bush.* Cambridge, MA: Harvard University Press.

Smith, Tom W. 1980. "America's Most Important Problem: A Trend Analysis, 1946–1976." *Public Opinion Quarterly* 44 (Summer): 164–180.

Smoller, Frederic T. 1990. *The Six O'clock President: A Theory of Presidential–Press Relations in the Age of Television.* New York: Praeger.

Sparrow, Bartholomew H. 1999. *Uncertain Guardians: The News Media as a Political Institution.* Baltimore: Johns Hopkins University Press.

Steele, Galen. 2008. "Strategic Factors Influencing the Issuance and Duration of Executive Orders." PhD dissertation. University of North Texas.

Steger, Wayne P. 1997. "Presidential Policy Initiation and the Politics of Agenda Control." *Congress and the Presidency* 24 (Spring): 17–36.

Stimson, James A. 1999. *Public Opinion in America: Moods, Cycles, and Swings*, 2nd ed. Boulder, CO: Westview.

Stimson, James A., Michael B. MacKuen, and Robert S. Erickson. 1995. "Dynamic Representation." *American Political Science Review* 89 (September): 543–565.

Stuckey, Mary E. 1991. *The President as Interpreter-In-Chief.* Chatham, NJ: Chatham House.

Suskind, Ron. 2004. *The Price of Loyalty.* New York: Simon and Schuster.

Towle, Michael J. 2004. *Out of Touch: The Presidency and Public Opinion.* College Station: Texas A&M University Press.

Tufte, Edward R. 1978. *Political Control of the Economy.* Princeton, NJ: Princeton University Press.

Tulis, Jeffrey K. 1987. *The Rhetorical Presidency.* Princeton, NJ: Princeton University Press.

Walcott, Charles E., and Karen M. Hult. 1995. *Governing the White House.* Lawrence: University Press of Kansas.

Wanta, Wayne, Mary Ann Stephenson, Judy Van Slyke Turk, and Maxwell E. McCombs. 1989. "How Presidents' State of Union Talk Influenced News Media Agendas." *Journalism Quarterly* 66 (Autumn): 537–541.

Waterman, Richard W. 1989. *Presidential Influence in the Administrative State.* Knoxville: University of Tennessee Press.

Wayne, Stephen J. 1982. "Great Expectations: What People Want from Presidents." In *Rethinking the Presidency*, ed. Thomas E. Cronin. Boston: Little, Brown.

Weiner, Terry. 2007. "Touching the Third Rail: Explaining the Failure of Bush's Social Security Initiative." *Politics and Policy* 35 (August): 872–897.

Welch, Reed L. 2000. "Is Anybody Watching? The Audience for Televised Presidential Addresses." *Congress and the Presidency* 27 (Spring): 41–58.

Welch, Reed L. 2003. "Presidential Success in Communicating with the Public through Televised Addresses." *Presidential Studies Quarterly* 34 (June): 347–356.

West, Darrell M. 1988. "Activists and Economic Policymaking in Congress." *American Journal of Political Science* 32 (August): 662–680.

Whitford, Andrew B., and Jeff Yates. 2003. "Policy Signals and Executive Governance: Presidential Rhetoric in the War on Drugs." *Journal of Politics* 65 (November): 995–1012.

Whitford, Andrew B., and Jeff Yates. 2009. *Presidential Rhetoric and the Public Agenda: Constructing the War on Drugs.* Baltimore: Johns Hopkins University Press.

Wittkopf, Eugene. R. 1990. *Faces of Internationalism: Public opinion and American Foreign Policy.* Durham, NC: Duke University Press.

Wildavsky, Aaron. 1966. "The Two Presidencies." *Trans-Action* 4 (December): 7–14.

Wilson, Scott. 2009. "Obama's Travel Mixes Policy, Politics." *Washington Post,* June 21, A1.

Wood, B. Dan. 2007. *The Politics of Economic Leadership.* Princeton, NJ: Princeton University Press.

Wood, B. Dan. 2009a. *The Myth of Presidential Representation.* Cambridge, UK: Cambridge University Press.

Wood, B. Dan. 2009b. "Presidential Saber Rattling and the Economy." *American Journal of Political Science* 53 (July): 695–709.

Wood, B. Dan, Chris T. Owens and Brandy M. Durham. 2005. "Presidential Rhetoric and the Economy." *Journal of Politics* 67 (August): 627–645.

Wood, B. Dan, and Jeffrey S. Peake. 1998. "The Dynamics of Foreign Policy Agenda Setting." *American Political Science Review* 92 (March): 173–184.

Wood, B. Dan, and Richard W. Waterman. 1994. *Bureaucratic Dynamics: The Role of the Bureaucracy in Democracy.* Boulder, CO: Westview.

Woodward, Bob. 2002. *Bush at War.* New York: Simon and Schuster.

Woolley, John. 2000. "Using Media-Based Data in Studies of Politics." *American Journal of Political Science* 44 (January): 156–173.

Yates, Jeff, and Andrew B. Whitford. 2005. "Institutional Foundations of the President's Issue Agenda." *Political Research Quarterly* 58 (December): 577–585.

Young, Garry, and William B. Perkins. 2005. "Presidential Rhetoric, the Public Agenda, and the End of Presidential Television's 'Golden Age.'" *Journal of Politics* 67 (November): 1190–205.

Zaller, John. 1992. *The Nature and Origins of Mass Opinion.* Cambridge, UK: Cambridge University Press.

Zaller, John R. 1998. "Monica Lewinsky's Contribution to Political Science." *PS: Political Science and Politics* 31 (June): 182–189.

Zaller, John, and Dennis Chiu. 1996. "Government's Little Helper: U.S. Press Coverage of Foreign Policy Crises, 1945–1991." *Political Communication* 13 (October–December): 385–405.

Zaller, John, and Stanley Feldman. 1992. "A Simple Theory of the Survey Response: Answering Questions versus Revealing Preferences." *American Journal of Political Science* 36 (August): 579–616.

Index

Achen, Christopher H., 195
Aday, Sean, 150
Afghanistan, 85, 144
Alvarez, R. Michael, 96
Amemiya, Takeshi, 100, 211n29
Andrade, Lydia, 61
Ansolabehere, Stephen, 54
approval ratings, presidential, 9, 14,
    16, 47; of George H. W. Bush, 109,
    128; of George W. Bush, 8, 46,
    158, 178, 218n39; of Carter, 109;
    and charisma, 31; and domestic
    travel, 158, 163; and economic
    conditions, 75, 103, 106, 109, 131,
    135, 210nn12,16; importance of,
    95; and Iraq, 101, 112, 116, 127,
    131, 146, 147; of Obama, 3, 178,
    218n39; and optimism, 12; of
    Reagan, 2; relationship to foreign
    policy, 75; relationship to presidential
    leadership, 12, 68–71, 72, 84
Arab-Israeli conflict, 208n12
ARX modeling, 135
Augmented Dickey Fuller tests,
    210n19, 211n25, 213nn11,12
Axelrod, David, 205n8

Bailey, Michael, 12
Barber, James David, 45
Barilleaux, Ryan J., 208n11
Barrett, Andrew, 6, 18, 49, 192; on Bush's
    domestic travel, 162, 167, 215n17,
    216nn15,17; on news coverage,
    17, 70, 78, 86, 123, 127, 159, 160,
    161, 162, 164, 167, 216nn15,17
Baum, Matthew A., 51, 124, 207n9;
    on Iraq War, 113, 150, 208n8;
    on news coverage, 4, 17, 60, 64,
    114, 117, 152, 198, 210n18; on

television audiences, 13, 49, 64,
    83, 85, 86, 90, 107, 198, 210n18
Baumgartner, Frank, 11, 18,
    22, 41, 43, 56, 92
Beckmann, Matthew N., 5, 163, 193
Begala, Paul, 159
Behr, Roy, 50, 54, 72
Bennett, W. Lance: on indexing by
    media, 55, 74; on Iraq War, 17,
    74, 145; on news coverage, 17, 55,
    56, 72, 74, 92, 124–25, 145, 150,
    198, 209n4, 210n18, 213n7
Biden, Joseph, 214n1
Bin Laden, Osama, 127, 144
Blumenthal, Sidney, 26, 205n1
Bogart, Leo, 63
Bond, Jon R., 28, 31, 68, 68–69, 73,
    192
Boorstin, Daniel, 161
Bork, Robert, 154
Borsuk, Alan J., 175
Bosso, Christopher J., 207n5
Boulton, Britanny Ann, 215n10
Boulton, Guy, 175
Box, George E. P.: impact
    assessment methods of, 100
Box-Jenkins time series methods,
    211n29, 213n16
Brace, Paul, 11, 56, 84, 210n15
Bradbury, Dieter, 168
Brody, Richard, 75
Brown, Scott, 27
Bumiller, Elisabeth, 160
Burns, James MacGregor: on
    followership, 34; on individual
    attributes and leadership, 31–32; on
    leadership and responsiveness, 5, 21,
    35, 51, 188; on opinion leadership,
    38; on power and leadership, 30;

Burns, James MacGregor *(continued)*
   and transactional vs. transformative
   leadership, 29–30, 207n8
Bush, George H. W.: approval ratings, 46;
   and clean air, 8; and the economy,
   101–2, 103, 105, 107, 109, 132,
   136, 140–41, 194, 207n1, 209n6;
   and federal spending/budget, 98;
   frequency of speeches, 101–2, 103,
   212n1; and Iraq, 9, 17, 102, 110,
   111, 112, 115, 127–28, 132, 144, 151,
   192, 194, 207n1, 209n6, 214n23;
   and Los Angeles riots of 1992, 59;
   as responsive to news media, 19,
   59, 207n5; size of audience for
   speeches, 91; Somalia policy, 59;
   speeches on the economy, 101–
   2, 103, 105, 107, 109, 128, 136;
   speeches on Iraq, 8, 111, 112, 115,
   128, 144, 151, 192, 212n34; "War
   on Drugs" speech, 50, 81, 209n1
Bush, George W.: approval ratings, 178,
   218n39; communication skills of, 7;
   and the economy, 25, 101–2, 103,
   107, 154, 157, 163, 165–70, 180, 184;
   and education reform, 166, 167, 168,
   216n14; frequency of speeches, 101–
   2, 103, 120; going local by, 9, 25,
   127, 154–55, 156–58, 159–61, 162,
   163, 164–74, 175, 178, 179, 184, 187,
   196, 215nn4,7,8,12, 216nn14,15,17–
   19,21, 217nn22,25,30; honeymoon
   period, 9; and Iraq, 8, 9, 17, 47, 86,
   91, 99, 112, 113–14, 115, 116, 118,
   144–45, 149–51, 152, 166, 171,
   186–87, 212n36, 215n4; as leader,
   17, 46, 149–51, 152, 163; "Mission
   Accomplished" speech, 86; and
   press conferences, 171; priority of
   foreign policy for, 46, 83–84, 144;
   and September 11th attacks, 96; size
   of audience for speeches, 50, 86, 91;
   and Social Security reform, 3, 8, 22,
   25, 56, 127, 145, 151, 154, 157, 161,
   164–66, 170–74, 178, 179, 180, 184,
   187, 196, 217nn23–25,27; speeches
   on the economy, 101–2, 103, 107,

   216n15; speeches on Iraq, 86, 112,
   113–14, 115, 116, 118, 144–45, 152,
   212n36; and tax cuts, 25, 154, 157,
   163, 165–70, 174, 175, 178, 179, 180,
   184, 187, 216nn15,16,19,21, 218n38

Campbell, Angus, 50
Campbell, Donald T., 100
Campbell, James E., 75
Canes-Wrone, Brandice, 68, 73, 95, 100;
   on agenda setting, 42, 122, 191,
   195; on approval ratings, 72, 95; on
   conditional opinion leadership, 38;
   on going public, 191; on legislative
   success, 23, 34, 41, 51, 191, 195;
   on news media, 57; on pandering,
   14, 37, 200; on policy leadership,
   200; on presidential domestic travel,
   158; on presidential prioritizing,
   13–14, 20–21, 35, 38, 70, 88, 174,
   180; on presidential responsiveness,
   15, 37, 39, 71; on presidential
   speeches, 42, 71, 88, 107, 122,
   191; on public agenda, 23, 41, 42,
   51; on public opinion, 39, 41, 202;
   on strategic leadership, 183, 196
Cannon, Lou, 1
Carter, Jimmy: and economic policy, 101–
   2, 212n31; and energy policy, 27;
   frequency of speeches, 101–2, 103,
   109; as leader, 27; size of audience
   for speeches, 85, 90; speeches on the
   economy, 101–2, 103, 109, 212n31
Cater, Douglass, 59
Chiu, Dennis, 55, 74
civil rights, 12, 72–73
Clines, Francis X., 91
Clinton, Bill: communication skills of,
   12–13, 28; and the economy, 19, 90,
   95, 101–2, 103, 104, 107, 132, 136–
   37, 143; frequency of speeches, 84,
   101–2, 103, 120, 212n1; and global
   warming, 16; going local by, 16, 25,
   154, 156–58, 159, 160, 174, 215nn7,8,
   216n13, 217n30; and health care
   reform, 3, 13, 27–28, 64, 126, 192,
   205n2, 216n13; honeymoon period,

Druckman, James N., 11, 12, 205n11
drug abuse, 50, 81, 86
Durham, Brandy M., 12

Eachus, Todd, 207n5
Eagleberger, Lawrence, 59
economy, the: and divided government,
    101, 106, 109–10; economic growth,
    12, 133, 136, 137, 213n15; media
    coverage of, 19, 25, 50, 60, 70, 72,
    94, 95, 96–97, 98–99, 103, 104–5,
    106, 108–9, 121, 127–28, 130,
    132, 133, 135–39, 151, 153, 166,
    168–69, 183–84, 186, 191, 210n14,
    211nn21,31, 212n3, 213n15, 214n21;
    misery index, 96–97, 101, 103, 106,
    110, 112, 116, 133, 146, 151–52,
    191, 210n17, 213n15; objective
    economy, 19, 68, 72, 96, 96–97, 133,
    135, 139, 151, 191, 210n16, 213n14;
    poverty, 133; presidential leadership
    regarding, 5, 19, 24, 75–77, 101–10,
    115, 131, 132–33, 134, 141–42, 143–
    44, 184, 189, 190, 191; presidential
    responsiveness regarding, 19, 25,
    75–77, 96, 98, 107–8, 109, 110, 117,
    118, 121, 125–26, 130–31, 134, 136,
    137, 138, 139–41, 147, 151, 153,
    185–86, 187, 190, 212n32, 213n15;
    presidential speeches regarding, 24,
    50, 68, 73, 86, 89, 90, 91, 93, 96,
    97, 98, 99–110, 120–21, 125–26,
    128, 130–31, 133, 136–37, 143, 153,
    183–84, 186, 189, 190, 194, 209n6,
    211n31, 212n3, 216n15, 217n29,
    218n1; public agenda regarding, 12,
    50, 57, 60, 72, 93, 94, 96–97, 98, 99,
    101–10, 121, 130–31, 133, 135, 136–
    41, 153, 154, 166, 169, 177, 178–79,
    183–84, 185–86, 187, 188, 189–
    90, 191, 192, 198, 201, 207nn1,7,
    208nn13,15,16, 211n24, 213n9,
    214nn18,21, 218n1; spending and
    budget issues, 19, 22, 25, 43, 57, 76,
    77, 98, 130–31, 133, 137, 138, 141–
    43, 144, 151, 186, 208n15, 209n6,
    213nn9,15. See also unemployment

economy of attention, 71–72
education, 19, 166, 167, 168,
    209n8, 216n14
Edwards, George C., III, 4, 26, 29, 38,
    39, 41, 46, 47, 73, 161, 183, 210n11;
    on agendas, 40, 43, 49, 56, 99, 124,
    180, 192, 194, 195, 197, 198; on
    Bush, 50, 160, 163, 169, 170, 173,
    196, 217n23, 218n38; on charisma,
    31, 206n3; on Clinton, 12–13, 27–
    28, 50, 160, 205n2; on Congress,
    56, 198, 207n2; on education
    levels, 209n8; on effectiveness of
    presidential leadership, 1, 19, 23,
    182; on foreign policy, 75, 146; on
    going public, 191, 193; on leaders
    and followers, 21; on leaders as
    facilitators, 32–33, 34, 35, 36, 42,
    87; on news coverage, 17, 18, 19, 61,
    62, 82, 99, 124, 126, 127, 146, 152,
    160; on political context, 32–34,
    68, 206n5; on presidential approval
    ratings, 210n12; on presidential
    power, 32; on presidential speeches,
    18, 50, 82, 84, 85, 89, 90, 91, 104,
    122, 123, 126, 133, 192, 209nn1,3,8,
    210n15, 211n26; on prospects for
    public leadership, 51; on public
    agenda, 36, 42, 52–53, 152, 218n38;
    on public opinion, 3, 8, 10, 12–
    13, 19, 20, 36, 195, 199, 205n2,
    209n8; on Reagan, 1, 2, 12–13,
    14, 50, 85, 195–96, 205n3, 209n9;
    on salience, 99; on Social Security
    reform, 170, 173, 196, 217n23;
    on strategic leadership, 196; on
    television audiences, 85, 209n3
Eisenhower, Dwight, 156
Eksterowicz, Anthony J., 159
Elder, Charles D., 40
Elliot, Philip, 214n1
Erbring, Lutz, 72
Erikson, Robert S., 15, 37, 39, 75, 96
events: international events, 59, 60, 61,
    68, 96, 103, 106, 112, 116, 118,
    131, 135, 145, 146, 147, 152, 190,
    191; new major policy events, 56,

town hall meetings, 174, 189, 217nn23,29
transactional leadership, 29–30
transformative leadership, 30, 32
Tribble, Sarah Jane, 218n33
Truman, Harry S., 6, 156
Tufte, Edward R., 75
Tulis, Jeffrey K., 11, 29, 187, 200, 206n7
two presidencies thesis, 68,
    73–74, 76, 94, 190

unemployment, 76, 77, 97, 133, 213n10;
    media coverage of, 19, 136, 137, 138,
    140, 141, 151, 210n14, 214n21;
    presidential responsiveness to
    public concern regarding, 19, 25,
    130–31, 136, 138, 139–40, 151, 186,
    213n15; public agenda regarding,
    19, 25, 130–31, 136, 137, 138–41,
    143–44, 151, 185–86, 188, 198,
    208n15, 213nn9,15, 214n21, 218n1
United Nations, 144–45, 215n8

Vanderbilt University: key word
    searches of TV News Archive
    at, 98, 133, 203, 211n21
vector autoregression (VAR) analysis,
    25, 134, 135, 141, 145–46, 149,
    172, 213n16, 214nn17,23
Vedlitz, Arnold, 134

Walcott, Charles E., 6, 16, 195
Wanta, Wayne, 57
Warber, Adam L., 206n4
Washington Post, 160, 161, 167
Watergate, 84, 107
Waterman, Richard W., 29, 207n2
Wayne, Stephen J., 36
Weber, Max, 207n8
Weiner, Terry, 173
Welch, Reed, 17, 46, 85, 86, 89, 90, 91
West, Darrell M., 209n3
White House: news correspondents
    assigned to, 54; Office of
    Communications (OOC), 6–7,
    16–17, 21–22, 23; Office of Media
    Affairs, 154; Press Office, 6, 7–8,
    16; press secretary, 7–8; public

relations operation, 1–3, 6–8,
    10–11, 16–17, 21–22, 23, 26,
    36, 54, 77, 79, 86, 120, 154–55,
    181–82, 195, 197, 205n2, 218n3
Whitford, Andrew B., 6, 15
Whitten, Guy D., 213n10
Wilcox, Clyde, 12
Wildavsky, Aaron, 68, 73, 94
Williams, John T., 134
Wilson, Scott, 163
Wilsonian leadership, 38, 207n3
Wittkopf, Eugene R., 73, 74
Wood, B. Dan, 21, 25, 68, 135, 188,
    207n2, 213n14; on agendas, 4,
    40, 197; on approval ratings, 69,
    210n12; on Congress, 56, 198; on
    the economy, 75, 96, 99, 206n1,
    210nn12,16, 211n24; on economy of
    attention, 71–72; on effectiveness of
    presidential leadership, 19, 182; on
    foreign policy, 57, 96, 146, 190, 191,
    208n12; on Granger causality tests,
    139; on international events, 190; on
    news coverage, 18, 19, 22, 56, 61,
    87, 92, 99, 105, 124, 126, 127, 146,
    152, 211n23; on political conditions,
    14; on presidential policies, 201; on
    presidential representation, 202,
    209n3; on presidential responsive-
    ness, 16; on presidential speeches,
    12, 13, 14, 15, 22, 124, 126, 133,
    190, 192, 211n26; on public agenda,
    129, 152; on public opinion, 8,
    12, 13, 15, 16, 20, 39, 214n20
Woodward, Bob, 113, 144
Woolley, John, 99, 211n21

Yates, Jeff, 6, 15
Young, Garry: on international
    events, 61; on presidential
    leadership, 182; on presidential
    speeches, 13, 22, 50, 64, 83, 85,
    91, 93; on public agenda, 4

Zaller, John, 75; on indexing by media,
    55, 74; on public opinion, 49, 51,
    90, 195; on resistance axiom, 69